THE NEW
DOLLS' HOUSE
DO·IT·YOURSELF BOOK

in ¹/₁₂ and ¹/₁₆ scale

THE NEW
DOLLS' HOUSE
DO·IT·YOURSELF BOOK

in ¹⁄₁₂ and ¹⁄₁₆ scale

VENUS AND MARTIN DODGE

David & Charles

A DAVID & CHARLES BOOK

Copyright © Venus & Martin Dodge, 1982, 1983, 1985, 1986, 1988, 1989, 1990, 1992, 1993

First published 1982
Reprinted 1983, 1985, 1986, 1988, 1989, 1990, 1992
New & extended edition 1993
Reprinted 1994, 1996
First published in paperback 1997
Reprinted 1998, 1999, 2001

A catalogue record for this book is available from the British Library.

ISBN 0 7153 0616 2

Colour photography by Jonathan Bosley

Typeset by Greenshires Icon, Exeter
and printed in Italy by Milanostampa SpA
for David & Charles
Brunel House   Newton Abbot   Devon

CONTENTS

INTRODUCTION

When *The Dolls' House DIY Book* was first published in 1982, we could not predict how popular the hobby was to become. In those days, dolls' houses were still regarded as children's toys and an adult who owned one was thought mildly eccentric. How things have changed! Nowadays the doll's house is back where it began – as an adult's toy – and perfectly sane and sensible people have discovered the joys of miniatures.

The book was always intended to be a guide for beginners based on our own experience of problem-solving, and we are pleased and grateful that it has proved so popular. It has been in print ever since it was published and we have had many delightful letters from readers and made many friends. However, the dolls'-house world has moved on and we felt that it was time to update and enlarge the book to include some of the new materials and methods which are available. There are now miniatures fairs, mail-order suppliers and dolls'-house shops all over the country and tiny treasures we could only dream of ten years ago are available everywhere. The original *DIY Book* was mainly in 1/16 scale as it was intended for people making dolls' houses for children, but as the hobby has developed, 1/12 has become established as the more popular scale and we felt that most people would prefer plans and patterns in 1/12 scale.

So, here it is, a completely revised and updated *DIY*! We have retained all the original material so anyone planning a child's dolls' house will still find patterns and plans in 1/16 scale but we have also re-drawn all the original projects in 1/12 scale, and added lots of new ideas which we hope both new readers and old will enjoy. All the projects are shown in colour photographs, and we have included lists of suppliers, useful books, and magazines.

The first seven chapters of the book offer advice on how to plan, build, decorate and furnish a dolls' house to your own design. The following chapters give plans, patterns and instructions to build specific projects including a cupboard house, a shop, and Victorian, Tudor, Georgian and modern houses with suggestions for variations for other periods and styles. There are also patterns and instructions for making simple dolls, a chapter on miniature gardening and advice for anyone renovating an old dolls' house,

We intend the book to be a guide, not a rigid set of rules – it offers methods we have used and found to work but they are not the only methods, you will have ideas of your own. Dolls' houses are dream houses, they reflect their maker's skill and personality, and the imagination of the builder is the only limit to the variety of dolls' houses which can be made and the way they are furnished. Our aim is to offer plans and methods which will enable any averagely-capable person to build and furnish a dolls' house of satisfying realism, and as few of us are

skilled craftsmen, most of the ideas are simple and straight forward enough for the absolute beginner to follow – no special skills or tools are needed, just the inclination and a little time – but we hope that the experienced dolls'-house person might also find our book helpful and perhaps discover a few new ideas.

If you are a complete newcomer to the small world of dolls' houses, you have chosen a good time to start! Twenty-five years ago, when we made our first dolls' house, not only did our friends think we were crazy but it was almost impossible to find the things we wanted. It was fun contriving dolls'-house furnishings from odds and ends, printing our own wallpapers and rugs and inventing methods for making furniture, but it was frustrating – especially when our abilities did not match our ambitions! Nowadays there are shops everywhere selling all the DIY materials you will need and dolls'-house fairs and shops countrywide where you can choose miniatures to suit every budget but you need to know where to find them. We strongly advise that you subscribe to one or two of the dolls'-house magazines (*see* page 188) – especially *The International Dolls House News*, which was Britain's first and, we think, still the best specialist magazine. The magazine will give you up-to-date information on what is happening in the miniatures world, the shops, the fairs, articles on old and new dolls' houses and on craftsmen and suppliers. After reading a few issues – and you can buy back issues – you will find that there is more to miniatures than you thought!

This is a hobby which can be enjoyed at many levels and in many ways. The collector with a valuable antique dolls' house enjoys the search for authentic antique miniatures to furnish it, the skilled craftsman enjoys the challenge of reproducing a piece perfectly in miniature but perhaps it is the beginner who has most fun! For you, everything is there waiting to be discovered and you will probably want to jump in with both feet! When you visit your first dolls'-house shop or fair, you will be amazed at the wealth of items on offer and may be confused by the wide variety of prices. If you go to one of the major fairs like The London Dolls' House Festival in Kensington or Miniatura in Birmingham you will see work produced by some of the finest craftsmen in this country and abroad – at prices to match – but there are many smaller events where you will see plenty of things at 'pocket money' prices; and most dolls'-house shops carry stock in all price ranges. It can be an expensive hobby if you choose to buy only the very best, but most of us like to make things for ourselves and only buy what we cannot make – or cannot resist! Most dolls' houses – like real houses – are a mixture of the home-made, the affordable and a few 'special' things. We believe that the recent surge in the popularity of miniatures might be due to the uncertain economic climate – dream houses have become less likely in real life so we are living out our fantasies in miniature! Whatever the reason, building and furnishing a dolls' house could be one of the most enjoyable things you will ever do and it doesn't have to cost very much.

The most important thing to understand is that there are no rules about what is 'right' or 'wrong' in a dolls' house – it is a fantasy, a toy, whether it is a simple play house for a child or the most elaborate mansion for a middle-aged collector. We each decide for ourselves what sort of house we want and how we furnish it and you should not be daunted by anyone who tells you that 'everything should be authentic, perfectly-scaled and in period' or 'everything should be home-made'. There are some odd snobberies in the miniature world as in the real world, and what one person considers absolutely essential, another person will consider completely irrelevant. So don't be afraid to 'do your own thing' – charm, whimsey and eccentricity are just as valid as authenticity and period accuracy. No two dolls' houses are the same just as no two people are the same and your idea of what makes a good dolls' house is just as valid as any 'expert's'.

You may find that your first efforts at house building or

Most dolls' houses are a mixture of the homemade, the affordable and a few 'special' things

furniture making are less than impressive – don't give up, few people get it right first time. Learn from what you did wrong and have another go – and remember that all the craftsmen whose work is so much admired were once beginners. You might like to take a course, either an adult education evening class in woodwork (ask at your local library) or one run by a miniaturist. You will find all kinds of courses advertised in the specialist magazines, the classes are usually small, and this can be an excellent way to acquire new skills and build confidence. You will also find a number of dolls'-house clubs advertised in the magazines. Clubs offer a warm welcome to beginners and you might find that sharing ideas, tools and skills adds another dimension to your enjoyment of the hobby.

A brief warning about plagiarism; all the plans and patterns in this book are designed for private use. It is illegal to use these patterns (or those in any other book) for commercial purposes without written permission (license) from the author. It is also illegal to copy the work of others for commercial purposes, or to sell (or permit to be sold) work which is an unlicensed copy.

Whether you are a first-time housebuilder or an old hand, we hope you will find as much pleasure in building a dolls' house as we do.

Venus and Martin Dodge
Dorset 1993

1 PLANNING

The first step in building a dolls' house is planning, first in your mind and then on paper, making decisions about the kind of dolls' house you actually want. If possible, during this planning stage, take advantage of the dolls' houses in museums and the various books on old dolls' houses in the library to gain inspiration. Consider subscribing to one or more of the specialist publications and, if possible, visit a miniatures fair or a specialist shop to collect ideas. Don't rush into it – you will be spending a lot of time and effort on your dolls' house, and a little research at this stage will help to prevent mistakes and ensure that you end up with the house you really want. Beginners especially will be surprised by the variety of old dolls' houses and the wealth of building components now available for making new ones. Often you do not know what you want until you see it, and simply knowing that you could have stained-glass windows or a wrought-iron balcony might inspire you to plan a more ambitious house.

SCALE

The first consideration is whether the dolls' house is to be for a child or an adult and a decision must be made about the scale. Traditionally, dolls' houses for children are built in 1/16 scale – three-quarters of an inch to one foot. This is the scale used by commercial manufacturers such as Lundby and Caroline's Home, whose furnishings and dolls' houses are available from toyshops. The 1/12 scale – one inch to one foot – is favoured by adult collectors, and the dolls' houses and furnishings sold by the specialist shops are in this scale.

The photograph on page 10 shows kitchen dressers in both scales to demonstrate the difference in size. The plans and furniture patterns throughout the book are given in both scales so you can choose whichever you prefer, but the scale must be consistent – 1/12 scale furniture will not fit into a 1/16 scale house. The exception is accessories, where carefully chosen items can be used for either scale. To demonstrate this, everything on both dressers is actually in 1/12 scale but the smaller size bowls, jugs and packets etc fit happily into the smaller scale.

The choice of scale is usually dictated by the amount of space available and whether the dolls' house is to be for a child or an adult. For a young child, the 1/16 scale is probably the best choice as it provides rooms accessible to children and is usually small enough to move and store easily. Also the accessories dear to a child's heart, like vacuum cleaners and telephones, are available in the cheaper commercial ranges in this scale. An adult or an older child would probably prefer a 1/12 scale house to take advantage of the wealth of 'collector's' miniatures which are now available. The choice is yours.

PERIOD HOUSES

If you intend to make a period house or cottage, it is often helpful to consult books on architecture to see how rooms in old houses were planned. The siting of staircases and fireplaces, the height of ceilings and size of rooms varied enormously from century to century. Building materials varied from area to area – for example, Cotswold stone, Devon cob or Cornish granite – as houses were generally built of the materials which were available locally. The size, style and placement of windows and doors changed as the fashions in building changed. A Tudor cottage would have smallish windows, often irregular in size and position because they were put in where they were needed and where they would fit between the upright timbers of the cottage. The fashion in the eighteenth century was for symmetry, with windows of equal sizes placed at regular intervals either side of a central front door. During Victorian times, as the land in towns became scarce and expensive, the tall, narrow town house with basement and attic became the general rule. Those elegant houses built in squares in the West End of London for the rich and fashionable, or the meaner versions in North or East London, were all designed to occupy the minimum area of land.

An historically accurate dolls' house can be a very satisfying project, involving research into architecture, interior decorating and furniture. It does, however, have some drawbacks. The first of these is the amount of time required for researching and tracking down exactly the right materials for the house. The purist finds that he cannot accept paper bricks and tiles, that greenish bottle glass simply does not exist in this scale, and that an inlaid marble floor is quite beyond his means! The most irritating aspect of building a completely accurate period dolls' house is probably the limitation on the furnishings and accessories you can put in it. It is frustrating to find a perfect miniature oil lamp or warming pan, and then to realise that it is useless because such things did not exist at the time your house was built.

However, dolls' houses are dream houses and for the majority of dolls'-house builders, historical accuracy is not a major consideration. We tend to pick a period, perhaps Victorian or Georgian, and aim for the flavour of the period rather than complete accuracy, allowing ourselves licence over such things as warming pans and four-poster beds. Perhaps the best of all possible worlds would be to build a period house which is now inhabited by a modern family and has been converted and modernised just as much or as little as you please. In this house the colour television could sit happily by the inglenook fireplace.

Fig 1 A few of the many styles to consider when planning your house

SHOPS

It is also worth considering at this planning stage whether a shop with living accommodation would suit you better than a house. If the building is small, with the shop on the ground floor, the living space would be limited unless you decide to have three storeys. A shop can be fun, both for the maker of the stock, who would find here an outlet for things that have no place in an ordinary house, and for the owner, perhaps a child for whom the shop doubles the play value. A Victorian draper's shop with elaborately trimmed bonnets, bolts of fabric, laces, ribbons and tiny dresses on dummies would give enormous satisfaction to the needlewoman, who could also turn her talents to the ruffled, quilted and embroidered furnishings of the apartments upstairs. A modern greengrocer's or baker's shop could be stocked with items modelled in clay or breadpaste – an ideal outlet for children's modelling talents. A miniature antique shop is another answer to the ancient versus modern dilemma, modern apartments upstairs and the shop downstairs providing the perfect setting for all the old-fashioned things which have no place in a modern house.

Fig 2 Consider a cottage or a shop

CASTLES

Consider also building a castle; the basic structure need be no more complicated than a dolls' house – a box-shaped house, given battlements, lancet windows and a Gothic door, painted or papered the appropriate grey stone colour. With most castles, the interiors are far more impressive than the exteriors, where the grim grey stone makes a marvellous background for glowing velvets, polished wood and tapestries. The imagination of the builder could run riot, devising heraldic banners, rich furnishings and miniature suits of armour. There might be a great hall with a stone fireplace, furnished with a massive table, carved chairs and tapestries. Upstairs could be a bedchamber with a four-poster bed, carved clothes chest and hooded cradle.

Kitchen dressers in 1/16 and 1/12 show the relative sizes of both scales. The 1/16 scale is used for children's dolls' houses, but the larger 1/12 scale is now more popular

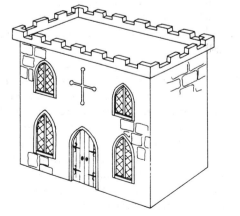

Fig 3 A simple box-shaped house can be adapted to make a castle

KITS

You might find the prospect of building a dolls' house daunting, though decorating and furnishing one appeals to you. If so, consider building a dolls' house from a kit. There are an enormous variety of kits available, ranging from tiny cottages to mansions, and most of them are very good. You will find them advertised in the specialist magazines and your local dolls'-house shop will probably stock a selection and be able to advise you on others (see Chapter 12 for further information).

CUPBOARD HOUSES

You may be more interested in making miniature furniture and furnishings, rather than the dolls' house itself, in which case a small cupboard will make a good home to display these pieces. The interior of the cupboard could be decorated in the same way as dolls'-house rooms. False doors and windows will add to

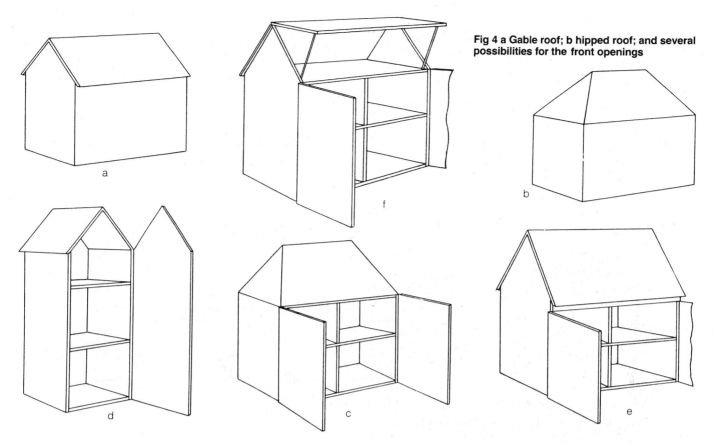

the illusion and, once the furnishings are in place, the cupboard becomes a dolls' house in the old tradition of the 'Baby houses' of the eighteenth century. (See Chapter 8.)

OUTBUILDINGS

Think also of possible outbuildings which would add interest and scope. An old cottage might have a lean-to extension used as a scullery or outside loo. A modern house often has a flat-roofed garage built onto one side. A period house might have a conservatory or stable. Porches add interest to the front of the house – a small gable porch for the front door of a modern house, or a deep, enclosed porch with seats for an old house.

PLANS

The next step is to work out some plans. These can be as detailed as you please, but simple scale drawings will suffice. The main reason for drawing plans is that dolls' houses are disproportionately tall – necessarily so, to allow access to the rooms, but annoying when designing the front of the house. You must decide how many rooms you want, how many floors, where the stairs will go, and fit all this into a basically box shape with the windows and front door in the right places.

Openings Usually a house which opens at the front is most satisfactory. A back opening allows you to make an elaborate front if you want to, but the house has to be kept in the middle of the room to allow you to get at it. The same applies to side openings; they allow for greater depth to the house, one room behind another, but access is awkward unless the house is kept in a clear space. The front-opening house can be kept with its back against a wall, and it does not have to be moved when you want to play with it. It does, however, limit you to one room depth.

Stairs Because of the extra height of the dolls'-house ceilings, you need more stairs than in a real house. As a general guide, the stairs rise at a 45° angle; therefore, to make a rise of 8in, you will need 8in depth. The stairs can rise in one flight to the next floor; or in a half-flight to a landing, followed by another half-flight doubling back or at right-angles. The amount of space needed for the staircase must be considered when planning the layout of the rooms and the depth and width of the house. Tape matchboxes together in various combinations and try them in different places, measuring the amount of space they occupy. If you find making a staircase beyond you, plan a house without stairs or fake them by having two or three steps which disappear behind a partition wall. If you have a staircase, remember that although some poetic licence is acceptable in a dolls' house, you must allow for a reasonably realistic stairwell, otherwise not only does it look wrong but the dolls will knock themselves unconscious!

Roofs There are two basic types of roof, a gable roof and a hipped roof, each with several variations. The hipped roof (Fig 4b) is often a good choice for a dolls' house because there is no overhang to hinder the opening of the front of the house, though it can be a little tricky to cut because the angles must be accurate to join the four pieces together. The attic space under a hipped roof is not usable as the roof must be fixed for proper support, but the whole roof can be hinged at the back to provide storage space. The gable roof (Fig 4a) can be placed either sideways or endwise-on to the house, depending on the width of the front; and the roof space can be used either as a room or for storage. The main problem with a gable roof is the overhang. If the gable is placed endwise (Fig 4d) with the attic used as a room, the front edges of the roof must end in line with the front edges of the side walls so that the front will hinge open freely. If the gable is placed sideways on (Fig 4f) there are several possibilities. The front section of the roof can be hinged at the ridge to lift before the fronts are opened, so that, propped up, it will provide an attic room. When closed, the fronts are held in place by the overhang of the roof.

Alternatively, a section of the front of the house at the top edge can be fixed permanently in place (Fig 4e), with the front cut to open below this fixed section. The roof can then be fixed in place with an overhang without hindering the front opening. With both styles it is sometimes effective to have the roof edge ending level with the top of the front wall (Fig 4c). This gives a rather 'tall' look to the house, but it dispenses with the overhang problem entirely. However, the type of roof depends on the style of the house and your own taste. There is no reason why your house cannot have a flat roof, dormer windows – or battlements.

Size The size of the house will depend on the scale, the number and size of the rooms and the style – the rooms in a cottage are smaller than the rooms in a Victorian town house. You will need enough space to put all the things you want in each room, but not so much that the rooms look bare even when fully furnished. The lack of a front wall limits the wall space for larger pieces. Generally, a cottage would be a little poky – a double bed, a washstand, a chest of drawers and the room was almost full – though a Victorian drawing room cluttered with furniture and knick-knacks still left enough space to move around in a crinoline!

Gauge the size of your rooms by the size of 'real' rooms, and if in doubt, allow more space rather than less. It is very frustrating not to have enough room for all the things you want to put in the house.

Drawing plans By this time you will either be thoroughly confused, or you will have a fairly clear idea of the kind of house you want. If the former, think about it some more: eventually it will all fall into place in your mind, and you will be ready to draw some plans (Fig 5).

A scale drawing of the front of the house is a good idea, lining up the windows with the rooms behind them and positioning the front door. Interior plans will need to show the depth, width and height of the rooms, position of stairs, stairwells, interior doorways and any windows on side walls.

If you intend to use commercial doors, windows or stairs rather than making your own, these should be considered in your plans. You may need to adjust the ceiling height to fit a commercial staircase or make larger or smaller holes to accommodate ready-made windows and doors.

As the exact measurements of rooms, ceiling heights, roof pitches, etc, are a matter of individual taste, the following sizes are offered only as a guide. In the 1/12 scale: the ground-floor ceiling is about 10in high, the first-floor ceiling about 9-10in high, and a room 14in square is fairly large. In the 1/16 scale: the ground-floor ceiling is about 8in high, the first floor about 7-8in high, and a room 10in square in this scale is a good size. Although the ceilings need to be high enough for you to see into the rooms without peering, too high a ceiling completely distorts the proportions. As an indication of size when planning doorways, stairwells and windows, the 'people' who live in a 1/12 house are about 5½-6in tall and the 'people' in a 1/16 house are 4¼-4½in tall.

A solemn warning at this stage: however meticulous your plans, dolls' houses have a way of developing personalities of their own. They never turn out exactly as designed!

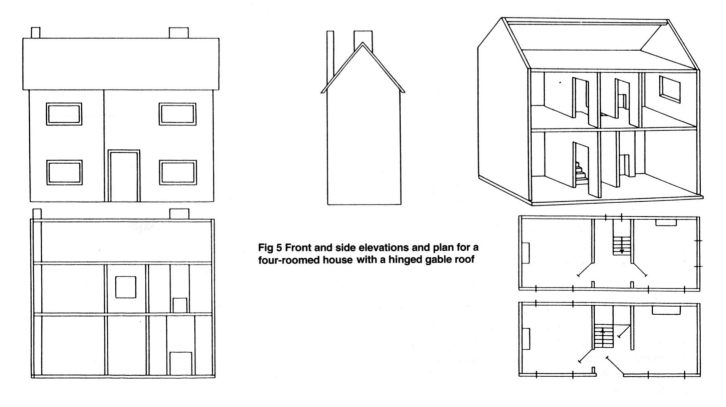

Fig 5 Front and side elevations and plan for a four-roomed house with a hinged gable roof

2 BUILDING

MATERIALS

The best material for building dolls' houses is plywood. This is available from DIY stores and builders' merchants in a range of qualities. Choose the best quality you can afford – preferably birch-faced marine ply, as cheap plywood can warp and splinter and is difficult to work with.

If you are building in 1/12 scale, you will need ⅜in (9mm) plywood for walls and floors and ⅛in (3mm) for the roof. In 1/16 scale, walls and floors should be made in ¼in (6mm) ply and roofs in ⅛in (3mm).

When you buy the plywood, check it carefully, make sure that it is as flat and un-warped as possible by sighting along all four edges. Choose pieces which have good smooth surfaces.

Most dolls'-house suppliers sell a range of 1/12 scale DIY components for housebuilding, including staircases, doors and windows, fireplace surrounds and chimney pots, and wood mouldings for skirting, cornice and architraves. These range from simple and inexpensive to very fine miniatures including windows which open and close, and stairs with proper treads, risers and stringers. There is a large choice of styles suitable for houses of different periods, from imposing Georgian front doors with pilasters and fanlights to small casement windows for cottages. There are also door, window and staircase kits available for those on a tighter budget, and a range of simple plastic fittings for 1/16 scale houses.

If you intend to use these commercial items rather than make your own, it is sensible to choose them before you begin building so you can ensure that everything fits. You may need to adjust a ceiling height, enlarge or reduce door and window holes or make a wider chimney breast to accommodate a fireplace surround. Ready-made windows usually have removable perspex glazing, ready-made doors can usually be re-hung to open on the other side, and staircases can usually be cut down to fit a lower ceiling height.

If you intend to make your own doors, windows and staircase, obeche or bass wood, balsa and wood strip can be found at some dolls'-house shops and in art and craft shops; and dowelling and triangular beading are available from DIY stores. Thin perspex for glazing windows is available from model and hobby shops and from picture framers. (See also the list of suppliers on page 186.)

ASSEMBLY

Draw the outlines of the house pieces onto the plywood using a sharp pencil and ruler, with space between each piece to allow for the thickness of the saw cut. Take care to get the lines straight, the right-angles exact and the measurements precise as this will save time and energy later. Draw in the window holes, doorways and stairwell. Mark each piece for identification, ie back, front, left side etc. Cut the pieces with a saw, aiming for a clean cut on the marked lines. Clean the edges of each piece with sandpaper or a small plane, taking care not to alter the dimensions of the pieces.

If you are using anything other than birch-faced ply, sand all the surfaces thoroughly before assembly. To cut the doorways, windows and stairwell, drill several holes side-by-side in each corner of the area to be cut out, and make a hole large enough to insert a keyhole saw by chiselling the holes together (Fig 6). Use the keyhole saw to cut along the lines you have drawn. By sawing on the lines, you then need the minimum amount of sanding to give a clean, smooth edge. Any awkward corners or curves are best cut with a fretsaw inserted through a hole drilled in a corner.

When all the house pieces are cut, with doors, windows and stairwells cut out in the relevant places, try the assembly by taping the various pieces together with masking tape. Check that floors fit closely and partition walls fit snugly together. Do not worry about small gaps, as these can be filled later. When you are satisfied that your pieces fit well together, sand all rough edges smooth and you are ready to assemble the house.

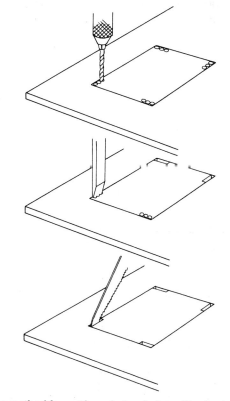

Fig 6 The method for cutting window holes with a keyhole saw

A selection of the materials and simple tools needed to build the dolls' houses in the book

Fig 7 The assembly of a simple four-roomed house showing the floor, partition wall and ridgepole in position

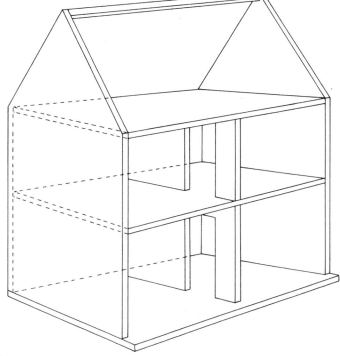

It is usually easiest to assemble the exterior of the house first – the back wall, side walls, base and top ceiling. We have found that glueing and pinning works well, using white woodworkers' glue and veneer pins, and it is a good idea to reinforce the corners with small screws. Fix the first side wall to the base, ensuring that the back edge of the wall is lined up with the back edge of the base and the wall is at a right-angle to the base. Fit the back into the right-angle made by the side wall and base, then fix the other side wall in place. Fit the top ceiling between the side and back walls.

FLOORS AND PARTITION WALLS
When the exterior is assembled, use a ruler and pencil to mark on the inside and outside of the three walls, ceiling and base the lines where the floors and partition walls occur. Follow these guidelines to ensure that the floors and walls are fixed accurately when you fit the interior.

Floors and partition walls can be inserted in several ways.

1 If the partition walls occur in the same place on each floor, put the partition wall in first, glueing and pinning

through the top ceiling, base and back wall. A cornice made of picture-frame moulding with the back planed flat, or similar, can be glued into each room at ceiling height, mitring the corners (Fig 8a). The floors are then glued and slotted in to rest on the cornice. (This method is used in the Victorian town house.)

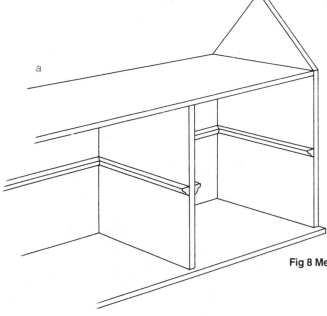

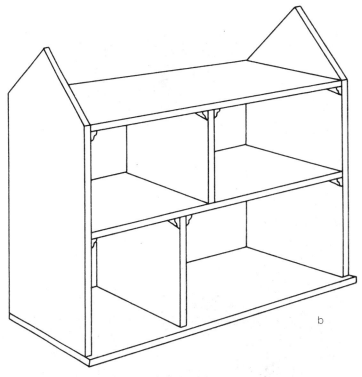

Fig 8 Methods for fixing the floors and partition walls using cornice ledges

2 Alternatively, if the partition walls occur in the same place on each floor but you do not wish to have cornices, cross-halving the floor and partition wall provides a strong method of putting both pieces in together. To cross-halve, cut a slot the same thickness as the wood to a point half-way across the partition wall at ceiling height, and half-way across the floor where it meets the partition wall. The two pieces are then interlocked (Fig 9) and put into the house together, glueing and pinning through the base, top ceiling and back,

Fig 9 Cross-halving the floor and partition wall together

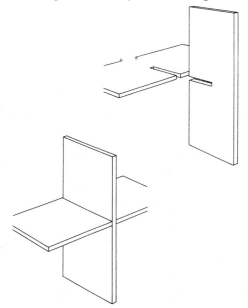

into the floor and partition. This is only successful when it is well done, and a snug fit of the two pieces is essential. (This method is used in the Tudor cottage.)

3 If the partition walls occur in different places on each floor (or if there is only one room on each floor), then the floor is put in first. This can be done with or without a cornice 'ledge' to rest the floor on, but if a cornice is used, small notches must be made to allow the partition walls to slot into place. Glue and pin the floor through the sides and back walls, then slot the partition walls in place, glueing and pinning through base, top, ceiling and back wall (Fig 8b).

It is easier to position the floor accurately if the ceiling height is marked carefully on the inside and outside of the house on all three walls, so that the floor lines up with the marks when it is put in place.

ROOFS

The roof of the house is usually fixed in place next, and again, depending on the type of roof, there are several methods.

Hipped roof (see Fig 4b)   The trickiest part of making a hipped roof is cutting it. The front and back pieces should be cut first, the top edges chamfered and the two pieces taped along this top edge. Tape these in place on the top of the house while the angles of the side pieces are measured, cut and tried in place. When the four pieces fit together properly, chamfer the edges where they join, glue and then tape over the joins. The roof is now ready to fix in place. (This method is used in the antique shop.)

Gable roof (see Fig 4a)   If the gable roof is to end at the top edge of the house with no over-hang, nor hinge, then it is relatively simple to fix. The two roof pieces are chamfered at the top edges where they join, and glued and taped together.

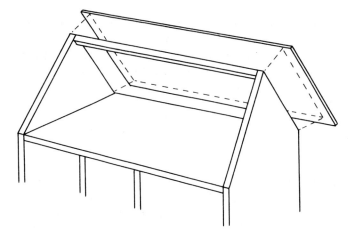

Fig 10 The back roof pieces fixed to the ridgepole and the gable-end walls

If the roof is wide, then the additional support of a ridgepole may be needed (Fig 10). This is a piece of ½in square or triangular beading screwed across the top between the gable ends of the house. The roof pieces are then laid over the ridgepole, and glued and pinned to the ridgepole and the tops of the gable-end walls.

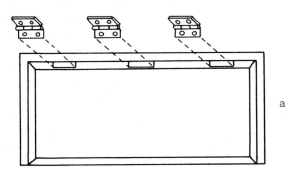

Fig 11 The front roof section, framed with wood-strip and hinged to the ridgepole

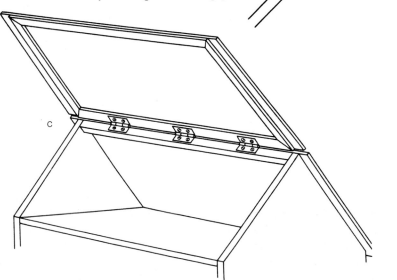

Hinged gable roof (see Fig 4f) With this method, a ridgepole of ½in beading is screwed between the tops of the gable ends. The back section of the roof is then glued and pinned flush to the ridgepole and the top of the gable-end walls (Fig 10). Before fitting the front, make a frame of ½ x ¼in wood-strip and fix it onto the underside of the section. The frame should be flush with the front edge, but set in about ⅜in at the sides and top edges. This frame gives rigidity to the roof section and provides a sufficient thickness to screw the hinges into (Fig 11a). To hinge the front roof in place, use either three hinges or a continuous length of piano hinge as preferred. The hinges should be rebated into both the ridgepole and the frame (Fig 11b) and the roof section fixed in place (Fig 11c). (This method is used in the Tudor cottage.)

Fixed overhang roof (see Fig 4e) When you wish to fix the roof permanently with an overhang at the front, it is necessary to open the front below this overhang. Therefore, to avoid a nasty gap at the top of the front wall, fix a piece the same depth as the overhang across the top edge of the front of the house. The roof is then attached in the same way as before, glued and pinned to the ridgepole and the top of the gable walls, and the opening front(s) of the house are cut to fit below the fixed piece. (This method is used in the modern house.)

CHIMNEY STACKS AND POTS

Chimney stacks and pots on the dolls'-house roof should conform to the chimney breasts used in the house (see Fireplaces). Modern houses need not have fireplaces or chimneys, but most older houses have both, even though the fireplace might be bricked up.

On a flat roof, a fixed gable roof or a hipped roof, the chimney stack can be made by cutting a block of balsa wood to the size required and notching the lower edge to fit the roof angle. Obviously the chimney stack should be sited above the chimney breast. On a hinged gable roof, where this method is impracticable, it is simplest to site the chimney breast and the stack towards the back of the house, so that the chimney stack can be fixed to the back part of the roof which does not lift. The bottom of the stack is cut to the same angle as the roof and stuck in place before or after the roof has been decorated.

The chimney stack should be brick-papered or painted before fixing in place, and a number of chimney pots appropriate to the number of fireplaces should be stuck in place on top of the stack. Large wooden beads which come in a variety of shapes make excellent chimney pots – they should be painted with matt terracotta paint for a realistic colour. Alternatively, you might prefer to model pots in Das or clay.

Exterior chimney breasts should be made tall enough to form the stack in one with the breast, merely needing the appropriate number of pots.

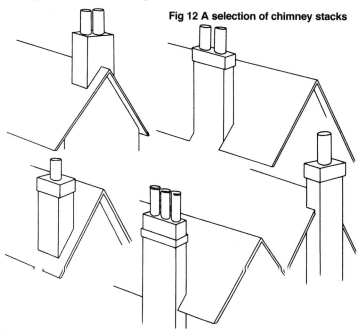

Fig 12 A selection of chimney stacks

FRONT OPENING

The front of the house can be hinged on at this stage or left until the interior of the house is completed. We generally prefer the latter, as access for decorating is simpler, and it is easier to fix the windows and door on the fronts before they are hinged. However, it is a matter of choice – the method for hinging the fronts is the same whether it is done now or later.

If yours is a tall, thin house, the front can open in one piece; but if the house is wider, it is better to cut the front into two hinged sections. The weight of a wide front opening can cause the hinges to sag, or even topple the house. If the front door is central, make the join to one side rather than trying to line up an exact fit through the door frame.

A large house needs larger hinges – usually 2in long by ½in wide, which should be recessed into the wood to give a good fit to the front. For a small house, 1in hinges are usually sufficient, but it is advisable to glue both the hinge and the screws in place with super-glue for extra strength, as the screws are essentially very small. Small cupboard hooks can be used to hold the fronts closed.

Lift-off fronts If you find the idea of hinging the front to the house too daunting, a lift-off front is a simple alternative. Choose a flat piece of plywood, and cut the front to fit in one piece. When the decoration is completed, the front is held in place by two or three cupboard hooks screwed into each side of the house.

STAIRS

There are various methods for making stairs, ranging from the craftsman's miniature with treads, risers and stringers, to amateurish matchboxes covered in brown paper. The method described here is one we have found simple but effective.

Use triangular beading (obtainable from most DIY shops), approximately ½in wide for a 1/16 scale house and ¾in for a 1/12 scale house, and cut into lengths the width of the staircase. Take care that these lengths are accurately cut. Glue the lengths, closely butted together, onto a piece of ⅛in thick obeche wood – when raised to a 45° angle they form quite realistic stairs. If a half-landing is used, this is generally the same width as the stairs. The top stair of the bottom flight and the bottom stair of the top flight, with edges chamfered flat, are stuck to the half-landing. The top edge of the top flight, chamfered flat, is glued firmly into the stair-well. If the stairs run up against a wall, they can be glued to the wall for extra stability, but if you wish to paint, stain, varnish or polish them, do it before you stick them in. It is also easier to carpet the stairs before you put them in place and to paint or paper the house before they are in, so we recommend that you make the staircase, check that it fits well but do not fix it in place at this stage.

It is simple, though fiddly, to make banister rails and posts from fine square or round dowelling. Cut and stick a newel post in place at the top and bottom of the flight of stairs. Cut a handrail to fit snugly between the posts and glue it firmly in place. Then cut each banister rail with the top edge at a 45° angle to fit between the stair tread and the handrail. If the banisters are cut, fitted and stuck in place one at a time, this should result in a good fit and a satisfactory result.

The stairs can be left open underneath, the flat obeche-wood backing providing a smooth finish for painting or papering; or they can be boxed in with a partition wall. The boxed-in area, provided with a door, forms a good under-stairs cupboard or even a loo.

A skirting board up the staircase finishes it properly. The simplest method is to cut a length of obeche wood the depth of the stair tread and stick it along the outside edge of the staircase. (This method is used in the Tudor cottage. See also the open-plan staircase in the modern house.)

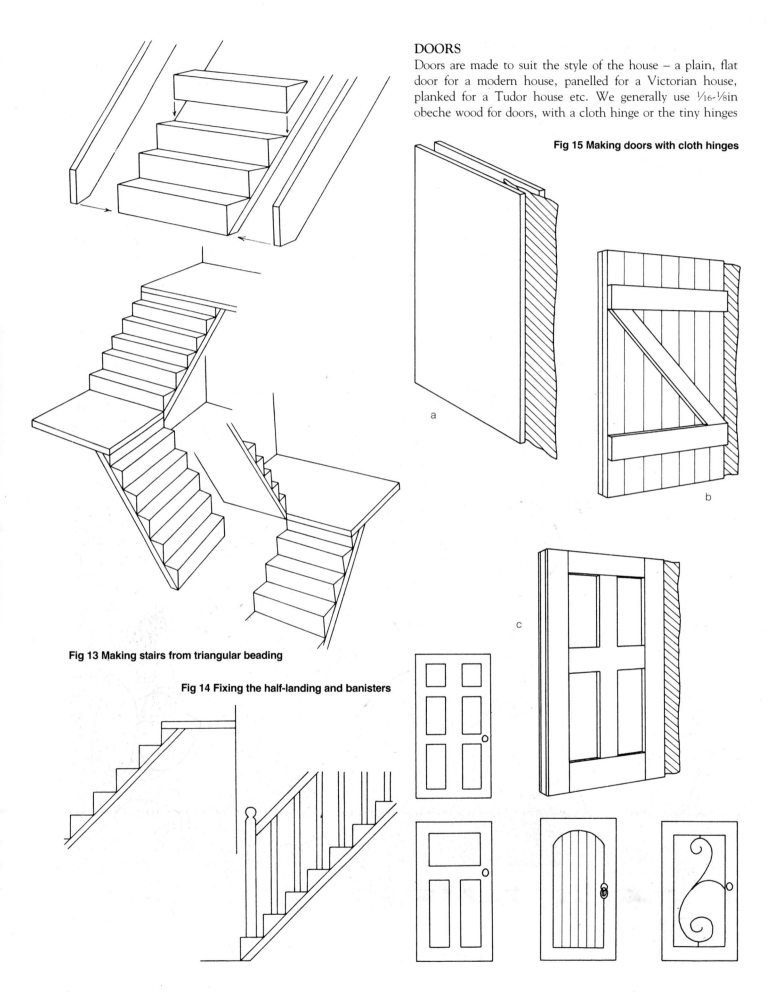

DOORS

Doors are made to suit the style of the house – a plain, flat door for a modern house, panelled for a Victorian house, planked for a Tudor house etc. We generally use 1/16-1/8in obeche wood for doors, with a cloth hinge or the tiny hinges

Fig 15 Making doors with cloth hinges

a

b

c

Fig 13 Making stairs from triangular beading

Fig 14 Fixing the half-landing and banisters

sold for dolls' houses. When making and hanging doors, remember to allow sufficient clearance to accommodate floor-coverings.

Plain door (Fig 15a)   This is made of two pieces of obeche wood, ¹⁄₁₆-¹⁄₈in thick as required. Cut the two pieces to the exact size of the doorway hole. If using a cloth hinge, cut a strip of black cotton tape about 1½in wide, a fraction shorter than the door. Stick the two door pieces together with the tape sandwiched between them, allowing about an inch of tape to protrude along one side. When the door pieces are firmly stuck, sand the edges smooth so that the door opens and closes freely. The door is hung by sticking the protruding strip of tape firmly to the wall on the side the door will open (Fig 16a).

The fireplace provides a focal point for the room. The fireplace surround should be chosen to complement the period style of the house

Planked door (Fig 15b)   This is made in the same way as the plain door. When the pieces are sanded, score both sides of the door with a pointed edge such as a scissor blade to indicate the planking. The characteristic Z pieces, cut from ¹⁄₁₆in obeche wood, are then stuck to the hinged side.

Panelled door (Fig 15c)   This is made by sticking ¹⁄₁₆in panel frames to both sides of a piece of ¹⁄₈in obeche wood, sandwiching the cloth hinge between the centre wood and the panelling on one side.

Door handles can be made from beads, brass upholstery tacks, map pins or the loops of large hooks and eyes bent to 90°; alternatively, turned wood or brass handles for dolls' houses can be bought from the specialist shops.

Door frames   Door-frame mouldings are best applied after wallpapering, as this gives a neater finish. Fine picture framing, thin wood-strips or commercial dolls'-house archi-

trave, mitred at the corners and fitted flush to the edge of the doorway, looks very convincing (Fig 16c). Any raw edges can be painted or stained to match the door frame, or the doorway edges can be faced with fine wood-strip before the doors are cut to fit.

A mitre block is very useful for cutting mitred corners on door and window frames and cornices.

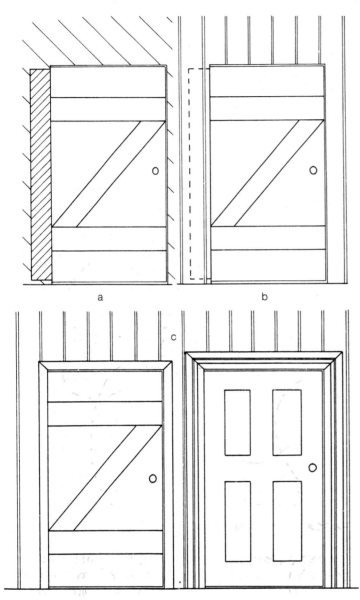

Fig 16 Fixing the cloth-hinged door in place

WINDOWS

Glazing dolls'-house windows with glass is impracticable to all but the most intrepid, but thin perspex, obtainable from art and craft shops, is an excellent substitute. It is expensive, but one square foot is enough to glaze most dolls' houses. The perspex is cut most easily by first scoring the cutting line with a Stanley knife and then cutting with a fine-bladed fretsaw. Cut the windows to the exact size of the window hole (a cardboard template makes this easier).

To fix the windows in place, glue a frame of fine square beading on the inside edge of the window hole, insert the 'glass' and sandwich with a similar frame of fine square beading glued to the outside edge of the window hole (Fig 17).

Window frames, again, are better applied after the wallpaper for a neater finish and can be made of the same moulding or wood-strip used for the door frames.

Glazing bars, appropriate to the house, should be stuck to both sides of the 'glass' for the best effect. Use a glue such as UHU sparingly and leave until tacky before sticking the bars in place – if they are to be painted or stained, this is best done before sticking to avoid getting paint on the windows.

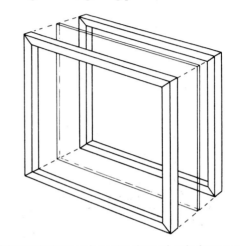

Fig 17 Making windows using mitred wood-strip frames and perspex

FIREPLACES

As in a real house, the fireplace in a dolls' house provides a focal point for the room and can give it a lot of character. Again the style of the house is one of the main considerations in deciding the kind of fireplace to install. The chimney breast could be external (Fig 18c), as in a lot of Victorian houses, or internal, which breaks up the box shape of the room. The fireplace can be sited on the back or side wall, but give the site careful thought – a chimney breast is not likely to occur in a downstairs room in the same place as a window in the room above! A corner fireplace can be an interesting feature, again breaking up the box shape of a room (Fig 18b).

An easy method for making chimney breasts is to use a block of balsa wood the width, height and depth of the required chimney breast. The fireplace opening is cut out with a Stanley knife and the chimney breast is then stuck firmly to the wall. A small piece of brick paper covering the inside and back of the opening adds realism. This method can also be used to make the large fireplace needed for period kitchens, where the chimney breast is wider and deeper and the opening larger to accommodate the kitchen range.

The fireplace surround again depends on the style of the house (Fig 19) – a simple beam for a medieval fireplace, or an elaborate marble chimney piece for a Victorian house. Most kinds can be made of obeche wood, stained or painted to represent other materials if necessary, or a stone or brick surround can be modelled from Das or similar clay. A brick or tiled hearth adds realism, and can be made from paper, clay or the tiny tiles sold for dolls' houses.

It is a good idea not to finish the fireplace until the room is

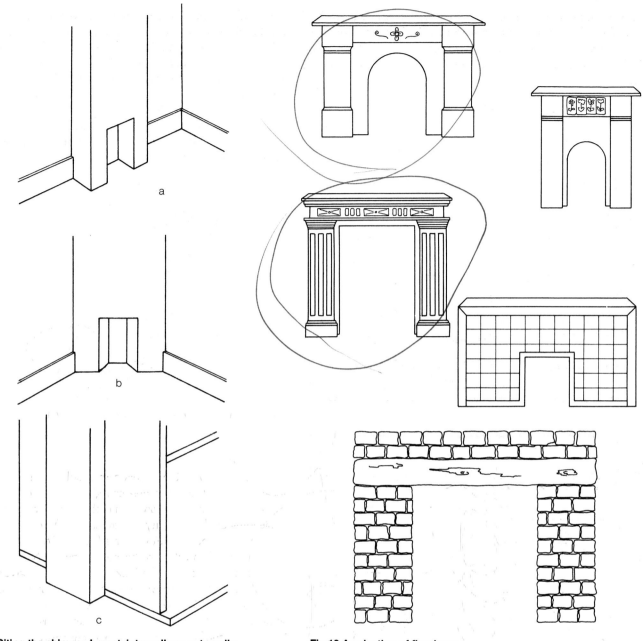

Fig 18 Siting the chimney breast, internally or externally

Fig 19 A selection of fireplaces

decorated as it is often easier to decide then on the style of fireplace which best suits the room. It is also neater to fix the fireplace surround after the room is papered.

SKIRTING BOARDS AND PICTURE RAILS

Simple skirting boards can be cut from thin obeche wood or woodstrip or choose commercial mouldings which are appropriate for the house – deep in old houses, smaller in modern ones. These too are best stuck in place after the room

has been papered and floored; and they should be stained or painted before being fitted. If the back wall is skirted first, the skirting on the side walls can be butted firmly against this, dispensing with any need to mitre the corners.

If your house requires picture rails, these can be made of fine dowelling or moulding or thin wood-strip, painted or stained before fixing and, again, stuck in place after the room is papered.

3 DECORATING AND LIGHTING

When planning a decorating scheme for your period dolls' house it is helpful to consult books on domestic architecture and interior design. Tastes and fashions have changed a great deal through the centuries, and correct details are an important part of a realistic period effect.

For example, mellow brick and oak timbers, doors and window frames are typical of a Tudor house; the Georgians favoured colour-washed stucco and white paint; and the

Victorians preferred coloured brick and dark paintwork. Roofing materials ranged from thatch through red clay or stone tiles to grey slate. Of course, there were many houses which did not conform to the fashion of their time, but the simplest way to achieve a convincing period effect is to use the architectural and decorative clichés then current. A square, red-brick house with white paintwork and a fanlight above a panelled front door is immediately recognisable as a 'Queen

Anne' house. Whether it is an 'original' or the modern copy so often found on housing estates depends on how you decorate and furnish the interior! The leaflets offered by manufacturers of paints are a good source of ideas for exterior decorating schemes, showing clearly the effect of different colours on different types of house.

A modern house also benefits from planning. Fashions have changed even in the last ten years, and house magazines show up-to-the-minute trends in decorating schemes, as do the paint manufacturers' leaflets and DIY magazines. Look around your area for examples of modern houses with pleasant decorative schemes and details. A housing estate with houses of basically the same design but each decorated to its owners' taste is a catalogue of ideas – details like shutters, porches and different colours make a surprising amount of difference.

Fashions in interior decoration come and go, but the 'English country house' style remains a favourite

The interior decoration of the house should also be in keeping with its style and period, unless you have a period house inhabited by a modern family, in which case the decoration can be as modern as you please. Each period had its tastes in colours, fabrics, floor and wall coverings. The Victorians liked heavy fabrics, dark colours and an air of opulent gloom; while pastel colours, striped papers, white paint and gilding were admired in Regency times. These are generalisations but a little research will provide the details, and there are houses of most periods which are open to the public and might provide inspiration.

MATERIALS

There is a wide range of commercial papers available for decorating dolls' houses, including brick and stone patterns for exterior walls and floors, tiles and slates for roofs and patterns suitable for any period interior. Most of these are inexpensive and readily available from art and craft shops as well as dolls'-house suppliers. The finer quality wallpapers can be expensive, the sheets are small and a large room might need three or four sheets, perhaps with a border. It is well worth considering life-size wallpapers, many of which are available with tiny patterns, often more appropriate than the dolls'-house papers and which can usually be acquired as 'free samples' from DIY superstores. Two feet, torn from the roll left open for customers to help themselves to a sample, will decorate any room and you can often bring home half a dozen samples to try in situ. The finer woodchip papers are also good for rough-plastered interior and exterior walls.

Consider printing your own wallpapers on good quality drawing paper. Look at wrapping papers, you might find one with a tiny pattern, but discard anything with a shiny finish which looks quite wrong. Lightweight cotton fabrics can be backed with lightweight iron-on Vilene and pasted and hung like wallpaper, a device often found in antique dolls' houses, or consider hanging your walls with pleated or gathered fabric for a very rich effect.

A little more expensive than paper, but very effective, are the embossed 'claddings'. These are available in sheets, patterned to represent brick, stone, tile, slate or pebbledash and the texture is very realistic. These are less widely available but your local supplier may be able to help or contact Hobbys (see Stockists).

If you prefer to paint your house, the small sample pots available from DIY shops are splendid. Choose matt emulsion in whatever colour you please, and a room or the whole exterior can be decorated at a very modest cost. Consider using some of the techniques used in life-size decorating such as dragging, marbling or stencils – these can all look very effective in miniature. You might paint the exterior of your house to represent brick, using acrylic colours over an undercoat of emulsion. Rule the lines of bricks lightly in pencil and paint them in a good variety of shades of colour so that they do not look too uniform. This is easy to do, but requires patience and a steady hand. Consider also papering the house with brick paper and painting in the individual bricks in a more realistic variety of colours.

For painting woodwork, household gloss is too heavy so we

prefer water-based acrylic colours or enamel model paints, available from art shops. Matt or satin finish is more subtle than gloss. Alternatively, you might stain the woodwork using household woodstain and finish with wax polish.

As a general rule, we recommend choosing the colours and materials for the whole house before you start decorating, to ensure that they harmonise, and to prevent a disappointing result from badly matched colours and patterns. This chapter offers ideas and methods for interior and exterior decoration, but the real deciding factor in any decorating scheme is your own taste. Fortunately, any mistakes in this scale are cheaply and easily rectified.

EXTERIOR

Whether you intend to paint or paper the exterior of the house, you need a good, smooth surface to work on so don't skimp on the sanding. Wipe away all traces of dust with a slightly-damp cloth.

Painting Paint the walls before the window and door frames. Use small household paint brushes to apply two or three coats of matt emulsion paint. Allow each coat to dry thoroughly, and sand lightly with fine-grade sandpaper if necessary, before applying the next coat. Paint the woodwork with small artists' paintbrushes and acrylic or enamel colours.

Papering Paint the woodwork before papering. Use household wallpaper paste to apply exterior papers and claddings – apply a coat of paste to the wall (or roof) first, then paste and apply the paper. Take care to line up rows of bricks or tiles, especially where a front opens in two sections.

Fig 20 Timbered effect for a Tudor house using veneer strips

Timbering If yours is a Tudor-style house and you want a half-timbered effect, this can be done by cutting strips of wood veneer (available from hobbies shops). Stain to the appropriate dark-oak colour and stick to the painted or brick-papered house with UHU or similar glue in a half-timbered or box-frame design. If the 'beams' are not too straight and even they look better (Fig 20).

Roof tiles Realistic roof tiles can be made simply, though it is a tiresome process. Cut strips of thin cardboard about ¾in wide, then make ½in deep cuts at ½in intervals along the lengths. Stick the strips to the roof, starting at the bottom edge and overlapping each layer by about ¼in over the one before (Fig 21). The roof is then given a coat of poster or acrylic paint – a mixture of scarlet, yellow and brown makes a good red roof-tile colour. When the paint is dry, a few individual tiles should be given slightly different colours. This method can also be used to make a scallop-tiled roof by cutting scallops along one edge of the cardboard strips and applying them in the same fashion. The same applies to stone roof tiles, cut larger at the eaves and smaller at the ridge. A coat of matt polyurethane spray varnish gives protection and makes it easier to clean.

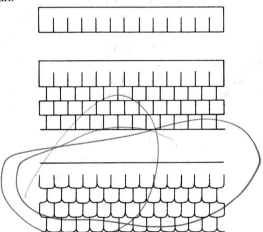

Fig 21 Cutting and fixing cardboard roof tiles

Thatching A thatched roof is difficult, but it can be done by sticking layers of natural raffia or bleached coir to the roof until a sufficient depth has been built up. Thatching is not recommended for a hinged roof – it is really only suitable on a house with a fixed roof and a fixed front top edge.

Bargeboarding Bargeboarding makes a nice finish on gable-end walls. Plain bargeboards can be made from picture-frame moulding, or more elaborate boards cut from obeche wood with a fretsaw. The boards are stuck in place under the roof edges (Fig 22), after painting or staining.

Plaques A small plaque of engraved metal, carved wood or clay, with the housebuilders' initials and the date, fixed to the front of the house adds a nice finishing touch.

INTERIOR

Interior decorating in a dolls' house is as much a matter of taste

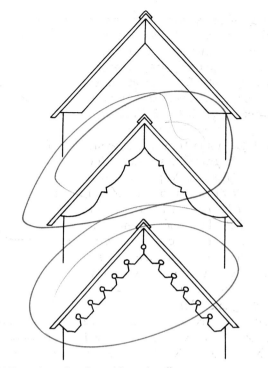

Fig 22 Bargeboarding for gable-end walls

as in a real house, but there are a few differences which are covered in this section. The most obvious difference is that an open dolls' house is viewed as a whole, and the effect is therefore usually more pleasing if the colours and patterns used in the individual rooms harmonise with each other.

Painting Before you begin decorating, especially if you intend to paint the walls, fill any gaps with a filler such as Polyfilla. Papering the walls with lining paper provides a really good surface to paint on, and hides any minor defects in construction. We have found that ordinary household emulsion paint with a matt finish works very well, using one or two coats as required. Unless the house is modern in style, avoid brilliant white as it looks quite wrong in any period house. Magnolia or ivory give a much softer 'white'. This also applies to ceilings: the quality of light reflected by brilliant white is too harsh and garish for any old-fashioned house. A similar rule applies to the gloss paintwork for an old house. We generally use acrylic paint or enamels, mixing white and cream or ivory gloss to get the right colour. Alternatively, the woodwork could be stained.

Wallpapering Wallpapering is simplest if you cover each wall in one piece. Make a paper template for each wall, marking around doorways, windows, and fireplaces. This will enable you to fit the wallpaper exactly and match any pattern, if necessary, with the minimum of fiddling. Start with the back wall, lining up the paper neatly at the ceiling, or where the picture rail occurs if you intend to put one in. Overlap the paper about ½in onto the side walls and floor and press it firmly into the corners. Then paper the side walls, again ensuring a neat edge along the top, papering just into the back corners, and overlapping the floor by about ½in.

This overlap onto the floor gives a clean edge when the

floor-covering is in place, which is particularly important if there are no skirting boards to cover little deficiencies in this area. If, however, you intend not to use a floor-covering, but rather to score and stain a wooden floor to represent floorboards, then obviously you will need to cut the wallpaper to end at the bottom of the wall.

Use a household wallpaper paste to stick the wallpaper, as glues and gums are not efficient. Apply a coat of paste to the walls and allow it to dry out. Then paste and apply the paper. If you find once it is in place that you dislike it, it is relatively simple to peel it off before it dries and start again.

Floor-coverings Unless you have a wooden floor which you intend to score and stain as floorboards, you will need some kind of floor-covering, even if it is later mostly concealed by rugs. One of the simplest finishes is plain brown wrapping paper. In an old house, with lots of rugs rather than fitted carpets, it looks very realistic.

Several of the Fablon or Contact designs make good tiles for a kitchen or bathroom. If the design is right but the colour is too bright, try toning it down with a coat of brown shoe polish. Some of these designs make convincing lino floors. Cork floor tiles can be cut to fit a modern house – they are rather thick, but if used all over the house this is not noticeable. There are floor papers made for dolls' houses, rather limited in design, available from art and craft shops. They include herringbone parquet, stone flags and tile patterns.

You could make your own floor-coverings, using thin card or paper with the design drawn in ink or paint. A good but rather expensive wooden planked floor can be made with the sticky-backed-veneer tape sold in DIY shops. This tape looks effective, can be stained and is easy to use, but make sure it is well stuck down. We made one impressive floor with the illustrations cut from the front of packets of woodblock flooring panels – they were just the right scale for the miniature woodblock floor. There are similar pictures of tiles or floorings in the leaflets advertising these products.

Paper floorboards A simple but effective method for making a 'wooden' floor requires a large sheet of good quality drawing paper and woodstain in the appropriate colour – we usually use light oak. Cover the work surface with several sheets of newspaper. Using a soft ½in wide artist's paintbrush, paint the woodstain onto the paper, working down the length of the paper in one direction only until the sheet is covered in stain. Leave for a few minutes then wipe off surplus stain with kitchen paper or tissue, again working down the length of the paper in one direction only, and leave to dry thoroughly. When the paper is dry, mark the floorboards in pencil with a ruler and score the marked lines with an empty ballpoint pen or stylus. Apply a coat of wax furniture polish and buff to a soft sheen. The floorpaper can then be cut to fit and stuck to the floor with wallpaper paste. This method can also be used to make a woodblock or parquet floor – if you have the patience!

Carpets Fitted carpets can be made from various materials. Felt is simple, but beware of over-bright colours. Fine

Georgian style interior decor in pastel colours with a printed tapestry and wood-stained paper floorboards

needlecord, printed or plain, looks good. Lightweight wool, denim or heavy printed cotton are all suitable. For a really plush effect, velvet is excellent. Take care to use a fabric which is not too thick – it will look clumsy and you will have trouble opening doors.

To make the fabric easier to manage, back it with lightweight iron-on Vilene, which will prevent the edges fraying and make it easier to cut and stick. Where possible, cut the carpet with a selvedge at the front edge. Use double-sided tape or UHU applied around all edges, to stick the carpet to the floor. Stair carpet can be made of any of the previously mentioned fabrics but felt is particularly good as it does not fray and tucks firmly into the angle of each stair. Also worth considering for stair carpet are woven braids and ribbons; if these are the right width and have a suitable pattern they look convincing. Simple stair-rods can be made by inserting black or brass-coloured hair grips, straight edge uppermost, after the carpet is stuck to the stairs. See also ideas for printed rugs in Chapter 6.

CURTAINS

When choosing materials for dolls'-house curtains, look out for fabrics which are fine but quite heavy. Natural fabrics like cotton or silk are usually better than crease-resistant man-made fabrics such as crimplene and polyesters; well-washed cotton is usually very good. It is difficult to get such small curtains to hang convincingly, but given patience it can be done and is well worth the effort.

It is realistic if the curtains open and close, so cut them large enough to cover the window when drawn, but not so large that they make big bunches either side of the window when open. The following method is the one we use for making and hanging curtains.

Hem the sides with as fine a hem as possible, and along the bottom edge with a slightly deeper hem. Turn the top edge over to form a casing and sew it down. Use a piece of fine brass tubing, fine dowelling or thin wood-strip as a curtain pole or track and thread it through the casing (Fig 23a). The curtain pole or track should be wider than the window so that, when open, the curtains hang clear of the window rather than obscuring it. Gather the curtains to each side of the pole and steam them with an iron to set the folds. To fix the track to the wall, glue tiny blocks of wood or square wooden beads to the wall, above and to either side of the window, then glue the ends of the curtain track to these wooden blocks (Fig 23b).

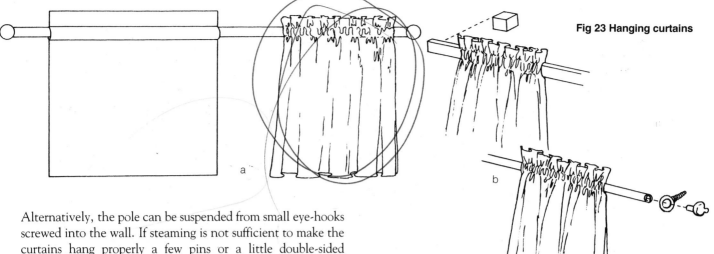

Fig 23 Hanging curtains

Alternatively, the pole can be suspended from small eye-hooks screwed into the wall. If steaming is not sufficient to make the curtains hang properly a few pins or a little double-sided sellotape will hold them in place and can be removed when they have given up the fight.

As an alternative to this method, the curtains could be hung from gilt jewellery jump rings as curtain rings, from a fine brass or dowelling curtain pole with small beads or brass knobs each end for finials.

Café-style curtains hung in tiers can look good; or the curtains can be looped back to each side of the window with narrow ribbon. Lace curtains can be made and hung in the same ways as the heavier curtains, either on their own for a light, airy effect or under heavier curtains as in Victorian houses. Wide petticoat-edging lace, left ungathered, also looks well as lace curtains. Lace curtains give the dolls' house a homely air, especially from the outside.

Curtain frills and pelmets can also be added where appropriate. A box pelmet can be cut from obeche wood and stained or painted and stuck to the wall; a frill to match the curtains can be stuck to a small block of wood fixed on the wall above the curtains (Fig 24).

When planning the curtains, make sure that the chosen fabric harmonises with the wallpaper, and consider using the same fabric somewhere else in the room, perhaps as a bedspread or cushion – this co-ordinated effect enhances the look of the room enormously.

ROLLER BLINDS
Roller blinds are an appropriate alternative or addition to curtains, not only for a modern house, but also for Victorian and Edwardian houses.

Fig 24 The style of the curtains should be chosen to suit the house

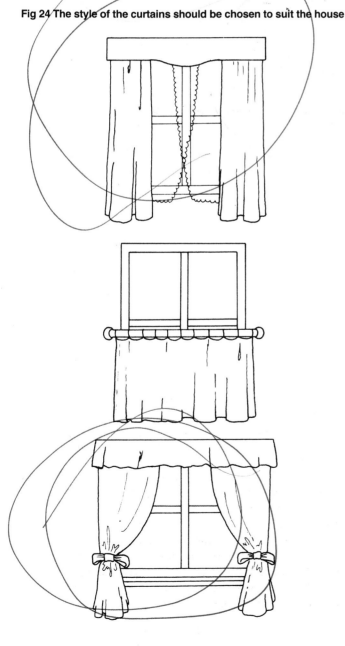

Fig 24b Simple roller blind, made of fabric, hung from a dowelling roller on small hooks

To make the roller, cut a length of dowelling approximately ⅛in thick the same width as the window, and push a small gimp pin into each end. The blind is best made from a firmly woven cotton fabric; dark blue, green or cream for the period effect, virtually anything you please for a modern house. Cut a rectangle of fabric to fit the window, soak it in wallpaper paste and allow it to dry flat. When the fabric is stiff and dry, stick the top edge to the roller with UHU or similar glue, then roll the blind tightly around the roller. The blind is hung by putting the two gimp pins in the roller through small eye-hooks screwed one each side of the window. Made by this method, the blind will pull down, but it will, of course, have to be re-rolled by hand.

If you are making a blind for a wide window, it may need the extra weight of a small strip of wood pushed through a narrow casing at the bottom edge. Old-fashioned blinds look good with a narrow cream-lace edging at the hem. A small cord made from cotton thread with a tiny bead on the end makes an effective pull.

FRONTS

When decorating the interior of the house, do not forget the inside of the fronts. These are usually dealt with in one of two ways. Either the fronts are divided into sections to correspond with the rooms behind them, and each section is decorated to match the corresponding room; or the entire inside front is painted or papered as one piece, taking one of the colours or papers used in the house or a different but harmonising colour or paper. The first method looks well on a tall narrow house with one room on each floor, but it can look rather 'bitty' on a larger house, where the second method is usually better.

Front edges The front edges of walls and floors can be painted or stained, papered with brick paper, or faced with woodstrip.

When the house is decorated outside and inside, the fronts can be hinged in place and the house is ready to furnish.

LIGHTING

Most people want their dolls' house to have lights but often find the prospect of installing them rather daunting. During the past ten years, the job has become easier with the advent of various systems designed specifically for dolls' houses. What you choose will depend on how much you want to spend – individual light fittings are relatively inexpensive, but buying sufficient does add up and the transformer is a fairly expensive item. There are light fittings available to suit any modern or period house, ranging from 'candlesticks' and 'gas lamps' to modern spotlights, so finding something appropriate for your house is not difficult. Most dolls'-house shops sell lighting systems and fittings and can advise you on installation, or refer you to someone who will install a system for you if you wish. Several suppliers, including Hobbys, (see Stockists) offer kits which include the necessary components and instructions for installation with a choice of lights.

If you intend to have lighting, it should be considered before you decorate as you may choose a system which requires the wires to be channelled under floors or copper tapes to be concealed by wallpaper. We strongly recommend that you 'shop around' and compare the prices and ease of installation of the various systems on offer, checking that the specific light fittings you prefer are compatible with the system you want to use.

The two most popular systems currently available use wire and copper tape. With the wire system, each light fitting has its own tiny bulb attached to a length of wire with a miniature plug on the other end. The plugs (which can be removed so that the wires can be fed through holes in the walls) are connected to multiple sockets, usually on the back of the house, which in turn are connected to the transformer and the mains.

With the copper tape system, a double run of narrow copper tape is applied to the walls of the house inside, where it is concealed by wallpaper, or outside, and the wires from each light are soldered or pinned into the tape. Both systems have advantages and disadvantages – the wire system is easier to install but copper tape is usually more discreet. It is a matter of individual preference but whichever you choose, the effect of a dolls' house with lights is quite magical and fully justifies the effort and expense involved in installing them.

While choosing light fittings, you might also consider the log or coal 'fires' which have flickering lights inside them and can be incorporated into your system.

Suggested Building and Decorating Guide

1 Draw all pieces on the plywood and cut out, including door, window and stairwell holes.
2 Tape pieces together to try assembly, making any necessary adjustments to ensure a good fit.
3 Assemble exterior, base, side walls, back walls and top ceiling.
4 Assemble interior floors and partition walls and fix in place.
5 Assemble the ridgepole and roof sections and fix in place.
6 Paper or paint exterior walls and front edges.
7 Paper, paint or tile the roof.
8 Hang doors and fit windows.
9 Cut and fix the chimney breasts in place. Cut and fix cornice. Fill any gaps.
10 Install lighting if required.
11 Line and paint the ceilings and painted rooms.
12 Wallpaper the rooms.
13 Fit floor-coverings.
14 Assemble, paint or stain and carpet the staircase and fix in place.
15 Stain or paint skirting boards, picture rails, door and window frames, and ceiling beams and fix in place.
16 Assemble, paint or stain and fix fireplace surrounds.
17 Paint or paper inside fronts.
18 Hinge fronts onto house and fix cupboard hook if required.

4 FIXTURES AND FITTINGS

Fireplaces, kitchen stoves and sinks and bathroom fittings are items which most people choose to buy rather than make as they have less appeal to the DIY enthusiast than furniture and are more difficult to make realistically. Most dolls'-house shops stock a wide range of fixtures in 1/12 scale suitable for modern or period houses in prices to suit all budgets and cheaper 1/16 scale items can be found in toyshops.

Fireplaces are available in most styles including Georgian basket or hob grates to complement the grander commercial 'marble' resin or plaster fireplace surrounds, and smaller Victorian fireplaces complete with surround are available to suit parlour or bedroom. When shopping, don't forget to take the measurements of your chimney breast and fireplace opening – or choose the fireplace first and build the chimney breast to accommodate it.

Kitchen ranges come in all shapes and sizes and if yours is a period house, it is worth doing a little research to find the right type. Many commercial ranges are the 'closed' type which came into use in the nineteenth century but a Georgian house will need the earlier 'open' range. There are good stoves available for 'gas' or 'electricity' from the early twentieth century to the present day, including both the older style and modern Agas.

Kitchen sinks are available in a range of sizes and the smaller ones can be used in 1/16 scale house as an alternative to a modern plastic sink. In 1/12 scale the choice is extensive, ranging from the shallow 'stone' sink found in early period houses to the deep 'Belfast' sink which came into use in the early twentieth century. Many sinks are sold complete with brick piers or wooden brackets and wooden draining boards, taps and wastepipes and most of them are inexpensive.

Bathroom suites are available in an enormous variety, from the modern plastic 1/16 scale to exquisitely detailed, transfer-printed porcelain 'Victorian' suites complete with elaborate plumbing and authentically detailed geysers.

WHITE METAL KITS

White metal kits are an excellent option for anyone who wants authenticity and realism, but would like to make their own fixtures and fittings. Phoenix Models (see Stockists) make a splendid range of kits which are available from most dolls'-house suppliers or by post. The range includes a number of period fireplaces and fenders, kitchen ranges and stoves, a pump and some excellent accessories. These kits, well-made and finished, make very impressive fixtures at a fraction of the cost of ready-made items.

The white metal kit comes with making-up instructions and is assembled with epoxy-resin or super glue (depending on how deft you are). Check the pieces and clean off any flashing before assembly and read the instructions carefully. Glue one piece at a time and allow it to dry before proceeding. Avoid putting too much pressure on the various parts as the white metal is soft and the model is not strong until it is complete. The items can be painted with enamel paints using fine artists' brushes or spray painted. Our own method for an extremely realistic finish for kitchen ranges is as follows. Spray the assembled range with two coats of matt black Humbrol enamel paint, allowing the first coat to dry thoroughly before applying the second. When the paint is dry, apply a coat of black-lead grate polish (available from hardware shops) with an old toothbrush – brushing the black-lead into all the nooks and crannies. Leave the polish to dry for a few minutes then brush it off with a second (clean) old toothbrush and polish with a soft cloth. This method can also be used on fenders and fireplaces, pumps and anything else which is required to resemble cast iron. Black-lead polish applied to unpainted white metal as directed will produce a polished steel effect – useful on grates and fenders as an alternative to brass enamel paint.

FIREPLACES

An empty fireplace, however elegant the surround, looks very bare. If you don't wish to have a grate, fill the fireplace with a vase of dried flowers, a paper fan or a firescreen. If, however, you prefer a grate, this should fit in style with the period of the house; for instance, the large open hearth in a Tudor house would have burned logs supported on firedogs.

Firedogs (Fig 25a) Simple firedogs can be made from soldering wire, or plastic-covered garden wire with beads stuck to the top for finials. Painted with matt-black enamel paint, these andirons look quite convincing supporting several logs in the hearth.

Fig 25 A selection of furniture for the fireplace

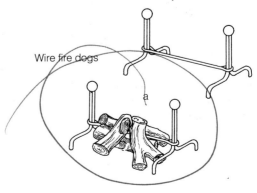

Wire fire dogs

a

An inexpensive white metal kit, finished with black-lead polish makes an impressive kitchen range

Basket grate (Fig 25b)   A basket grate can be made from fine wood-strip. Only the front of the basket need be made as, when it is fixed in place and filled with logs, only the front is visible. Cut the cross-bar to fit the width of the grate and the upright bars high enough to hold the fire in place. Stick the uprights to the cross-bar and paint the grate front with matt-black enamel paint. Cut a small block of wood approximately ⅛in thick to fit into the fireplace and paint this block matt black to match the grate. The basket front is then glued to the block and pushed into the fireplace.

Fireback (Fig 25b)   A finishing touch for the basket grate is a fireback. This can be cut in thick cardboard or thin obeche wood and painted matt black. It can be stuck to the back wall of the fireplace or to the back of the wooden block.

Metal grates (Fig 25c)   Soft lead strip, of the type sold for stained-glass window kits, or other soft metals, perhaps cut from tin cans, can be used to make a variety of grates in different styles. A small support block of wood cut to fit the fireplace opening, with a straight or curved front edge as required, will shape the grate and support it. Cut the metal strip to fit around the wooden block, ensuring that it is deep enough to contain the fire, and stick it in place. The grate can be left in its natural colour or painted with black enamel paint and black-leaded. A small knob, perhaps a glass-headed pin, pushed into the front looks effective.

Fenders (Fig 26) This soft metal can also be used to make fenders. Cut a piece of soft lead strip or metal long enough to enclose the front of the fireplace. The top edge can be cut into a curved shape and the fender painted with brass-coloured enamel paint. Alternatively, the gilt metallic braid for trimming lampshades makes a rather grand fender stuck to the soft metal. Square wooden beading can be used instead of metal strip – use it either as support for a braid fender or painted or stained to make a simple wooden fender.

Fig 25

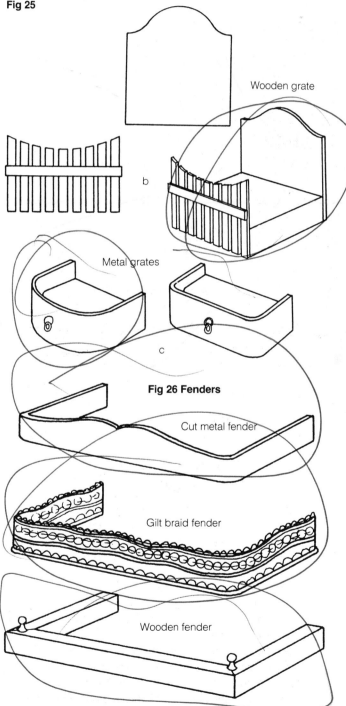

Wooden grate

b

Metal grates

c

Fig 26 Fenders

Cut metal fender

Gilt braid fender

Wooden fender

Hearths A fender generally encloses a tiled hearth. Tiles can be cut from magazine illustrations, hand painted or modelled in clay. If you use paper tiles, a coat of varnish (colourless nail varnish works very well) will make them look more realistic. A few of the same tiles might be used to decorate the fireplace surround.

Fires The finishing touch to the fireplace is, of course, the fire. It is simple to cut some small twigs into short lengths for a log fire. Arrange them in the grate, and glue them lightly in place. A few more logs in a log basket or piled beside the fire look good.

A coal fire is a little more fiddly as, to look convincing, it should be laid like a real fire, but with the component parts glued in place. Stick a small scrap of crumpled newspaper to the wooden firegrate base, then glue slivers of wood (matchsticks split in half) to the newspaper for kindling. You could use tiny pieces of real coal or imitations like crushed black sweets (black fruit gums, left in the fridge for a while, will crush well) or black glass beads. Stick each piece of coal in place, almost covering the sticks and paper. The finished result should be realistic enough to need only a match to set to it to burn!

Flames Realistic flame effects are difficult to achieve, so we generally lay a coal or log fire as if ready for lighting. If you want a burning fire though, the simplest method is probably to stick a picture of a burning fire from a magazine to the back of the fireplace opening; then lay the fire in front of the flame picture, using blackened logs or coal and red-tinfoil sweet papers, or tinsel to give the impression of a burning fire. An ingenious electrician might be able to contrive a red light bulb in the fireplace, discreetly hidden by logs or coal, which would look effective.

LIGHTS
The light fittings in this section are designed for effect, rather than practical use, and concentrate on old-fashioned methods, such as candles, oil lamps and gas lights.

Candles (Fig 27a) Candles, one of the earliest forms of lighting, are appropriate to any period house. The small

Fig 27 Candlesticks, oil lamps and gas brackets

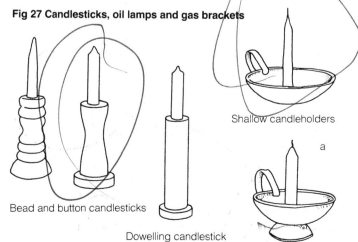

Bead and button candlesticks

Dowelling candlestick

Shallow candleholders

a

candles sold for birthday cakes are the simplest, but they are rather thick – this looks well in a castle where thick candles are appropriate, but in a house they look like birthday-cake candles! The best solution is to dip your own candles, by repeatedly dipping a fine wick into melted candle wax until the required thickness is built up. If this is rather more effort than you wish to make, cocktail sticks cut to the right length and painted ivory look quite effective glued into candlesticks.

The candlesticks might be brass or china ones bought from dolls-house shops, or home-made ones, using tubular-shaped beads, fine brass tubing, or dowelling and buttons. Long tubular beads, stuck to small buttons and painted to represent china will make a fine pair of candlesticks with convenient holes for the candles. Dish-shaped buttons, painted to represent pewter or brass, make good shallow candleholders, preferably with a wire-loop handle stuck to one side. Lengths of dowelling stuck to buttons and painted to imitate brass or china make simple but effective candlesticks; the candle must be stuck firmly to the top of the dowelling or drill a small hole to take it.

Oil lamps (Fig 27b) The designs of oil lamps vary, but the basic parts are a base which holds the oil, a chimney and a globe or shade.

Simple but pretty oil lamps can be made from beads, buttons and jewellery findings. Choose crystal or opaque beads of the appropriate size for the base and globe of the lamp, plus a prettily shaped button for it to stand on, and cut a short length of empty biro refill for the chimney. Super-glue the pieces together, taking care that they are straight – start at the bottom of the lamp and build upwards. Glue the base bead to the upturned button; add a short piece of biro refill, followed by the globe of the lamp, and a longer length of refill on top. The base bead and button could be painted with white-gloss enamel paint to represent china and decorated with painted flowers or transfers, or the base could be enamel-painted to imitate brass. Coloured glass or opaque white glass beads look pretty, and typically Victorian, as both bases and globes.

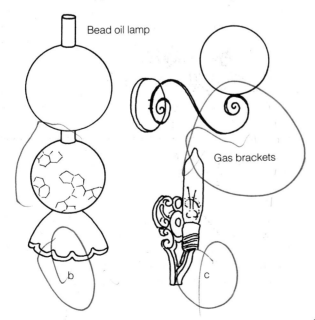

Bead oil lamp

Gas brackets

b

c

Gas lights (Fig 27c) Gas lighting became general in town houses by the 1850s, though country people still had only oil lamps and candles. Gas brackets, which were usually placed on either side of the chimney breast, can be made from fancy picture hooks (sold in art and craft shops) glued to the wall, or plastic-covered wire bent into a scroll. The wire should be painted brass colour and attached to a button (using its holes) with fuse wire. The button is then stuck to the wall. The gas lights can be made from fairy-light bulbs or faceted glass beads glued or wired to the brackets.

Commercial lights It is worth considering the commercial dolls'-house light fittings, even if your house is not wired for electricity. It is simple to remove the wires from the lights, and many of them are designed to fit into period houses. The oil lamps and chandeliers are particularly effective, even when they do not light.

KITCHEN RANGE

A simple, but effective, kitchen range can be made from a tin – the smallest size of 'Colmans' mustard is the perfect size; another possibility is a Spam tin.

Fig 28 Kitchen stove made of a mustard tin and fitted into a deep fireplace

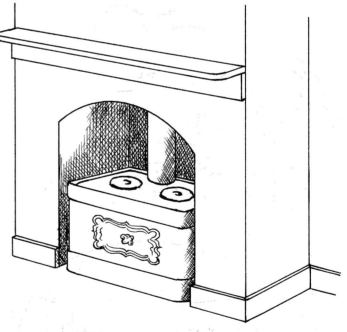

Clean the tin. If it has a lid, this can provide a base to stand the stove on. If the tin is too tall, cut a piece off the open end with scissors. Turn the tin upside-down and paint it all over with matt-black enamel paint, except for the raised rim around the now top edge which is left unpainted, and polish with black-lead.

The metal label from an aftershave lotion such as Brut (or a similar fancy metal label, perhaps a buckle) with the centre painted in black enamel, leaving the raised pattern around the edge unpainted, is then stuck to the front of the stove to represent the oven door. A black map pin can be pushed through to represent the door handle. The stove pipe is made from a felt-pen casing or a piece of dowelling, black enamel painted. This is glued to the centre back of the top of the stove, and the end of the pipe disappears up the chimney. Hot plates are made of silver-coloured washers, stuck one either side of the stove.

Although the oven door does not open, this stove is convincing and suitable for a variety of old-fashioned kitchens. It could be sited in a large fireplace opening or used as a free-standing range against an outside wall, in which case the chimney pipe should seem to disappear through the wall.

KITCHEN SINKS

Kitchen sinks can be made of metal or plastic lids, wood or clay, all of which, painted in the appropriate colour, are quite effective. The simplest kind is made from a shallow rectangular metal lid, for example, the lid of a Vaseline jar, which is the right size and shape for an old-fashioned pottery sink. Paint the lid with several coats of enamel in a matt yellow-brown colour to represent pottery, or a creamy-white gloss for the fire-clay found in Victorian kitchens (Fig 29).

If you have no suitably shaped lid, or if you wish to make the deeper sink which came into general use during the 1920s, a box of obeche wood will make a good sink. Use the directions given in the section on furniture-making for a dower chest or blanket box to construct a small box of the shape and size you require. Sand the top edges and all the corners smooth and rounded and give the sink several coats of white gloss enamel paint.

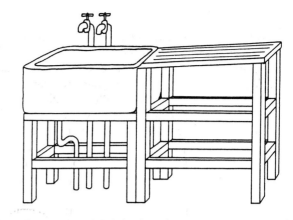

Fig 30 Deep sink and draining board mounted on a wooden frame

takes about twelve hours), paint the sink as described above.

Mount the sink on a frame made of fine square beading (Fig 30), or on brick piers made of suitable small blocks of wood painted to represent bricks or covered in brick paper (Fig 29).

Draining boards should be appropriate to the sink; for example, the oldest kind of shallow pottery sink would have a slate or stone slab as a draining board. A roofing slate will split easily, and a piece the required size can be cut with a hacksaw. Alternatively, a piece of obeche wood, preferably with grooves cut with the point of the scissors, would be suitable for the deeper fireclay sink. The draining board can be supported on small wooden brackets stuck to the wall, or mounted on a wooden framework like the sink.

Taps and pipes Taps and pipes add the necessary finish to the kitchen sink. The plumbing in old houses was usually obvious, so a waste-pipe and at least one tap are required. The pipes can be made of fine dowelling painted lead-grey and stuck to the wall behind the sink. This will serve for a simple straight pipe, but to get some interesting bends in the pipes, it is best to use either lead strip, which is easy to work and already the right colour, or fine brass tube which can be bent to the required shape with pliers.

Taps are rather more tricky and we have not yet discovered a simple method. There are, however, several possibilities, depending on the materials at hand. A tap from a piece of miniature, modern, bathroom furniture might be utilised if given a coat of brass-coloured paint. Various plastic oddments can be used for taps, for example, those left in plastic model kits when the components have all been broken away from the supports make credible tap shapes when painted and glued in place. Gilt jewellery findings, or even broken scraps of gilt jewellery, can be glued with super glue into a tap shape; for example, the wing-shaped piece from the back of an ear-ring stuck above a barrel-shaped necklace catch. If all else fails, inexpensive pipes and taps in white metal or brass are available from the specialist shops.

BATHROOM FITTINGS

Bathroom fittings are only appropriate to a house of the late nineteenth or the twentieth century, as until then bathrooms did not exist. Modest households managed with a tin bath used in front of the kitchen fire and hung on the wall when not in use. An oval-shaped lozenge tin with a wire-loop

Fig 29 Shallow sink mounted on brick piers

The most realistic sinks are modelled in clay. You can use ordinary clay which will need firing, or – more practically – Das or a similar material which dries hard without firing. Clay is easiest to work when it is 'leather dry' – so work it to make it malleable, then leave it to dry a little before beginning your modelling. The sink can be modelled using the finger-pot method, but, unless you are experienced in working with clay, it is simpler to roll it out like pastry and cut a bottom and four sides with a knife. Use the clay or Das fairly thick as this will give substance to the sink and make the pieces easier to handle. Assemble the four sides and the bottom and join them by damping the edges liberally with water, using a small paintbrush. When the clay is almost dry, use the paintbrush and water to smooth the surfaces and round the top and sides of the sink. When it is completely dry (with Das this usually

The deep white Belfast sink and the Aga cooker have been used in kitchens for more than seventy years and are completely at home in the modern kitchen of this period house

handle and the top edges gently splayed outwards will make a reasonable tin bath. Grander households had hip baths (try a china soap dish or Das model), usually decorated with flowers. Curious slipper baths, shaped like large shallow bowls, were also used in the bedroom – these could again be modelled in Das or, possibly, the sugar bowl from a dolls' tea-set would serve.

The early bathroom fittings were elaborately made of cast iron or porcelain. It is possible to adapt a modern plastic bathroom set with two coats of creamy-white, gloss enamel paint, to make it look like porcelain, and boxing of mahogany-stained obeche wood (Fig 31). The bath and basin look quite acceptable when the taps are painted with brass paint, and perhaps a flower decoration applied (paint or transfers). The loo needs more effort: firstly, the low-level cistern must be cut away with a craft knife, then the seat must be painted brown

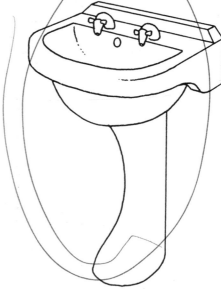

Fig 31 Modern commercial washbasin, boxed-in for a Victorian effect

to represent wood and the painted flower decoration applied to the painted bowl. If the cistern is the appropriate size, it can be painted matt grey and mounted on the wall on wooden brackets above the loo. If, however, the original cistern is unusable, a replacement can be made from a plastic box, such as a cut-down sweet container, painted and mounted as above. A pull made from a short length of jewellery chain with a bead handle is stuck to the side of the cistern.

The intrepid or experienced clay modeller might try making an old-fashioned bath, loo and basin in Das, using the finger-pot technique and 'leather dry' clay. The ingenious might try using various containers such as the plastic pots which contain individual portions of jam, painted with several coats of enamel paint.

A geyser (Fig 32) To complete the bathroom fittings, mount a geyser on a corner shelf over the bath. A piece sawn from thick dowelling or the top of a broom handle (shorter and fatter for the Victorian bathroom, longer and thinner for the Edwardian effect), will make the cylinder of the geyser. Paint this with copper enamel. Pipes can be made of lead strip or brass tube, pushed and glued into small holes drilled in the cylinder. Here, as in the kitchen, the plumbing should be obvious and should be seen to connect the geyser to a gas pipe. A small spout, a piece of tube or lead strip glued into a hole in the cylinder, should be positioned so that hot water can pour into the bath.

Furnish the bathroom with bath mat, towels, sponge, loofah, soap and toilet roll, made from pieces of the life-size items, and the realism is complete.

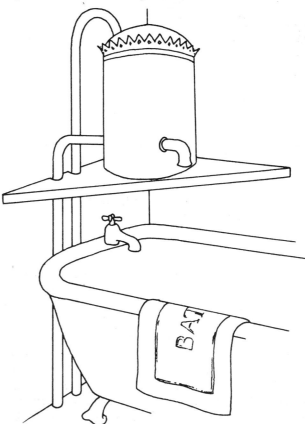

Fig 32 Geyser mounted on a corner shelf above the bath

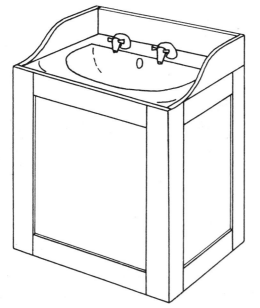

5 FURNITURE

As with building and decorating, tastes in furniture have changed considerably through the centuries as a result of fashion, need, and increasing prosperity. Medieval trestles, benches and straw-mattressed box beds gave way to Tudor chairs, tables and buffets with carved bulbous legs, and massive curtained four-poster beds. The great houses of the eighteenth century required suitably elegant furniture to grace them; the nineteenth century brought its classical revival; and Victorian taste found expression in solid carved mahogany and over-stuffed horsehair.

Each generation, as far as means allowed, refurnished in the latest style, and each period had its typical pieces, like the Tudor chest, indispensable in its time for both storage and seating but rarely found in later houses. Regency is typified by the Grecian sofa, upholstered in striped fabric with bolster cushions; the Victorian parlour is immediately evoked by a round pedestal table or mahogany chiffonier. Modern houses too are subject to changing tastes: the chrome and glass popular in the sixties and the stripped pine of the seventies are still to be found in most modern houses. Furniture catalogues and homes magazines are the best sources of reference.

However, few people have the resources or the inclination to redecorate and refurnish as often as fashion changes, so most homes are a mixture of old and new.

When choosing furniture for your house, consider the space each piece will occupy in the various rooms. It is frustrating to make a piece of furniture and then find that you cannot arrange the room to fit it in – careful planning will avoid this problem. For example, in a bedroom the bed is the largest piece of furniture, and occupies the most space, so if the bed is placed first, the smaller pieces can be planned to fit around it. If you have the bed against one wall, a window in another wall and a chimney breast on the third wall, there is probably nowhere to put a wardrobe! As in a real house, doors need enough space to open without obstruction, and cupboard doors and drawers should be accessible. By placing the largest pieces first, and planning other pieces to fit into specific spaces, eg a chest of drawers or a bookcase in an alcove, a pleasing arrangement of furniture can be built up.

Some pieces show to better advantage in one position than another; for example, a kitchen dresser filled with plates, cups and saucers, looks best viewed from the front where the details can be seen most clearly – this aspect must also be considered when planning the room layout. Dolls'-house rooms are more like stage sets than rooms – they are three-sided boxes, designed to be looked at from the front – so the furniture has to be arranged for the most pleasing effect rather than the most practical arrangement.

This chapter covers the basic tools, materials and methods we use to make furniture. Patterns may be taken from the project chapters, which include scale patterns for all the pieces in the houses. These patterns can be adapted, if required, to a variety of period styles – by using a thicker wood, adding a pediment, staining or painting to a different finish, and other such minor alterations. The projects cover a wide range of furniture pieces, which are simple to cut and assemble using the methods described here. Alternatively, you might prefer to draw your own furniture patterns.

The various pieces of furniture fall into categories, eg hinged cupboards, tables, upholstered furniture, etc, which are dealt with individually after the basic method. The notes on tools and materials apply to all the wooden furniture in this chapter.

TOOLS AND MATERIALS

Tools The tools we recommend for making wooden furniture are: a razor-toothed saw (small saw with a fine-toothed blade which will cut cleanly through wood); a fretsaw with a fine blade, for cutting curved pieces; a craft knife with a supply of new blades; a try-square for marking accurate angles; a mitre block for cutting angles; a white wood-glue and a fine-grade abrasive paper such as flour paper (Fig 33).

Materials You can, of course, make dolls'-house furniture in almost any wood if it can be planed to a suitable thickness and the grain is small. For beginners, however, obeche or bass woods which are obtainable from dolls'-house suppliers and art and craft shops are a good choice. They are easy to work with and can be stained to imitate almost any wood. Obeche and bass are sold in sheets approximately 3in wide and 2ft 6in long in thicknesses ranging from $\frac{1}{16}$in to $\frac{1}{4}$in. Choose pieces which are not warped and have a good small grain – the grain can vary considerably from piece to piece. The most useful thicknesses for making miniature furniture are $\frac{1}{16}$in, $\frac{3}{32}$in and $\frac{1}{8}$in.

A good selection of wood stains is available from DIY shops, together with matt and gloss polyurethane varnishes. If you intend to varnish your furniture, avoid a too-glossy finish by diluting the varnish with a little white spirit. For painting furniture, we recommend acrylics or enamel paints, using a coat of gloss over an undercoat of matt. The undercoat should be allowed to dry thoroughly and sanded before the top coat is applied. We do not recommend household gloss paints, as these are too dense for painting such small pieces. We prefer the subtle effect of polished wood, so we generally finish wooden furniture with a coat of amateur French polish and several coats of a good wax polish.

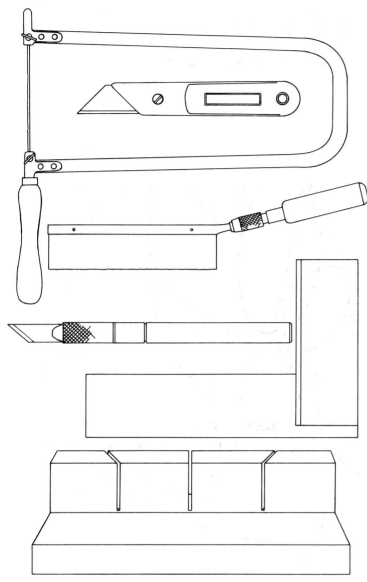

Fig 33 **The basic tools for making wooden furniture**

Firstly, draw the furniture plans onto the wood, using a sharp pencil ensuring that the grain of the wood lies in the correct direction on each piece. Use a set square to mark the right-angles. Cut the pieces out, using a razor-toothed saw for straight lines and a fretsaw for curves. When cutting across the grain of the wood, scoring the cutting line first with a craft knife will provide a clear groove to guide the saw. Sand each piece carefully, using abrasive paper wrapped around a small block of wood to avoid rounding the edges of the pieces. Check that the pieces fit well together, and then stain them before assembly, as wood stain will not 'take' over glue. Applying the wood stain with a soft cloth gives a better finish than brushing it on. When the stain is thoroughly dry, glue the pieces together, supporting them if necessary until the glue is dry. Varnish, paint or polish are applied when the piece is assembled. For the best results with polish, carefully apply one coat of amateur French polish to the well-sanded piece with a small paintbrush or soft cloth. When this is dry, sand carefully again and then apply several coats of wax polish, well-buffed between each coat.

If care is taken at each stage in the assembly, especially with the finishing, the result should be a realistic piece of miniature furniture.

Shelf units (Fig 34)   This method for making a shelf unit can be used for hanging wall shelves, the top part of a kitchen dresser or a free-standing wall unit or bookcase – only the sizes vary.

First, cut the back of the shelf unit to the required height and width. This is generally cut in the thinnest wood available, and the piece can be scored lengthwise with a scissor blade to represent planking. Next, cut the side pieces the same height as the back piece and the full depth – the back will fit inside the side pieces. The top and bottom are cut to fit, or, as for the kitchen dresser, to overhang at the top edge. The shelves are then cut to the required width and depth.

The plain shelf unit is suitable for a bookcase or a simple kitchen dresser, but if the sides are cut with a fretsaw into a curved shape and a similar curved piece is fixed under the top front edge, it becomes a more elaborate dresser top. A curved pediment can be added for a Chippendale effect.

Recommended products   The following list of tools and products are those which we use and recommend. The first-time housebuilder might find it helpful to know which products to buy when faced with a variety of similar brands in the DIY or art and craft shop.

Xacto razor saw
Eclipse fretsaw (12in)
Xacto craft knife and blades
Swan Morton craft knife and blades

Evostik woodworking adhesive
UHU all-purpose clear adhesive
Blackfriars French polish
Blackfriars button polish
Blackfriars wood stains
Goddards cabinet makers' wax polish

METHOD
The following directions apply to all the pieces of wooden furniture described in this section.

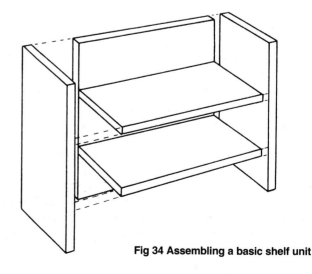

Fig 34 **Assembling a basic shelf unit**

Remember when planning the furniture for a small bedroom that the bed occupies a lot of space

Drawer units (Figs 35 and 36)   The shell of the drawer unit is the same as the shelf unit, except that it is generally deeper. Whether the drawer unit is to have one or six drawers (or any other number!) the shell is made, assembled and stained before the drawers are made.

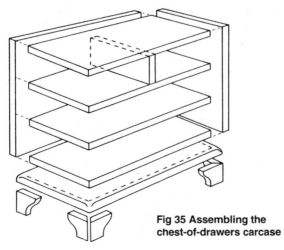

Fig 35 Assembling the chest-of-drawers carcase

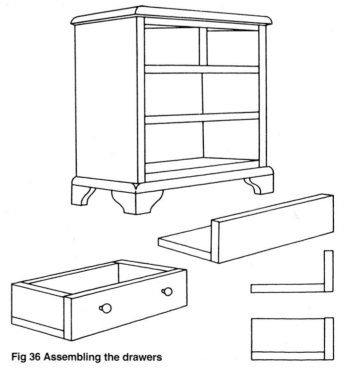

Fig 36 Assembling the drawers

Simple wooden furniture made from the patterns in the book

To make the drawers, cut the drawer fronts first – to fit as snugly as possible into the drawer spaces. The base of the drawer, cut to the same width as the drawer front and trimmed to fit into the drawer space, is glued to the drawer front. The side and back pieces are then cut to fit onto the base to complete the 'box'. Made this way, the drawer should fit well, but glide easily in and out of the drawer space. Drawer handles can be made from map pins, beads, the loops of hook and loop fastenings (these need to be pulled apart slightly with pliers), pieces of dowelling or fine square beading. Tiny, brass, turned or drop handles for dolls'-house furniture are also sold by the specialist shops.

A set of four, five or six drawers, one above another, makes a chest of drawers. Two drawers, side-by-side, can be incorporated into a kitchen dresser. One small drawer can be used in a kitchen table or dressing table.

Cupboards (Fig 37) Cupboards are all basically boxes with hinged doors. There are tiny brass hinges available from the specialist shops, but the following simple method uses dressmakers' pins for hinging.

The back, sides and base of the cupboard are made the same way as shelf and drawer units, but the top is not fixed on at this stage. If shelves are required inside the cupboard, they must be cut to allow space for the doors to close in front of them. The door or doors are cut to fit as snugly as possible into the front. A fine hole is bored with a dressmaker's pin in the top and bottom corners of the door, as close to the edge as possible, taking care to work gently so as not to split the wood. The pins are then pushed into the holes and snipped off with about ⅛in protruding. The doors are positioned on the front of the cupboard and small holes bored in the base to receive the pins. The top of the cupboard is then fitted, and small holes made to receive the pins. When these are correctly positioned, the top can be fixed in place. It may be necessary to sand the hinged edges of the doors slightly rounded to ensure that the doors swing open freely – check this before the top is glued in place. For handles, see suggestions for drawer handles.

Cupboards with one door will make broom or bedside cupboards, depending on size. With two doors, they can be used as base units for kitchen dressers, wardrobes or sideboards, etc. Combinations of shelf, drawer and cupboard units can make kitchen dressers, sideboards or modern wall units. They can also be used to make built-in furniture for a modern house.

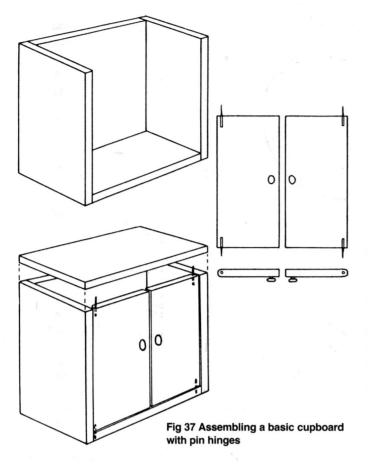

Fig 37 Assembling a basic cupboard with pin hinges

Tables (Fig 38) The basic design and method for a table with four legs can be adapted to a round, square, rectangular or oval top as required, or, with the legs shortened, a coffee table or stool.

Cut the table top from wood of a suitable thickness, appropriate to the style of the intended table. The legs are cut from square beading or dowelling, and can be 'turned' by whittling with a craft knife, but it is important that they are all exactly the same length! A frieze of wood (thinner wood than that used for the table top) is cut in four pieces to fit the underside of the table a little way in from the edge. The amount of the overhang will depend on the style of the table. The frieze is stuck in place to form a rectangle: either 'closed',

so that the table legs are stuck inside the corners; or 'open', so that the table legs fitted into each corner complete the rectangle. After the pieces have been sanded and stained, assemble the table upside down, supporting the legs straight while the glue dries. The frieze will help to hold them in place, but additional support may be needed. On certain styles of table, stretchers cut from the same beading or dowelling look well. These are cut to fit between the legs when the table is completed, stained and glued into place.

The basic table can be varied enormously by the way it is finished. The traditional dining table, whether square, rectangular, round or oval, usually has a highly polished wooden top. The traditional kitchen table, usually rectangular with heavy legs has a well-scrubbed wooden top. The modern dining table could be the round-topped, white-painted kind, and the modern kitchen table might have a formica or Fablon top. Glass-topped coffee tables can be made from a piece of perspex with well-sanded edges.

This method can also be used to make stools by cutting a smaller top and short legs. If the seat is to be upholstered, cut a small piece of foam or wadding to fit the seat, cover it in fabric and glue it in place.

Refectory tables and benches (Fig 39) The top of an old refectory table is of thick wood, thinner if it is one of the modern pine type. Cut the narrow, rectangular top piece and the two legs from the same thickness of wood. The top of the table can be scored with a scissor blade to represent planking. The legs can be plain rectangular pieces, or cut with a fretsaw to a curved shape; they are fixed in place under each end of the table, in from the edge. A stretcher is cut to fit between the legs and glued in place.

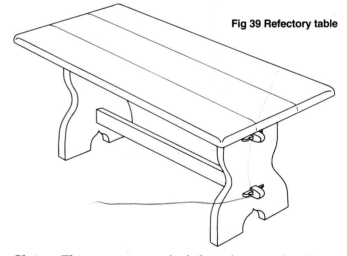

Fig 39 Refectory table

Chairs There are many methods for making wooden chairs; here we describe three of them.

The first chair (Fig 40) is made of thickish wood, in three pieces; the back (including back legs), the front, and the seat, which is glued between the back and front. The style of the chair can be varied by the choice of stain or paint, the shape of the back and the use of upholstery, made by cutting small foam or wadding pads to fit the seat and back, covering these in fabric and sticking them in place. Stretchers, if appropriate, can be cut to fit and glued in place between the legs.

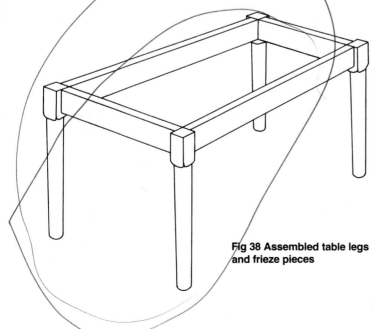

Fig 38 Assembled table legs and frieze pieces

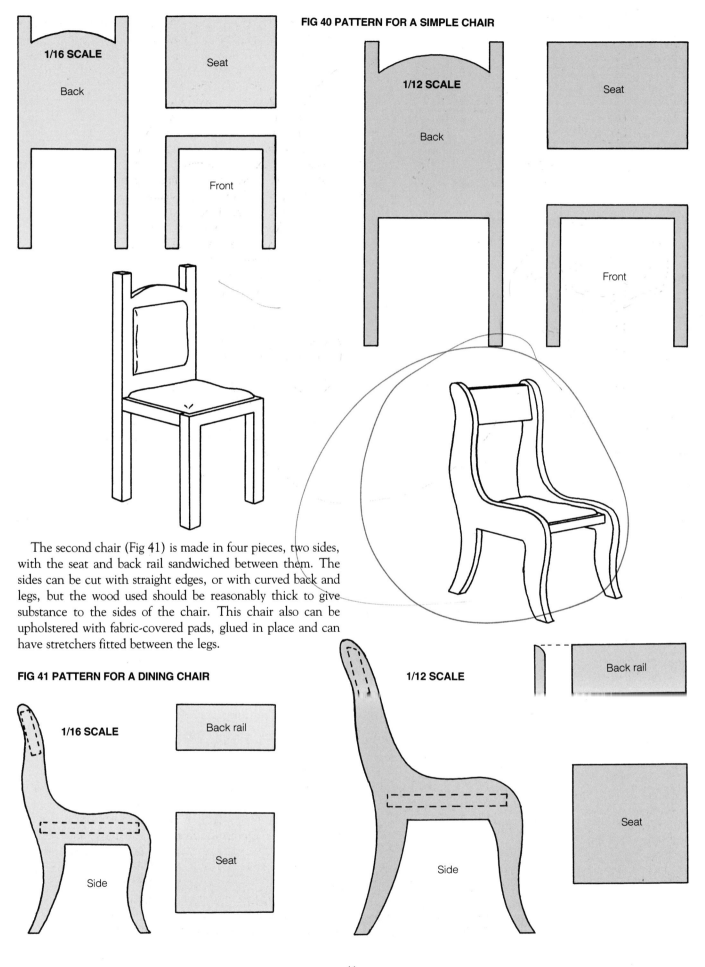

FIG 40 PATTERN FOR A SIMPLE CHAIR

1/16 SCALE

Back

Seat

Front

1/12 SCALE

Back

Seat

Front

The second chair (Fig 41) is made in four pieces, two sides, with the seat and back rail sandwiched between them. The sides can be cut with straight edges, or with curved back and legs, but the wood used should be reasonably thick to give substance to the sides of the chair. This chair also can be upholstered with fabric-covered pads, glued in place and can have stretchers fitted between the legs.

FIG 41 PATTERN FOR A DINING CHAIR

1/16 SCALE

Back rail

Seat

Side

1/12 SCALE

Back rail

Seat

Side

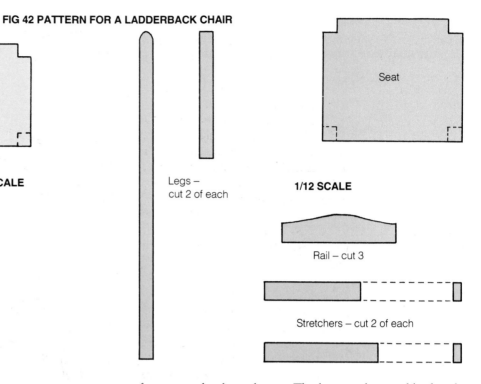

FIG 42 PATTERN FOR A LADDERBACK CHAIR

Legs – cut 2 of each

Seat

1/16 SCALE

Rail – cut 3

Stretchers – cut 2 of each

Legs – cut 2 of each

1/12 SCALE

Rail – cut 3

Stretchers – cut 2 of each

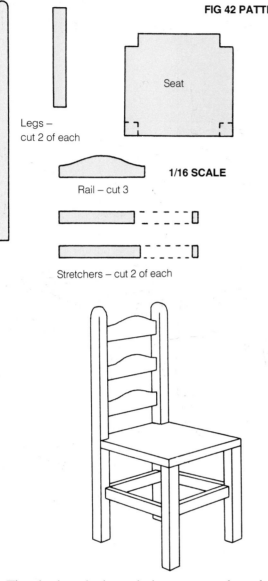

The third method is a little more complicated than the previous two, but can be used to make a variety of chairs in the ladderback style (Fig 42). The legs can be cut from fine square beading or dowelling; the rails from dowelling, beading or wood-strip, either used flat or steamed over a kettle and bent to a curved shape (while it dries, tape it around an object which has the correct curve eg a jam jar). The seat can be either a solid wooden one, or dowelling rails infilled with woven raffia to imitate a rush seat.

Cut the back legs to the length of the finished height of the chair, and the front legs to the height of the seat. If the seat is to be a wooden one, cut a square piece of wood and from the back corners cut out square notches the size of the back legs. Glue the front legs under the front edge of the seat and the back legs into the notches cut into the seat. Ensure that the legs are straight as the glue dries, and that the chair stands firm without wobbling. The back rails and the stretchers are then cut to fit and glued in place between the legs. If the seat is to be a rush one, the front and back legs are cut as before and stretchers of dowelling or beading are cut to fit between the legs, back, front and two sides. These are glued in place, making a frame. Raffia is then woven over and under the

frame to make the rush seat. The leg stretchers and back rails are then glued in place. If the chair is made of round dowelling, cocktail sticks or toothpicks can be used for the stretchers, drilling small holes in the legs to take the ends.

Dower chest or blanket box (Fig 43) The dower chest is made of a medium-thin wood, the lid slightly thicker. Cut the base, front and back the same length. Cut the two ends the width of the base plus the thickness of the back and front. Stick these together to form a box, with the base inside. The lid is cut slightly larger than the box so that it overhangs. Cut a second piece of wood to fit snugly into the open top of the box and glue it to the underside of the lid – or the lid could be hinged in place with tiny hinges.

The front and sides of the chest can be panelled with a fine wood-strip mitred at the corners, or a stencilled design could be painted on the front and lid. Given a coat of brightly coloured paint, the chest would make a good toy box for the nursery. Used without the lid, with bead feet or rockers, it would make an old-fashioned cradle.

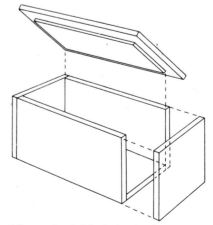

Fig 43 Assembling a simple blanket or toy box

BEDS

The bed in its simplest form is a divan, but even in a modern house it is made more interesting by the addition of a headboard and footboard.

As a rough guide for size, in the 1/12 scale house the bed will be about 6¼ x 3in for a single bed, or 6¼ x 4½in for a double bed. In the 1/16 scale house a single bed is about 5 x 2½in and a double bed 5 x 3½in. These measurements can, of course, be altered slightly to suit individual taste or to fit a bed into a specific space in the dolls' house. As a general rule, modern beds are lower than old-fashioned ones but this is a matter of taste. The example shown below is made in obeche wood, but it could be adapted with a padded headboard, or abandoned in favour of a brass bedstead made from brass tubing soldered together. (Brass tubing can be bought from hobby shops – or use metal knitting needles or even dowelling painted with enamel paint.)

Basic bed (Fig 44)   Cut a base of the appropriate size from wood. The headboard and footboard are cut to the same width as the base, and two side rails about ½in deep are cut the same length as the base. The pieces are sanded, stained and assembled with wood glue: the side rails are stuck to either side of the base, the head and footboards are then glued to each end. The bed-posts, cut from square wooden beading, are then fitted into the notches left between the side rails and head and footboards. Ensure that all four bedposts are properly aligned.

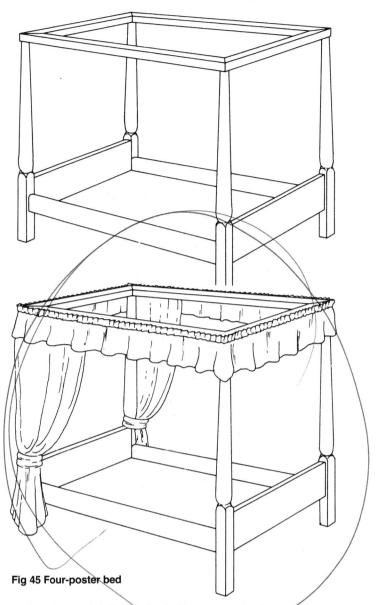

Fig 45 Four-poster bed

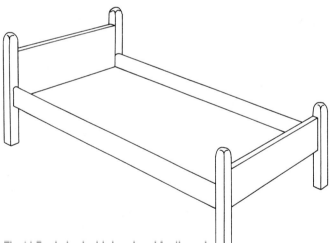

Fig 44 Basic bed with head and footboards

Half-tester   A half-tester bed is made in the same way except that, instead of a headboard, a rectangle of wood the same width as the bed and approximately the same length is glued upright to the head end of the bed. The roof of the half-tester is approximately one-quarter of the length of the bed, and is glued to the back piece to form a right-angle. The back piece can be stained, painted or covered in fabric to match the bed curtains.

Four-poster (Fig 45)   A four-poster bed can be made using dowelling, fine square beading or paintbrush handles for the posts with a frame of fine square beading to support the canopy. It can have a backpiece, as for the half-tester, or a headboard.

Curtains and frills for the half-tester or the four-poster are made using the same method and fabrics as for window curtains. The curtains are cut and narrowly hemmed to the required length and width, then gathered at the top edge and stuck in place on the side of the tester roof or the top frame of the four-poster with fabric glue. They look best if they are looped back to the head of the bed with narrow ribbon or a strip of matching fabric. If you wish to roof over the four-poster bed, this can be done with wood (or cardboard) or fabric. Cut the wood to exactly the size of the canopy frame, stain it or cover the underside with fabric and glue in place to the canopy frame. Alternatively, cut a rectangle of fabric slightly larger than the frame, turn a narrow hem all-round and glue the fabric to the frame, stretching it taut. A frill, although not essential, finishes the bed properly. Cut a long, narrow strip of fabric, hem the bottom edge, turn in and gather the top edge and stick in place over the curtains, around the sides and front of the half-tester, or the canopy frame of the four-poster.

Bedclothes   A mattress can be made by stuffing a cotton bag with wadding or cotton-wool, but has a better shape if the sides are boxed with a narrow edge of stitching. If you wish, the mattress can be 'buttoned' with French knots. If the mattress is made slightly smaller than the base, this will allow space for the bedcovers to be tucked in, and the side rails will hold everything firmly in place.

Sheets and pillowcases can be made of fine cotton; old handkerchiefs are perfect – white or cream for old houses, but almost anything goes in a modern house. Double beds look better with two small pillows rather than one large one. Blankets, perhaps cut from and old vest with edges ribbon bound or blanket stitched, are suitably lightweight. Alternatively, Viyella, flannel or winceyette all make good blankets.

An eiderdown or bedspread adds the finishing touch: an eiderdown should be of lightly padded, fine fabric: a bedspread matching the bed or window curtains looks good. A miniature patchwork quilt can be quite a challenge, but well worth the effort – choose firmly woven, cotton fabrics, but if your sewing skill is not up to the real thing, a fake can be made by drawing small squares onto a plain-coloured cotton and filling them in with various coloured felt pens.

UPHOLSTERED FURNITURE

For the upholstered furniture described in this section, use a cardboard base, thin foam or wadding for padding, and fabric covers. The finished results, if the pieces are carefully made, are realistic, but it is important to use the correct materials. The cardboard should be good-quality art cardboard (available

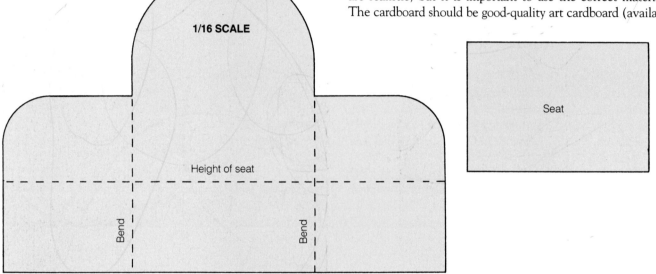

FIG 46 PATTERN FOR AN UPHOLSTERED ARMCHAIR

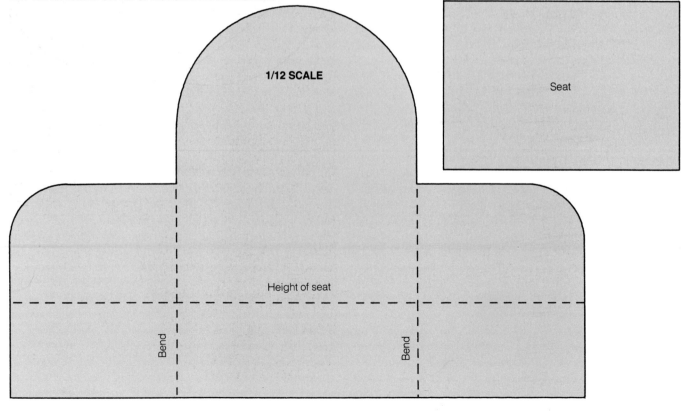

44

FIG 47 PATTERN FOR AN UPHOLSTERED SOFA

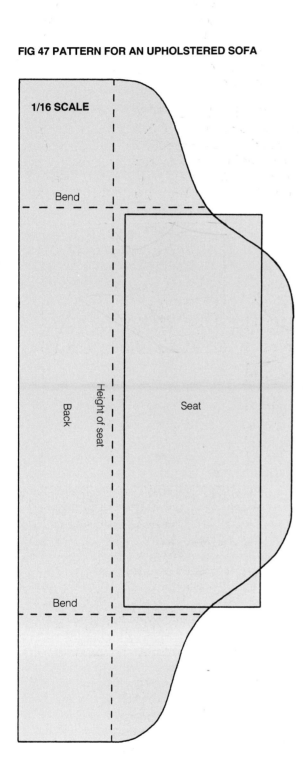

1/16 SCALE

Bend

Bend

Back

Height of seat

Seat

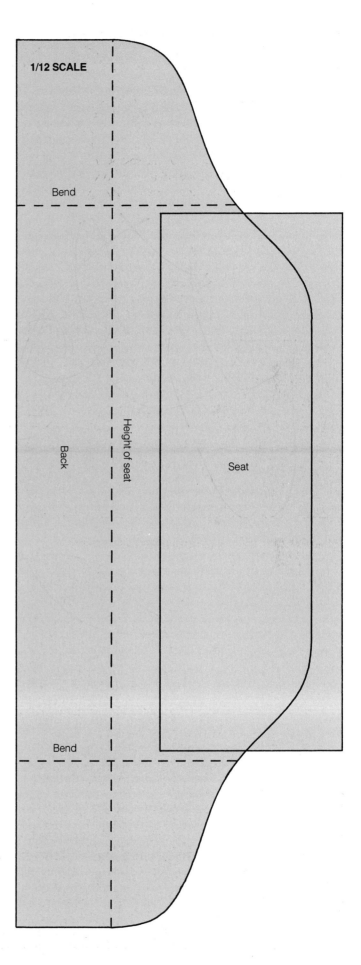

1/12 SCALE

Bend

Back

Height of seat

Seat

Bend

Upholstered wing chair and sofa, simply made of padded cardboard and covered in cotton print

from art shops) – cereal packets or cardboard boxes are not suitable. The foam should be about ⅛in thick, and is preferable to wadding. The choice of fabric for the covers is important – avoid anything thick, heavy or with a large pattern. It is worthwhile finding colours and patterns in the right scale and style for the house. Felt is a useful fabric to work with as it does not fray and stretches easily; very fine velveteen, cotton, and fine wool or silk are all suitable, but man-made fabrics such as crimplene are not, as they stretch too much. The choice of shape and fabric will make the piece suitable for the type of house you are furnishing.

Cut a cardboard base from the pattern; then cut a piece of foam or wadding the same shape but about ½in larger all-

round. Cut two fabric covers, one on the straight grain of the fabric, one on the bias grain, also about ½in larger all-round than the pattern. The outline of the pattern is used as the sewing line on the fabric covers.

Score the two vertical dotted lines on the pattern onto the cardboard base, using a scissor blade – this allows the arms of the chair to bend forward. Glue the padding to the inside of the chair, rolling the ½in overlap over the edges and glueing it to the back all the way round. This will give a padded inside and padded edges to the chair (Fig 48a).

Sew together the two fabric covers, right sides inside, using small tight stitches to make a strong seam. Clip the curves and turn the cover right side out. With the bias-cut side of the cover to the inside of the chair and the straight grain to the outside, gently stretch the cover over the padded cardboard. The raw edges at the bottom are turned in and slipstitched

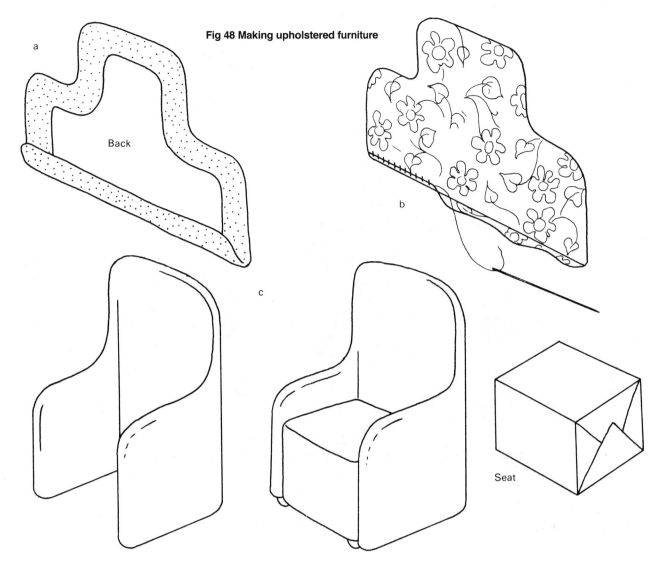

Fig 48 Making upholstered furniture

a

Back

b

c

Seat

closed. The more tightly the cover fits, the better the chair will look, so use the exact pattern line (the outline of the cardboard base) as your sewing line and pull the cover down as tightly as possible when slipstitching the edges (Fig 48b).

The seat of the chair is made by cutting a block of balsa wood to fit inside the back and arms, to the height required. The block is padded and covered in fabric like a parcel, with the ends glued firmly in place with fabric glue; the back and sides of the block are glued and put in place inside the chair. Pins pushed through from the outside will hold everything in place until the glue is dry (Fig 48c).

If you want a frilled skirt on the chair, cut a strip of matching fabric long enough to go around the chair one-and-a-half times and a little deeper than the finished frill is to be. Seam the short edges together and turn a small hem on one long edge. Turn the other long edge in and crease the fold, then run a row of small gathering stitches as close to the fold as possible. Place the frill on the chair and pull up the gathers to fit. Distribute the gathers evenly and slip stitch the top edge of the frill in place.

Obviously, the neater the work, the better the finished result will be – care taken with the cutting, sticking and stitching is well rewarded. To neaten the underside of chairs, sofas or stools, a small piece of felt can be glued on to cover any raw edges, and small blocks of wood or wooden beads can be stuck under each corner for feet. As trimming, narrow lampshade braid or russian braid piping can be sewn or glued in place. Cushions in a matching or harmonising fabric, or scatter cushions, made of small pieces of fabric or ribbon, can be arranged along the back of the sofa, or tucked invitingly into the corner of an armchair.

6 ACCESSORIES

The dozens of tiny accessories which give a dolls' house character and charm are often the easiest things to make and find, and can be one of the most pleasurable aspects of dolls'-house making. The dolls'-house shops stock a wealth of tiny treasures but they are by no means the only source of supply. Look at the commercial dolls'-house ranges in toyshops, which includes pictures, mirrors, rugs and ornaments suitable for 1/12 as well as 1/16 houses. Browse in gift shops and department stores, stationers, cake decorating suppliers and garden and hardware shops.

MATERIALS
The secret to successful DIY accessories is hoarding! You will need scraps of fabrics and trimmings, beads and buttons, wood scraps, paper cutouts, tiny dried flowers and all the little oddments which seem to have no particular use until inspiration strikes.

Small-print cotton fabrics, narrow ribbons and lace and tiny trimmings can be bought from dolls'-house shops or by post from The Dolls'-House Draper (see Stockists). A wonderful selection of beads is available from Janet Cole whose catalogue can be bought at newsagents, including W H Smith. Hoard scraps of wood, dowelling and woodstrip left over from furniture-making and look at the picture-frame mouldings, available from dolls'-house suppliers, which can also be used to add a decorative finish to furniture. Consider some of the jewellery-making supplies on sale in art and craft shops, cake decorations and key ring novelties. A catalogue from the Tate Gallery will provide pictures suitable for any period house, and catalogues showing small pictures of products will provide package labels. Dralon furnishing velvet and tapestry make good rugs or carpets, and old sample books can often be scrounged or bought cheaply from upholsterers or furnishing fabric shops. Table mats in woven straw or fabric can also make good rugs.

You will need small sharp scissors and a product like Fraycheck, which is painted onto the raw edge of fabric to prevent it fraying, and craft and fabric adhesives which dry clear and virtually invisible will make things easier. These things are all available from art and craft shops and haberdashery (notions) departments.

Many accessories for the dolls' house can be made from tiny pieces of the real thing including dusters, household sponges, bath sponge, soap and loo paper – even a passable pair of rubber gloves! Tiny dried flowers make the most realistic arrangements because they are real, and tea, sugar, flour, etc look completely convincing in tiny storage jars.

Cheap and cheerful accessories from the toyshop can be transformed with paint or transfers. Pink or yellow plastic saucepans and kettles look quite different when given a coat of copper enamel paint, and a plastic tea-set will look like china if you paint it with white-gloss enamel and perhaps add a tiny painted pattern or transfer. A toothpaste cap painted with matt terracotta paint looks like a flower pot, and a cheap white-metal figure looks like parian or marble after a coat or two of white enamel paint.

PHOTOCOPYING AND LASER PRINTING
Modern printing techniques offer a wealth of possibilities for the miniaturist, though for the best results you need a professional printer with good machines – cheaper machines produce smudgy copies and poor quality colour. If you want to make your own wallpapers, you need only draw or paint one sheet and have copies made – in black and white, and colour with paint or felt pens, or colour the original and have sufficient colour photocopies made to decorate the whole room.

Most photocopiers can enlarge or reduce the size of copies which is very useful in a miniature world! Reduction photocopying can be used to reproduce birth or marriage certificates, favourite pictures, package labels or shop signs and advertisements. It is also a good way to make properly-scaled wallpaper from wrapping paper – for example, the William Morris patterns which are available from National Trust shops.

Colour laser printing, which reproduces an image from paper onto fabric, is the technique used to print on T-shirts. It is a little more difficult to find a printer who has this machine – try the Yellow Pages. You may have a little difficulty persuading the printer to do the job (they have not usually considered anything but T-shirts) but reassurance that you will pay whatever the result generally settles the issue. The result will depend on the original picture and to some extent on the person operating the machine, we have had some very good results and some not so good, so you must be prepared to gamble. It is expensive but the machine can handle paper up to A4 size (the size of a large dolls'-house carpet) and carefully chosen subjects and good results more than justify the cost.

You need a good clear picture of the item you want to reproduce – this might be your own drawing or painting, or a magazine cutout, and a piece of fabric (approximately 12 x 8in) to print onto. The fabric must be natural and a light colour, white and cream are best. The fabric should also be appropriate for the item you are going to reproduce – for example, a bedspread would be best on cotton lawn, a tapestry on fine linen and a rug on cotton velvet. The original picture is first copied in reverse then the copy is printed onto the

Fig 49 Patterns for rugs made of printed felt or needlepoint in either scale

surface of the fabric in inks. The ink is stable and can be washed and ironed, but the colours are usually a little darker and less sharply defined than the original.

As the machine can print A4 size, it is most economical to mount small items together on a sheet of A4 paper. They should, of course, be items you want printed onto the same fabric, for example, a bedspread and a set of cushion covers to be printed on lawn or several small rugs to be printed on cotton velvet. Remember to leave enough space around each item for cutting-out, seaming or hemming. Original pictures can also be reduction photocopied before printing, so you could have a piece of fabric printed to match a wallpaper – from the same sheet of wrapping paper.

A selection of accessories for the laundry, including a mangle and clothes airer made from kits

Note:

A word of warning about copyright; it is OK to reproduce your own work and anyone else's work when they have been dead for fifty years, but it is against the law to reproduce other people's work without their specific permission. Though it is unlikely that anyone would object to you reproducing a picture of their bedspread or fabric purely for your own use, it would be illegal to do it commercially.

RUGS

Rugs can be made in a variety of ways, ranging from a simple rectangle of cloth to beautifully worked petit-point. Suitable pieces of wool, weaving or velvet, etc can be cut to the appropriate size, the shorter edges fringed and a piece of heavyweight iron-on Vilene or carpet tape placed on the back to prevent fraying and give the rug weight, so that it lies flat. A piece of short-pile fur fabric or a wide braid with suitable pattern, similarly backed, looks effective. If you plan to work a petit-point rug, choose the finest available canvas and use fine embroidery wool or silk. Designs for rugs can be copied from pictures in magazines, or you could design your own, drawing it on to the canvas with felt pens.

One effective and simple method for making rugs, is to draw with felt pen on felt. Use good-quality felt in a light colour, cut to the required size and backed with carpet tape. Draw on the design with pencil or light-coloured felt pen. Choosing felt pens which are not too bright or garish, in colours which harmonise, fill in the design. Work the colour well into the

Simple accessories made from beads and buttons, raffia baskets, rugs and cushions, and other made and 'found' items

felt all-round the edges, to give the effect of pile. A large rug with a complex pattern can be quite time consuming, but if the design and colours are well-chosen the end result will justify the effort involved. A suitable rug or carpet for any period or style of house can be made by this method.

Braided rugs Braided rugs are made by plaiting three strands of wool (tapestry wool is the right thickness and the colour range is extensive) and coiling the plait into a spiral, starting from the centre and working outwards, stitching each round to the previous one with tiny stitches. Plait as long a length of wool as you can comfortably work with to cut down the number of joins, and keep all joins to the underside of the work. The rug will be circular or oval depending on whether it is started by coiling the first few rounds into a circle or sewing them straight up and down. When the rug has reached the required size, finish it by tucking the end to the underside and stitching it in place. A backing of carpet tape or iron-on Vilene will prevent any curling up at the edges.

PICTURES, CLOCKS AND MIRRORS

Magazines are an excellent source of miniature pictures, especially advertisements for prints, which are often found in the colour supplements. Other sources include postage stamps, cigarette or tea cards or your own miniature originals. Try to find pictures which are appropriate to the style of the house – Picasso looks very strange in a Victorian house! Look out for pictures of clock faces of a suitable size.

Pictures can be framed by sticking them onto thin card and using fine wood-strip, mitred at the corners, stuck around them. The surplus cardboard is then cut away and the frame can be painted or stained. Flat buttons with a raised rim make good picture frames and are suitable for wall clocks. Brooch mounts make elaborate frames for a more opulent house. Small standing picture frames can be made in any of these ways, with a block of wood stuck behind the picture to hold it upright.

Pictures can be glazed by using the thin acetate sheet used for packaging, cut to size and held by a fine smear of glue at the edges; but the majority of pictures look better unglazed, as light tends to reflect from the acetate, obscuring the picture.

Any of these framing methods can also be used for mirrors. We generally have mirrors cut to the required size at a glass merchant's. Most glass merchants will do this, it is not expensive, and you end up with a suitably thin mirror with bevelled edges and exactly the right size. Handbag mirrors or mirror tiles are too thick and tin-foil is unrealistic.

Mantel clocks can be made from a block of wood, with a clock-face picture stuck to the front, perhaps framed by a brass curtain ring. Old watches can be used to make dolls'-house clocks, but they are usually too large for anything but a grandfather clock.

Pictures, wall clocks and mirrors usually look best stuck onto the wall, rather than attempting to hang them. Use double-sided Sellotape or a small piece of Blue-Tac or Gripwax.

BOOKS, MAGAZINES AND RECORDS

For making miniature books, magazines and record covers, pictures in magazines are again an invaluable source of materials. If you need a set of books to fill a shelf, cut a block of wood to fit the shelf space and cover it neatly with a magazine picture of a set of books. Advertisements for encyclopaedias show sets of books in about the right size. Alternatively, the wooden block can be covered with plain-coloured paper and the spines of the books drawn in with felt pen.

Individual books can be made by covering blocks of wood in a similar way, or, more realistically, by cutting pages and a cover from thin paper, folding them in half and stitching the spine. If the books are pressed under a heavy weight for a couple of days they will flatten to the proper shape. Magazines can be made by the same method, perhaps using a miniature picture of a magazine from an advertisement for the cover. Given a lot of practice, a magnifying glass and a fine-nibbed pen, you can write your own text and illustrations in the books and magazines!

Record clubs often advertise themselves in magazines by showing a whole page of record covers. These could have been designed especially for a dolls' house as they are exactly the right size, printed clearly and in colour. Cut the page out and stick it to a sheet of firm cardboard. Choose your record collection, and simply cut out the ones you want!

BASKETWARE

The methods described here can be used to make virtually any kind of basket, from a tiny workbasket to a large log basket, using the appropriate thickness of raffia strands (Fig 50). Use natural garden raffia, or the artificial kind sold in art shops.

Cut three strands of a suitable thickness for the item you are making – fine for a small workbasket, thicker for a laundry or log basket. Use the raffia strands as long as you can comfortably work with, as this will reduce the number of joins needed. Knot the three strands together at one end, then plait them together, knotting the other end to finish.

Starting at the centre base of the item you are making and working outwards and upwards, coil the plaited raffia around and around, oversewing each coil to the one before with a strand of fine raffia. Join in new lengths if necessary, keeping all the knots to the inside. When the basket is finished, oversew all-round the top edge to neaten it and make it firm. Handles can be made by sewing plaited raffia loops at the appropriate place.

A workbasket can be filled with a few tiny balls of wool and a piece of knitting worked on dressmaker's pins (sand the points off the pins before you begin), or a piece of miniature embroidery and some cottons wound around tiny lengths of fine dowelling. A pair of scissors from a charm bracelet adds the finishing touch. The log basket can be filled with twigs of the right thickness sawn into roughly ½in lengths. The laundry basket could have neatly folded washing; the wastepaper basket, miniature rubbish; the shopping basket, tiny groceries.

Thick strands of plaited raffia can be used to make rush mats, either round or oval – a piece of carpet tape stuck to the underside will prevent any tendency to curl up. It can also be used to make a baby's moses basket or rush cradle, a dog or cat basket, an Ali-Baba linen basket – and probably several other

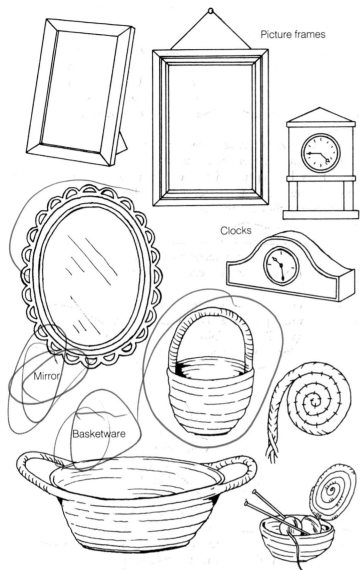

Fig 50 Picture frames, clocks, mirrors and basketware

Wooden beads make excellent door knobs, feet for furniture, or finials for curtain poles. The barrel-shaped ones make good planters, biscuit barrels, flower vases or beer kegs. It is possible to wire and glue together a series of small wooden beads to make a turned leg for a piece of furniture or a newel post for the stairs.

Shallow, flat buttons with rims make good plates. Fill the holes with Polyfilla and give the buttons a coat of enamel paint and perhaps a tiny painted pattern or transfer. Bowl-shaped buttons treated the same way make bowls (sand the bottom if necessary); wooden ones make salad or fruit bowls. Crystal-glass buttons make ashtrays, glass dishes or serving dishes depending on size. Small black or coloured buttons make bases for bead vases or small ornaments. Buttons stuck one on top of another, perhaps a metal button with a crest on top of a plain-coloured one, make tobacco jars, storage jars or pill boxes. The large metal buttons with raised patterns make wall plaques, or, given a coat of copper enamel paint and a dowelling or cocktail-stick handle, a warming pan to hang on the wall. The dome-shaped buttons with a raised pattern, with the shank cut off and painted the appropriate colour, make jelly moulds, cakes or puddings.

Fig 51 Bead and button items, books, magazines and record covers

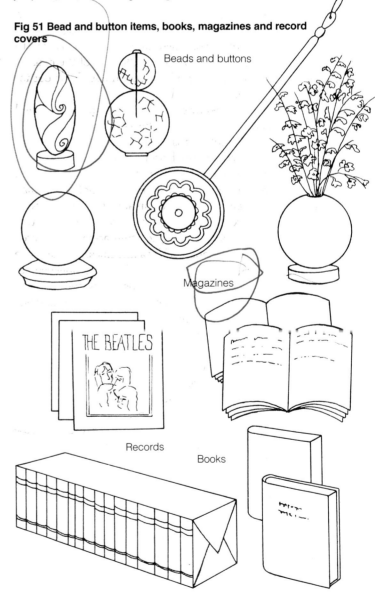

things we haven't thought of yet!

Although it is harder to work with, we prefer natural raffia to the artificial kind for mats and baskets, as the colour deepens with age to a beautiful gold, and it looks and feels better.

BEAD AND BUTTON ITEMS

From the enormous variety of beads and buttons available, numerous dolls'-house items can be made (Fig 51). Look around the local haberdashery department and art and craft shop, and raid friends' button-boxes for supplies. One of the super-glues is best to stick these bits and pieces together, as it will stick glass to plastic or metal, or practically anything else (including people, so use it with care).

Small glass beads, stuck together with a pin through the middle, make perfume bottles or decanters. Sand the bottom if necessary to make them stand properly. A large glass bead, with its bottom sanded, or stuck to a button base will make a crystal flower vase, with tiny dried or artificial flowers glued well into the hole. Coloured-glass or patterned beads can be used on their own or stuck together to make vases, bottles, paperweights, pots, jars or ornaments.

53

FABRIC ITEMS

Scraps of fabric, ribbon and lace will provide the dolls' house with numerous small items of household linen. As with the soft furnishings, the choice of fabric is important. Natural cottons, lawns and silk are generally more use than heavier man-made fabrics, as they both hang and crease better.

Tablecloths can be made in lightweight cotton, cut either rectangular or round to suit the table and hemmed narrowly, or the edges could be frayed out. If you have difficulty getting the cloth to hang properly, damp it before putting it over the table and crease it firmly at the table edge. Tiny napkins can be made in matching or contrasting cotton fabric. Cut the squares carefully on the grain of the fabric and turn tiny hems, fray or blanket stitch the edges as preferred.

Towels are easily made from cotton tape, which comes in a variety of colours and widths. If the ends are cut carefully on the grain they can be neatly hemmed or frayed into a fringe. Crêpe bandage, calico and felt are also good to use as towels. If required, coloured borders or patterns can be marked onto the fabric with felt pen. When making towels for the bathroom, don't forget to cut squares for flannels and bath mats as well. Tea-towels for the kitchen also look well made from coloured cotton tape; or look out for small rectangles of pattern in a cotton print to make modern tea-towels. If hemming these items is beyond you, paint a thin line of glue or Fraycheck along the edge to prevent the fabric from fraying.

Small pieces of lace trimming can be used to make doilies, table mats and antimacassars. Round motifs cut from lace trimming make table mats suitable for any kind of house, and no Victorian parlour is complete without a selection of antimacassars on every chair and doilies under every potted plant! Scraps of pretty ribbon make excellent cushions. Don't stuff the cushion too much, or it will not tuck into the corner of a chair. Narrow embroidered ribbon would make a good bell pull to summon the maid from the Victorian kitchen. Plain-coloured ribbon gathered along one edge makes an ideal valance for the bed, a skirt for the dressing table or a pelmet frill for the curtains (embroidered ribbon also makes attractive pelmets if it matches the curtains). Wide ribbon is an excellent choice for simple curtains, needing hemming only at top and bottom.

FOLDING SCREEN

A folding screen was generally found somewhere in a Victorian house, either to block a draught or to undress modestly behind, and is easy to make and effective. Cut three or four panels of thick cardboard or thin obeche wood – approximately 4 x 1½in for a 1/16 scale house or 5½ x 2in for a 1/12 scale house. The panels are hinged together with strips of ½in wide black cotton tape, cut slightly shorter than the panels. Glue the tape to the panels, leaving a slight gap between each panel. Frame each panel on both sides with fine wood-strip, mitred at the corners. If required, paint or stain the wooden frame. The panels can be decorated with fabric or paper, cut to fit and stuck in place, or, more interestingly, with scraps of pictures. This last method is time consuming and fiddly, but rewarding, as the completed scrap screen is quite charming. Scraps on one side only, with a patterned

paper on the other side, reduces the amount of work, and a coat of varnish (paper varnish is the best for this kind of work) will protect the end product.

WOODEN ITEMS

Fine wooden dowelling, cocktail-sticks, square beading and scraps of thin obeche wood can be used to make a variety of wooden items. Use a craft knife with a sharp blade to cut the wooden pieces, with a metal ruler as a guide for cutting straight edges. With such small pieces, painting is often fiddly, but felt pens will colour wood effectively and are much easier to use.

A set of coloured pencils can be made from cocktail-sticks, by cutting lengths ½in long from the pointed ends of the sticks. Colour the points and most of the sticks with different coloured felt pens, leaving a small amount of bare wood around the point to represent the sharpened part of the pencil. A set of these pencils look effective in a mug or glass on the dolls'-house desk.

Square beading, ⅛in or ¼in thick, can be cut into cubes to make children's building blocks. Colour each face of the blocks in different coloured felt pens, perhaps drawing letters of the alphabet or simple pictures (an apple or fish) over the colour.

Fine round dowelling and obeche scraps can be used to

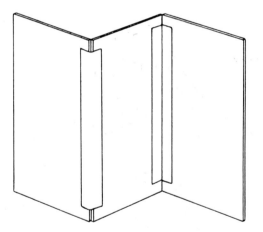

Fig 52 Making the folding screen

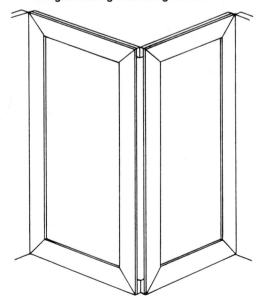

make a roller towel for an old-fashioned kitchen, a set of coat pegs and wooden kitchen tools. The roller towel is a length of dowelling with a tiny gimp pin pushed into each end. This is supported by a piece of thin obeche wood, cut a little wider than the roller. Two small eye-screws are screwed into the obeche wood to hold the gimp pins at each end of the roller. A towel made from a length of cotton tape, 1in or 1½in wide, is seamed at the short ends and slipped onto the roller.

The set of coat pegs can be made in any length. Cut a board from obeche wood, as wide and deep as you require, and drill holes of the same diameter as the dowelling pegs at regular intervals. Cut the dowelling pegs to even lengths of approximately ¼in and glue them into the holes – the coat pegs can be stained. This set of pegs might also be used for hanging pots and pans or cooking tools in the kitchen.

With a little skill, a rolling pin with handles can be whittled from round dowelling, but if this is beyond you, glass-headed pins, cut short, can be glued into holes drilled into the ends of a length of fine dowelling. This rolling pin looks well on a pastry board cut from a piece of obeche wood. A similar board, cut to shape, will make a modern chopping board. Drill a fine hole through the handle, and cover one side with a picture, varnished to represent melamine. A square board of obeche wood could be ruled into squares and coloured to represent a draughts or chess board. Small slices of dowelling would make draughts, but whittling a chess set in this scale would be quite a task!

MOPS AND BROOMS

Very fine dowelling is used for the handles of mops and brooms, the top end sanded round. For the head of the mop, cut strands of soft white cotton thread such as crochet cotton about 3in long. Holding the bunch of cotton threads together in one hand, push the handle down into the middle of them. Bind the threads tightly to the handle halfway down their length, with cotton or fusewire. Shake the mop so that all the threads hang downwards and trim them to the required length. For a 'witch's' broom, use bristles or the finest twigs you can find and bind them to the handle close to the top of the bunch, then trim roughly to the right length (Fig 54).

A modern broom can be made by cutting the head off a toothbrush and sanding the cut end to match the other. A hole is drilled in the centre of the head and the dowelling handle glued into place. Small hand or hearth brushes can be made from mascara brushes or the small ones sold for cleaning sewing machines, cut down to the required size.

FOODS

Dolls'-house foods can be modelled in bread paste (equal amounts of flour and salt with a little water) and Das or similar self-hardening clays, and painted with poster or acrylic colours, but are more easily made in Fimo (available from art and craft shops). Fimo is a self-coloured modelling material which is easy to work with and comes in a wide range of colours which can be mixed to make the exact colour of any fruit, vegetable or almost anything else so does not need painting. Modelled items are baked in a domestic oven to harden. If you model all the items you want – this can be done over a period of time as the Fimo will not harden until it is baked – they can all be placed on a baking sheet together which is more economical than baking one or two items at a time. When modelling it is usually best to choose things which have simple, recognisable shapes and it is helpful to have the lifesize item in front of you to copy, and keep a doll by you to check the size.

A loaf of bread – perhaps a cottage loaf – on a bread board is simple and looks at home in any kitchen. A pie is easily made if it is modelled in the dish, lining the dish with clay as a real pie dish is lined with pastry, and using tiny beads or balls of clay for the fruit filling. Flute the edges of the pastry lid for the finishing touch. A string of sausages (joined by a cotton thread through the middle), eggs, a chicken or a ham, or a cake, are all good choices (Fig 54).

Packets of foodstuffs such as corn flakes can be made by cutting labels and packet fronts from magazine advertisements and wrapping them around blocks of wood. Look out also for various seeds from garden plants, which look like miniature vegetables. Clarkia seed pods for example look exactly right as tiny cucumbers – these things are not suitable for children's houses!

Pasta, salt, flour, lentils, rice and other stuffs which will not deteriorate or go sticky can all be used as dolls'-house foodstuffs

Pencils

Building blocks

Chopping boards

Games board

Roller towel

Coat pegs

Fig 53 Small wooden items

Fig 54 Brooms, mops, sacks and modelled foodstuffs

given a coat of paint, make a variety of containers or dishes. A toothpaste cap becomes a flower pot; a small tin lid, a tin tray. Washing-up-liquid bottle caps make flagons; shallow screw caps make dishes or baking tins. Oddments of metal, nails, screws, rivets, washers, cotter pins, etc can all be used. Washers make rings for kitchen stoves, cotter pins make firedogs for the hearth. A certain kind of rivet is perfect for a dolls'-house poker complete with handle. The secret is to look at all these bits and pieces with a dolls'-house maker's eye. What does the shape remind you of? What would it look like painted brass or copper or black?

Key rings often have useful things attached, perhaps a tiny teddy bear or a pair of football boots. Pencil sharpeners are sometimes disguised as globes or cash registers, even kitchen stoves! Charm bracelets carry lots of things which would fit very happily into a dolls' house.

Cake ornaments are useful, from the white wedding-cake pillars, which make good pedestals for busts or jardinières, to the miniature trains or cars which will fit into the nursery. Cake-size bunches of artificial flowers fit dolls'-house vases, and tiny marzipan fruits will last quite well if you varnish them. Christmas-cake trees can stand in tubs outside the front door, or be decorated with beads for a Christmas tree.

Souvenir shops sell lots of tiny items – miniature Limoges vases or china potties, small brass kettles and candlesticks. Some games include pieces with dolls'-house possibilities (eg Monopoly), and odd wooden chess pieces with the tops cut off make excellent turned pedestals for tables. Knights from a small chess set make ornaments or book-ends. Miniature lead soldiers and horses for battle games look very effective polished up for ornaments. A clear greenish-glass marble mounted on a black button stand makes a good crystal ball for the Victorian parlour. Tiny shells found on the beach make pretty dolls'-house collections.

Empty vaccine bottles (ask for them at your doctor's surgery) make storage jars for the kitchen, or a sweet shop. The smallest empty perfume bottles find a place as decanters. Pill boxes make pretty work or jewel boxes. Christmas crackers often contain miniature toys for the nursery. Broken jewellery might make brooch-mount picture frames, ear-ring ornaments or charm-bracelet door-bells. An empty lipstick case will make an umbrella stand to hold walking sticks, made from cocktail sticks with bead handles.

Half a ping-pong ball makes a good modern light fitting for the bathroom when stuck to the ceiling. Thin split-bamboo table mats can be cut down to make rush matting. Those perfumed sachets, about an inch square, prettily embroidered and lace trimmed, which are sold in haberdashery departments, make beautiful cushions or nightdress cases. Miniature china animals look particularly good as dolls'-house ornaments.

The possibilities are endless!

in the appropriate containers, and miniature bottles can be filled with vinegar, cochineal, or paint and water for wine and milk.

'FOUND' ITEMS

The number of dolls'-house items which can be contrived from odds-and-ends is limitless. Lids and caps from bottles and pots,

7 GARDENING

MATERIALS

Even if you do not plan to make a garden for your dolls' house, you may want to have a climbing plant around the porch, some window boxes or shrubs in tubs by the front door.

The dolls'-house shops sell a range of craftsman-made plants in pots or containers and you may choose to fill a garden with these but they are expensive, and with the right materials plants are not difficult to make. The first source of supply is the range of trees, plants and hedging sold for model-railway landscaping. These are in a smaller scale than dolls' houses so the trees will make bushes and the bushes will make plants. The model shops also sell flocked paper 'grass' which makes splendid lawns and lichen or reindeer moss in a variety of shades of green which makes good plant material. Tiny dried flowers, which are available from florists and garden centres, make the most realistic flowering plants and you will need as large a selection as you can find in natural colours. Look out for twigs which can be used for stems and branches and stones which could be used for a rockery. Cake shops sell pillars in plaster or plastic which will make pedestals, birdbaths or sundials, and small fir trees used for decorating Christmas cakes make small conifers and can be decorated with beads for miniature Christmas trees. The dolls'-house 'claddings' which are available from the specialist shops in various brick patterns make good paths, and the pebbledash patterns make good gravel paths or 'mud' for the flower beds. The specialist shops also sell garden tools and terracotta flower pots, planters and wooden tubs.

You will need small, sharp scissors, a pair of wire cutters and a craft knife. One of the craft glues which dries clear is best for plant-making and UHU or a similar strong, tacky glue for holding plants to walls.

CLIMBERS

Simple but very effective climbers can be made with sprigs of dried plant material. Try the plant sprigs in place to choose the most suitable pieces, arranging them so that they branch out naturally and trim off any pieces which spoil the arrangement. Glue the sprigs in place where they touch the wall or porch with UHU or a similar tacky glue. These are fragile and will not last very long before they fade but it is quick and simple to replace them.

Climbers can also be made by glueing suitable small twigs to the wall and glueing clumps of lichen or moss to the twigs. Add flowers, glued one at a time into the lichen.

SHRUBS IN TUBS

Tubs can be made from bottle caps or spray can lids. Paint the lids with acrylic or Humbrol enamel paint and if you wish, mark and paint staves and bands to represent wooden tubs. Fill the tubs with brown oasis or similar plant arranging material, or brown plasticine, to represent mud. Choose railway-model trees or bushes and if necessary shorten the wire stems. Push the stems into the oasis and glue if necessary.

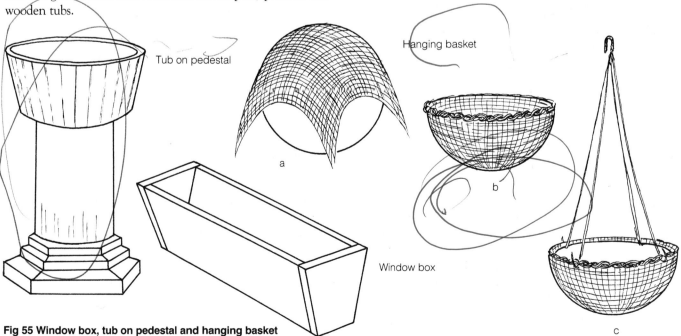

Tub on pedestal

Hanging basket

a

b

Window box

c

Fig 55 Window box, tub on pedestal and hanging basket

57

A small, walled garden with plants, garden tools and a birdbath

Plants in tubs Similar tubs, filled with oasis can be planted with lichen or reindeer moss glued in place. Cut and glue tiny dried flowers, and push the stems into the oasis one at a time. If you want your tub on a pedestal, cut a wedding-cake pillar to the required length and glue the tub onto the cut end.

WINDOW BOXES
Make the window boxes in ³⁄₃₂in thick obeche or bass wood (see Chapter 5) to fit the width of the window. Stain or paint the boxes – green is traditional – and fill with oasis. Glue the boxes in place beneath the windows and fill with lichen and flowers, glued in place.

HANGING BASKETS
To make the hanging baskets you will need a small piece of embroidery canvas and a mould of the appropriate size; a ball or large marble for a round-bottomed basket or a bottle cap or similar for a flat-bottomed basket. Cover the mould with cling-film or polythene and soak the canvas in craft glue or wallpaper paste. Press the canvas around the mould and leave to dry. Ease the basket off the mould and trim the top edge with small sharp scissors. Reinforce and neaten the top edge with plaited canvas threads glued in place and paint the basket dark green if required. Use fine wire or canvas threads to hang the basket and fill with lichen and flowers. Brackets for hanging baskets can be bought from the specialist shops.

MAKING A GARDEN
The garden can be made to complement a dolls' house or as a separate project and can be any size you wish. It is made on its own base and is not attached to the house so that it does not impede the front openings.

If you make a front garden for your house, consider the front door when planning the arrangement of walls, path and flower beds and the period of the house when designing the style of the garden, For example, a cottage garden with a brick path suits the Tudor cottage, but a Georgian house needs something a little more formal.

To make the garden, cut a base in ¼in or ⅜in plywood and sand all the edges. If you want walls, cut these in plywood and glue and pin them to the base using white woodworkers' glue and veneer pins. The archway shown above was drawn onto

the plywood with a compass, cut with a fretsaw and glued to the walls. The walls may be painted with two or three coats of matt emulsion paint or painted to represent brick or stone. Walls could also be papered with brick or stone dolls'-house exterior paper or 'cladding' applied with wallpaper paste. (See Chapter 3.)

Cut a path in brick or pebbledash cladding and glue to the plywood base with craft glue. Cut flocked paper grass to fit, coat the back liberally with craft glue and smooth onto the plywood, butting the edges against the path and allow to dry. Cut flower beds in brown pebbledash cladding and try in place. With a craft-knife, cut through the grass around the flower bed and peel it away from the base. Glue the back of the flower bed and press it in place in the cut-out space so that the edges of grass and flower bed are flush.

Arrange the lichen or moss and railway-model plant materials on the flower bed and glue in place with craft glue. Cut, glue and place tiny dried flowers, one at a time, in the lichen. Arrange climbers, and glue where they touch the walls. Drill holes into the plywood base to receive railway-model trees and bushes, shorten the stems if necessary and screw the trees into the drilled holes. Arrange and glue railway-model hedging beside the path if required.

Wedding-cake pillars can be painted with acrylic or poster colours to resemble stone to make a birdbath or sundial. Cut a plate and gnomon for the sundial in card or thin metal and glue in place and fill the birdbath with water or resin. Try the pillar in place, cut out the area of grass around the base and peel away. Glue the base and fit into the cut-out.

If you wish to make a door or gate for your garden, consult Chapter 2. The garden tools shown in the picture are inexpensive miniatures from a specialist shop. The deckchair

A larger garden with walls, terrace and steps made from modelling clay

59

is from our book *Making Miniatures*, where anyone with green fingers will find lots more gardening ideas. (See Books, page 188.)

The garden shown on page 58 is small and there is not room for more, but if you make a larger garden there are a number of possibilities. You could include a garden bench, made from a kit (see the Tudor cottage) or made in obeche or bass wood. A stone bench can be modelled in Das or similar clay to rest on small pilasters cut from cake pillars and painted matt grey. A standard rose bush can be made from a small polystyrene ball, with a twig pushed and glued into the ball as a stem. Coat the ball with craft glue and lichen and add tiny dried flowers. Plant the rose bush in a tub or glue the stem into a hole drilled into the garden base.

Embroidery canvas, stiffened with craft glue and painted dark brown or white, will make a trellis for climbing plants or can be glued to wire hoops to make an arch.

You might like to model a wishing well in Das or similar clay or build a bird table in obeche or bass wood. A pond can be made in a shallow plastic box or lid, painted grey and filled with weeds and pebbles and resin 'water'. The pond can be set into a hole cut in the base or surrounded by a small modelled wall. Make a rockery with small stones glued together and plant material tucked into the crannies.

Railway-model hedging will make excellent 'clipped box' hedging for a Tudor knot garden, with brown pebbledash cladding paths.

Look in the specialist shops for small statues, garden gnomes or other ornaments to decorate your garden, and don't forget a few 'human touches' like the occasional weed in the path or forgotten tools in the flower bed.

THE LARGER GARDEN

The larger garden shown on page 59 is made in the same way as the small garden, on a plywood base with back and side walls. The raised terrace and the steps are cut in balsa wood – with a cut-out for the pond – and glued onto the base. The walls, terrace and steps are covered with brick and stone made from Das modelling clay. Roll-out the Das (like pastry) with a rolling pin to approximately ⅛in thick and cut pieces to cover each wall, the steps and the terrace. Mark the bricks and stones with a pointed tool and leave to dry. When dry, the Das sheets are glued to the wall, steps and terrace with UHU or similar glue and painted with acrylic or poster colours. The pond is made as described above, and glued into the cut-out in the terrace. The gate, plant troughs and flower pots are from a dolls'-house shop and we have added a garden bench, a sundial, a rockery and a tree stump cut from a small tree branch. The flower beds and climbing plants are made as described earlier and the ivy, strawberry pot and delphiniums are from a dolls'-house shop. Plastic cake decorations, painted with acrylic paints, make convincing statues or small animals in the garden, and a larger plastic animal could be painted and mounted on a cut-down cake pedestal to make an impressive statue. (Anyone who would like detailed plans and instructions for making this garden will find them in *Making Miniatures* see page 188.)

8 THE CUPBOARD HOUSE

Making a dolls' house in a cupboard is a very old-fashioned idea. In the seventeenth century, the early Dutch 'Baby Houses' were toys for rich women, many of whom were married at fourteen or fifteen, and were displayed with pride in the drawing room. In England too, during the eighteenth century, these adult toys were often made in cupboards. The Baby Houses usually contained valuable collections of exquisite craftsman-made miniature furniture, silver, porcelain and paintings and many of them have survived to be admired in museums. This is the ideal dolls' house for anyone who does not want a traditional house or is more interested in decorating and furnishing a house than in building one.

THE CUPBOARD

First, find your cupboard! The choice will depend on how many rooms you want, how much you want to spend and what is available. You will probably be working in 1/12 scale as this type of dolls' house is most likely to appeal to an adult with sophisticated taste, so you need something which will make well-proportioned rooms of perhaps 12–18in wide by 8–12in deep with a ceiling height of 9–12in. This is most likely to be a wall-hung cupboard or perhaps the top part of a dresser or a bookcase, and there is a fairly wide choice of old cupboards available in antique shops and junk shops. Take a tape-measure with you when you go shopping and be prepared to keep a fairly open mind. You may find it simpler to telephone the shops in your area, describing what you want and asking if they have anything suitable. (Such a call offered us four possible cupboards in a shop that we might not otherwise have tried.)

Your cupboard should have shelves at the right heights for ceilings (or adjustable shelves) and sufficient space on each shelf for the things you are likely to want to include. If you are planning a period house, room sizes and ceilings should be credible for the period, for example, Georgian houses generally have spacious rooms with high ceilings but if you want a Victorian cottage it should have small rooms with lower ceilings. The cupboard could have a glazed door so that you can see the contents, or a wooden door so that the dolls'-house interior is a surprise. The door or doors should open fully, or be removable, for access when decorating.

LINING

You may choose to decorate the interior of the cupboard, but if it is an antique which would be spoiled by wallpapering or painting it should be lined with cardboard. Use good quality poster board, available from art shops and cut the pieces to fit with a craft knife and metal ruler.

Measure and cut card to fit the ceiling of each room

(turning the cupboard upside-down makes this easier) and fix the card in place with narrow double-sided sellotape along each edge. Measure and cut card to fit the back walls of each room and fix with tape, then measure, cut and fix the side walls. If you intend to use flooring or fitted carpet; measure, cut and fix lining on the floors. Check that the lining does not impede the cupboard door closing and trim the card if necessary. When the card is in place, the decorating is applied to the lining and will not damage the cupboard in any way.

Chimney breasts Measure and cut chimney breasts in balsa wood (see Chapter 2). Cut out the fireplace opening and glue the chimney breast in place.

Doors and windows False doors and windows can be simply glued to the wall but they are more convincing if they are properly built into a false wall. Measure and cut a piece of ¼in thick plywood to fit the side or back wall of the room. Cut out the doorway or window hole and fit the door or window, and the door or window frame. You can use commercial doors and windows from a specialist supplier or make your own using the instructions in Chapter 2. As there is nothing for the door to open onto, it is better not to hinge it but simply to glue it in place. Windows might have a 'view' cut from a magazine or greetings card pasted onto the card lining behind them. It is easier to paint or stain the window or door and frame before the false wall is fixed in place. Glue the back of the false wall and fix it in place to the lining.

DECORATING

See Chapter 3 for instructions for decorating. Cut and fit the cornice, mitring or butting the corners as you prefer, and glueing it to both the wall and ceiling card lining. Paint the cornice and ceiling with two coats of emulsion paint (turning the cupboard upside-down makes this easier).

Paper the walls with lining paper if you intend to paint them, or dolls'-house wallpaper or life-size paper as you prefer, applied with wallpaper paste and leave to dry. Paint the walls with two coats of emulsion paint.

Fit the fireplace surrounds. These can be bought from dolls'-house suppliers, but if you prefer to make your own see Chapter 2 and the house plans.

Measure and cut the skirting boards. Paint or stain and glue in place with UHU or similar glue.

Measure, cut and fix floor coverings. Floor papers can be applied with wallpaper paste, fitted carpet with double-sided tape around the edges.

In an antique cupboard it is not practicable to make holes

A small antique pine cupboard gives no hint of its dolls'-house interior

kitchen. The proportions lend themselves very well to a Georgian house so the elaborate plaster fireplace surrounds and the decorating scheme are elegant and timeless.

The house is inhabited in the present day by a couple who prefer traditional fixtures like the Aga cooker and the Belfast sink, and antique furniture. The sink, with its brass taps, is available from dolls'-house shops, and this Aga and a modern version are available from Gable End (see Stockists) both as a kit or ready-made to order in all the Aga colours. The pine fireplace surround and the kitchen units built in around the sink are made in stained bass wood, using the methods described in Chapter 5, and have small brass knobs painted with gloss enamel to represent china. The fireplaces and fenders in the drawing room and bedroom are good quality brass miniatures from a specialist shop.

The furnishings in this house, as in any English country house, are a mixture of styles and periods and range from fine-quality craftsman-made pieces to cheap imported items. In the bedroom, the fine brass bed has a duvet and bedding made as those in the modern house. The wooden furniture can be found in our book *Making Miniatures* and the pictures are cut from a Marks & Spencer catalogue. In the drawing room, the sofa and chairs (Dijon) are inexpensive imported pieces, the bureau bookcase, pedestal table and chess set and table are our own. In the kitchen, the miniature packages (Thames Valley) give the room a sense of 'life', the clock is made from a kit, the kitchen table and small cupboard (Carol and Nigel Lodder) are craftsman pieces, and the dresser, chairs and small table can be found in *Making Miniatures* (see Books). The rugs, ornaments and accessories in the house are all available from most dolls'-house shops and suppliers.

The cupboard house is scented by the miniature pot-pourri in the blue bowl in the drawing room made by crumbling real pot-pourri and dried lavender as fine as possible. Sprigs of lavender or perfumed sachets can also be used to scent any dolls' house – as the front is usually kept closed, the perfume lasts well.

VARIATIONS

If you choose a wider cupboard which has room for more than one room on each shelf, you will need to make partition walls. Line the cupboard with card as described earlier and plan where you want the partitions. These need not occur in the same place on each floor – for example, you might divide the top floor into a larger and a smaller room for bedroom and bathroom, leave the middle floor as one large room for a parlour and divide the ground floor into equal sized rooms as kitchen and dining room. In a wide cupboard there may be room to make a central hallway with a flight of stairs and rooms opening from each side.

Mark where you want the partitions in pencil on the card liner, back wall, floor and ceilings, as a guide for fitting.

Cut the partition walls in ¼in plywood and cut out doorways. Doors can be hinged on to open from one room to another, but remember to allow sufficient clearance for floor coverings and it is easier to decorate doors and frames before the partition is fitted. Coat the back, top and bottom edges of the partition with UHU or similar glue and slide into place,

for wiring lights so any lights must be non-functional, but if you wish to have working lights see Chapter 3, and use any of the kits available for dolls' houses.

FURNISHING

The cupboard house shown opposite was designed in the spirit of a Baby House, as an adult's toy and is based on the houses shown in magazines like *Country Living* and *Ideal Homes*, including all the clichés such as the Aga, the green wellies and the labrador. We decided, for fun, to give the house a 'lived-in' air as a change from the orderliness which usually prevails in houses in *Country Living* and in dolls' houses so the bed is unmade, last evening's chess game is still in progress and the washing-up is not done.

The cupboard is an English antique pine one with a very nice brass lock – most of the Baby Houses had locks to prevent the servants and children helping themselves to the contents. The cupboard is 27in tall, 16in wide and 11in deep and makes three large, well proportioned rooms. We have fitted a false wall on the right side with windows in the bedroom and drawing room and a door in the kitchen. The chimney breasts are wide and shallow in the upper rooms and deeper in the

following the marked guidelines and supporting if necessary until the glue dries. At this stage, the partition walls are not very secure but when cornice, wallpaper and skirting are fitted into each room the partitions will be properly supported. Finish the front edges of the partition walls with paint, wallpaper or woodstrip as you prefer.

If you use a cupboard which has no intrinsic value, the

The interior of the Cupboard House, decorated and furnished in *Country Living* style

outside could be decorated to represent a house. Windows and door can be painted on or could be cut in the cupboard door, and any of the ideas for exterior decoration in Chapter 3 could be applied to the cupboard house.

9 THE ANTIQUE SHOP

The Antique shop is the ideal project for anyone who wants to display a small collection of miniature furniture and accessories. They can be shown to better advantage in this situation than in a room setting, where many pieces would be placed against a wall and obscured.

The shop is designed in 1/12 scale and is simple to make, even for the beginner. It is basically a box with a front, divided at the centre and hinged to open at both sides. The hipped roof is made separately and fits inside the pediment around the top of the box. We have used a ready-made door and windows from Blackwells (see Stockists) in mock Georgian style as we felt these were most appropriate, but any other ready-made door and windows may be substituted for these. If you prefer to make your own see Chapter 2 for instructions. If you use a different door and windows, check the measurements before cutting as the dimensions given on the patterns may need adjusting.

MATERIALS
⅜in plywood for walls, floor and ceiling
thick posterboard or art card for the roof
picture-frame moulding for the pediment
four 1in hinges to hang the fronts
wood glue, veneer pins and masking tape
door and large window for the front
small window (optional) for the side

CUTTING
Draw the pattern pieces onto the plywood using a sharp pencil and ruler. Ensure that all right-angles are correct, the measurements are precise and label each piece to avoid confusion when assembling. Cut the pieces including door and window holes and smooth all edges with a small plane or sandpaper. Tape the pieces together with masking tape to check that they fit properly and make any necessary adjustments.

ASSEMBLY
Glue and pin the back onto the base. Glue and pin the sides onto the base and to the back. Glue and pin the top onto the sides and back, ensuring that all joins are square. Note that the base and top protrude to allow for the fronts.

The door and windows are more easily painted before they are fitted and glued into the side and fronts, and the shop is more easily decorated before the windows and door are fitted and the fronts are hinged in place.

Cut the pediment in picture-frame moulding. Cut the front piece first, with mitred ends and glue to the top front edge of the box, ensuring that it does not obstruct the front openings. Cut and fix the side and back pieces, with mitred ends, to line up with the front piece. The pediment rises above the top of the box, making a frame to hold the roof securely in place.

ROOF
The roof is cut to fit inside the pediment. Cut the pieces in poster board and tape the back and front pieces butted together, with masking tape, along the ridge on the underside. Try the back and front roof in place, resting inside the pediment, and tape the ridge join on the outside. Try the side pieces in place and trim if necessary to ensure that they fit properly, then with the roof pieces in place, tape the sides to the back and front. Reinforce the joins with tape on the underside and outside so that the roof is rigid. Do not glue the roof in place until the shop is decorated and the lighting installed.

DECORATING
We decorated the exterior of the Antique shop with embossed 'cladding' in dark red brick and grey slates from Hobbys (see Stockists), but any dolls'-house exterior papers or emulsion paint would be equally suitable. The interior can be papered or painted as you prefer, but lining paper will provide a better surface for painting on, including the ceiling. The front edges of the box and the edges of the two fronts can be painted or covered with brick paper, lapped round from the exterior, or faced with thin woodstrip. Note that if you use woodstrip you may need to plane the edges where the fronts meet a little before applying it to ensure that the fronts close properly. We decorated the interior of the Antique shop with a commercial dolls'-house wallpaper and used cornice, skirting and architrave mouldings from Hobbys.

Exterior Decorate the exterior first. Paint the pediment with two coats of acrylic or gloss or satin finish enamel paint, covering the front, top and back edges.

If painting the walls, sand thoroughly and apply two or three coats of emulsion paint allowing each coat to dry before applying the next. Paint the edges if required, extending the paint about ½in onto the interior walls.

If papering, apply a coat of wallpaper paste to the walls, then paste and apply the paper (or cladding), wrapping and trimming to lap around the edges if required and extend about ½in onto the interior walls. If you wish to apply wood strip to the edges, cut and stain the woodstrip and glue in place then apply the paper, trimmed to fit without lapping. Trim around the door and window holes and take care to ensure that any brick pattern lines up, especially where the fronts meet.

Paper the roof in separate sections for the most realistic effect, using the roof patterns to cut the paper and taking care to line up the slates or tiles as neatly as possible. We added embossed hip tiles over each join and ridge tiles along the top.

Paint the door and windows with acrylic or satin-finish enamel paint. Note that the acrylic glazing used in ready-made windows should be removed for painting. Fit and glue the door and windows in place with UHU or wood glue.

Interior Apply a coat of wallpaper paste to the walls and ceilings. Turn the box upside-down to rest on the pediment and apply lining paper to the ceiling. Cut cornice moulding with mitred corners and glue in place to the walls and ceiling. Paint the ceiling and cornice with two coats of matt finish emulsion paint.

Paper the walls (with lining paper if you intend to paint) applied with wallpaper paste and apply two coats of emulsion paint if required. Cut and stain or paint skirting and glue in place with mitred corners. Paper (and paint) the insides of the fronts, trimming the paper to fit just inside the edges and taking care to line up any pattern. It is not practical to fit cornice and skirting on the fronts as this would impede their closing.

Cut architrave mouldings, if required, with mitred corners, stain or paint and glue in place around door and windows. We framed the small side window and door and the top and sides of the shop window, fitting a shelf on brackets at the lower edge.

Cut and fit the floor covering and glue in place. Note that the flooring should be cut to line up with the side walls and not extended to the front edge. We used a self-adhesive wooden floor (Hobbys) stained with light oak woodstain and finished with wax polish, see Chapter 3 for other flooring ideas.

FINISHING

Cut a shelf, if required, in obeche or bass wood and small brackets in moulding. Glue the brackets to the underside of the shelf. Cut a rail in fine wood strip with mitred corners and glue to the sides and back edges of the shelf. Paint the shelf and glue to the wall beneath the window.

Hinge the fronts onto the box, rebating the hinges in both fronts and side-front edges and fixing with super glue and small screws.

Install the ceiling light by drilling a hole in the ceiling to feed the wire through and glueing the light fitting to the ceiling. Tape the wire across the top of the box to the centre back leaving the end protruding under the roof to plug into the transformer.

Interior of the Antique shop, displaying a collection of fine quality craftsman-made miniatures

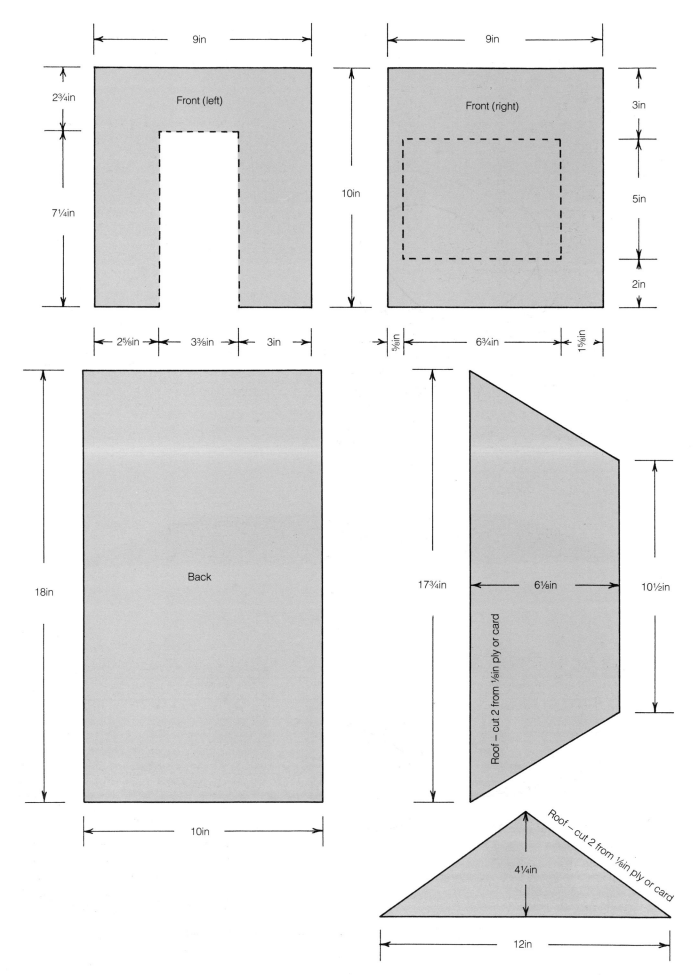

9in

Front (left)

2¾in

7¼in

10in

2⅝in 3⅜in 3in

9in

Front (right)

3in

5in

2in

⅝in 6¾in 1⅝in

18in

Back

10in

17¾in 6⅛in 10½in

Roof – cut 2 from ⅛in ply or card

4¼in

Roof – cut 2 from ⅛in ply or card

12in

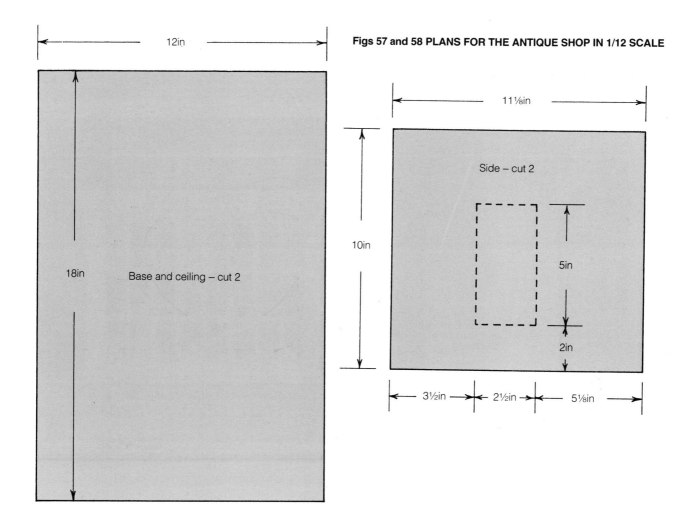

12in

18in

Base and ceiling – cut 2

11⅛in

10in

Side – cut 2

5in

2in

3½in

2½in

5⅛in

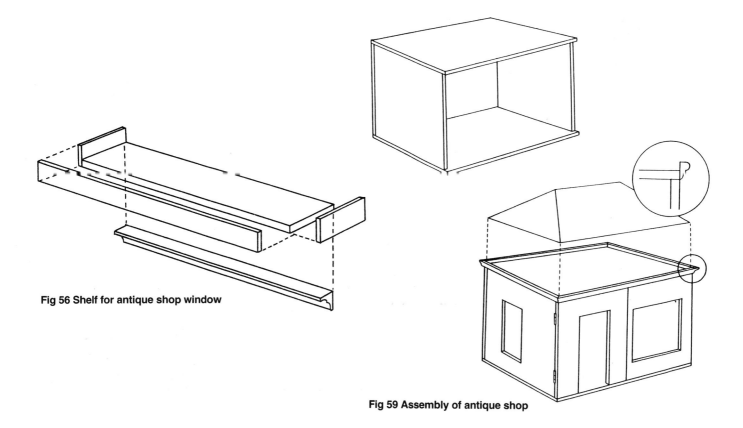

Fig 56 Shelf for antique shop window

Fig 59 Assembly of antique shop

Exterior of the Antique shop – desirable shop premises, suitable for most trades

Run a line of glue around the top of the box, inside the pediment and fit the roof in place. If you prefer, the roof can be removable by attaching a small tape or ribbon loop to the back edge so that it can be lifted off.

Our 'Cobwebs' sign was made with Letraset on card, framed with picture-frame moulding and glued in place above the window. Directions for making the hanging basket and plants in containers can be found in Chapter 7. The pavement is made from plywood covered in pebbledash effect, dolls'-house cladding, and the credit card and open/closed signs in the window are magazine cut-outs.

FURNISHING
The items displayed in the Antique shop are fine quality craftsman-made miniatures. The painted dresser and the porcelain on it are made by Carol and Nigel Lodder, the rocking horse and ship by Brian Nickolls and the trunk by Bob Bradshaw. The other furniture pieces are our own and the shop's proprietor was made to commission by Sunday Dolls. Similar items and accessories can be found in the specialist shops or you might enjoy a day spent at a miniatures fair choosing items to stock your shop. If you prefer to make the stock, the patterns for the Victorian town house and the Tudor cottage can be used to make 'antique' furniture, and the methods described in Chapter 6 to make accessories.

VARIATIONS
If you are a beginner to miniatures and want to 'try your hand' before embarking on a dolls' house, the plans for the Antique shop can be used to make a room box. If you omit the pediment, roof and fronts, adapt the side window, and add a chimney breast and a false door, you will have a large, well-proportioned room which can be furnished in any way you please.

The shop can be adapted to any trade; shop fittings, shelves and counters can all be found in the specialist shops or made in obeche or bass wood and the shop stocked with bought or made items. A Victorian draper's shop would be an enjoyable project, with shelves filled with fabrics and trimmings, tailor's dummies and hatstands, a cheval mirror and elegant chairs for the customers. Consider an old-fashioned grocer's shop with sacks and boxes of provisions, bottles and tins on the shelves, scales with weights and a cash register, or a toy-shop stocked with tiny dolls and teddies, toy animals, cars and trains. More unusual ideas include a furniture-maker's or restorer's workshop, a photographer's or artist's studio or an art gallery displaying paintings and sculpture. Miniature carpentry tools, artists' materials or photographic equipment are available from specialist shops to lend realism to the project, and if you choose a background to complement your own skills most of the contents can be your own work. For example, an art gallery might display your own miniature paintings or photographs and a milliner's shop could be stocked with your own elegant creations.

10 THE VICTORIAN TOWN HOUSE

The Victorian town house is a simple project, ideal for the first-time housebuilder. It has three rooms, no internal doors or staircase and a fixed gable roof. The tall, narrow shape takes up little space, but the rooms are quite large and well-proportioned with high ceilings which make viewing and access easy.

The windows in the side wall make the rooms light and the fireplaces on the back wall provide focal points in each room. The house front opens in one piece, hinged on one side or, if you prefer, could be made simply to lift off.

The furniture patterns are for simple pieces which can be made in obeche wood, stained to represent mahogany and pine or painted, and instructions for accessories are given in Chapter 6.

The plans and patterns are all given in both 1/16 scale and 1/12 scale so you can choose whichever you prefer, but of course you should use the same scale throughout.

The house shown on page 76 was decorated with commercial dolls'-house papers, old brick and slate patterns for the exterior and the same wallpaper pattern in different colours for the bedroom and parlour – the kitchen was painted magnolia.

We used commercial mouldings for the cornice and skirting boards and fine woodstrip for door and window frames. The floors are commercial papers, parquet in the bedroom and parlour and tiles in the kitchen. Similar papers and mouldings are available from most dolls'-house shops or from Hobbys (see Stockists) by post, but any of the decorating suggestions in Chapter 3 might be used as alternatives.

You may find it helpful to refer to Chapter 2 on building before beginning.

MATERIALS
¼in plywood for the house in 1/16 scale
⅜in plywood for the house in 1/12 scale
⅛in plywood for the roof (in either scale)
cornice (or picture frame) moulding for the ledges
commercial moulding or woodstrip for skirting
1/16in perspex for the windows
⅛in and 1/16in obeche wood for the front door
fine woodstrip for door and window frames and glazing bars
three wooden beads for the chimney pots
two ½in hinges for the door
three 1in hinges for the front
balsa block for the chimney breast and stack:
  4 × ½in in 1/16 scale or
  5¼ × ¾in 1/12 scale
wood glue, veneer pins, masking tape

Exterior of the Victorian town house – small and easy to build, a good choice for the beginner

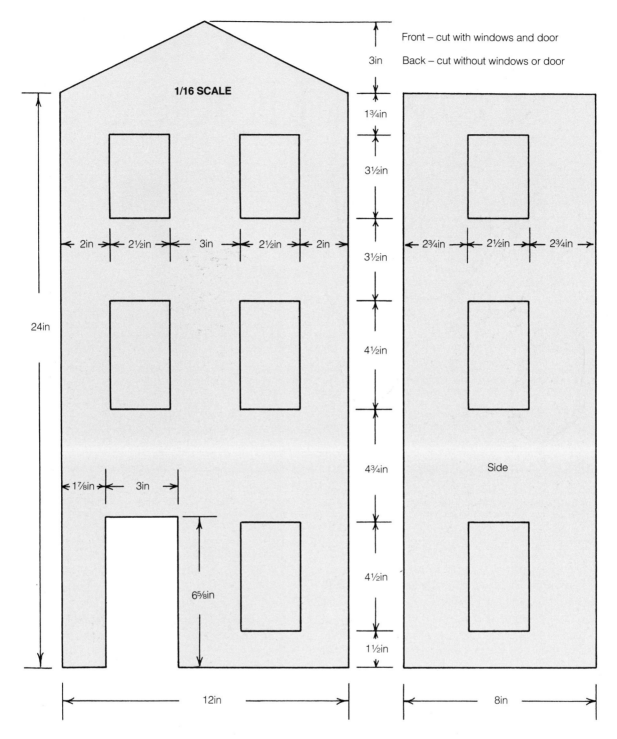

FIGS 60 AND 61 PLANS FOR THE VICTORIAN TOWN HOUSE

CUTTING (PLANS: FIGS 60 AND 61)

Draw all the pieces onto the plywood using a sharp pencil and ruler. Ensure that all the right-angles are correct and the measurements precise. Label each piece in pencil, ie back, side, roof, etc, to avoid confusion when assembling. Cut out all the pieces, including doorway and window holes. Chamfer the apex edges on both roof pieces. Draw lines on both the insides and outsides of the back and side pieces showing where the floors occur.

Tape the pieces together with masking tape to check that they fit properly, and make any minor adjustments.

ASSEMBLY

Glue and pin one side to the inside edge of the back. Glue and pin the base inside the side and back, then glue and pin the other side to the base and the back.

Glue and tape the two roof pieces together at the apex, on the underside, and glue and pin the roof to the back and sides. The roof should overhang at the front, and fit flush with the wall at the back. When the roof is fixed in place, use masking tape on the outside of the apex to strengthen the join (Fig 63).

Cut and fit the cornice ledges (plain moulding for the kitchen and a more elaborate one for the parlour), mitring the

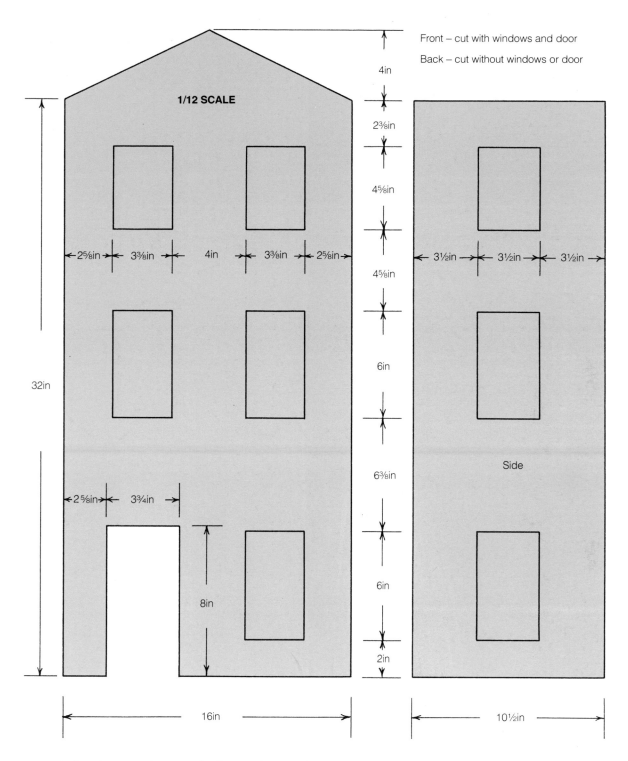

1/12 SCALE

Front – cut with windows and door

Back – cut without windows or door

4in

2⅜in

4⅝in

4⅝in

6in

6⅜in

6in

2in

32in

←2⅝in→ ←3⅜in→ 4in ←3⅜in→ ←2⅝in→

←3½in→ ←3½in→ ←3½in→

←2⅝in→ ←3¾in→

8in

Side

16in

10½in

corners, and glue them in place on the lines indicating the floor levels. Leave a gap in the centre of the back wall of the kitchen to accommodate the chimney breast. Glue the side and back edges of the floors, and slide them in to rest on the cornice ledges – when the glue is dry, tap pins through from the outside, using the marked lines as a guide.

Cut the kitchen-fireplace opening out of the block of balsa wood, and cut the balsa wood exactly the height of the kitchen. Glue the back of the balsa block and push it into place against the back wall. Cut a piece of cornice moulding the same width as the chimney breast and stick to the ceiling and the front of the chimney breast.

EXTERIOR

At this stage, paper the exterior. We chose red brick and grey slate as typical of a Victorian town house, but you might prefer different papers or paint finishes. Paper the roof, lapping the paper round the front edge to the underside, and the house, lapping the paper round the sides to the inside. Cut strips of paper about 1½in wide to paper over the front edges of the floors, lapping them onto the floors and the ceilings, and underneath the base.

Paper the front of the house, lapping the paper round all sides to the inside, and through the door and window holes. Line up the bricks on the front with the bricks at the sides.

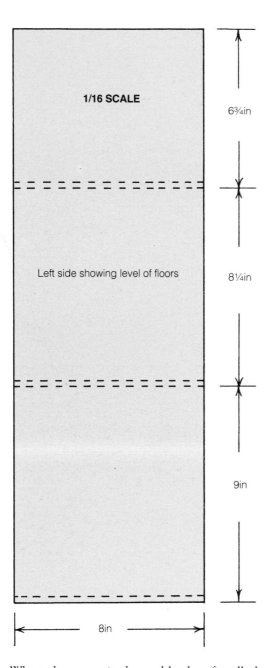

1/16 SCALE

Left side showing level of floors

6¾in

8¼in

9in

8in

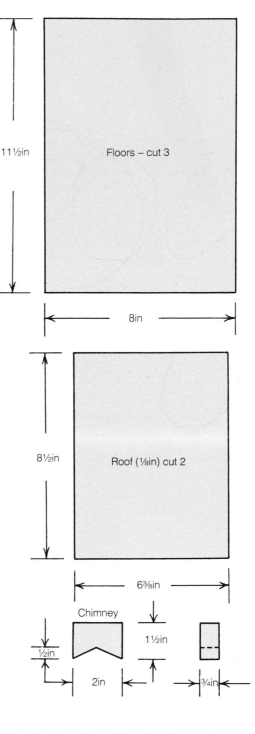

11½in

Floors – cut 3

8in

8½in

Roof (⅛in) cut 2

6⅜in

Chimney

½in

2in

1½in

¾in

Windows When the paper is thoroughly dry, fix all the windows in place. If the window frames are to be painted or stained, do this before cutting. Make a frame for each window from the fine woodstrip, mitred in each corner and stuck to the inside front edge of the window hole. When each frame is complete, cut and insert the perspex window and make a similar frame on the inside to hold it in place. If you wish, the windows can be given an outer frame of fine wood-strip, mitred at each corner, (we have done this on the interior – after wallpapering – but not on the exterior). Stick on the glazing bars, firstly the horizontal ones, then the verticals, representing sash windows – for the best effect they should be stuck to both the outside and inside of each window.

Door The edge of the doorway is faced with wood-strip (painted first) and the door is cut to fit easily into the faced opening, with sufficient clearance to open over the ground floor.

Make the door from ⅛in obeche wood, panelled with ¹⁄₁₆in obeche on both sides, sand carefully and paint it on both sides. Hang the door from ½in hinges fixed to the left-hand side and recessed into the wood. These hinges are too small to fix with screws so we use fine pins.

To avoid splitting the wood, mark the holes through the hinges onto the door and use a fine drill or dressmaker's pin to drill the holes. Use super-glue to hold the hinge to the door and on the pins pushed through the hinges. Repeat this process to hinge the door to the doorway, recessing the hinges into the door frame.

Chimney The chimney stack is made from a block of balsa

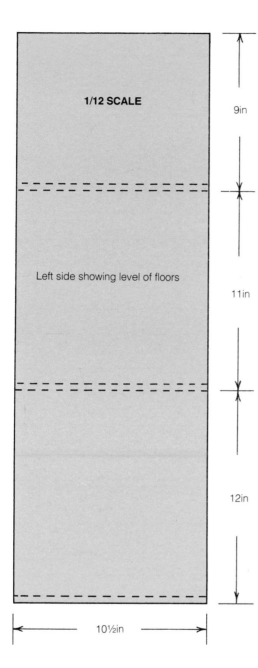

1/12 SCALE

9in

Left side showing level of floors

11in

12in

10½in

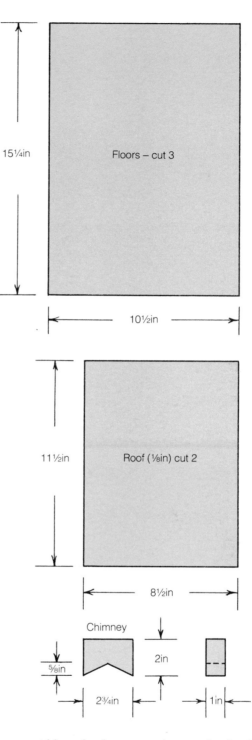

15¼in

Floors – cut 3

10½in

11½in

Roof (⅛in) cut 2

8½in

Chimney

⅝in

2in

2¾in

1in

wood, the bottom edge notched to fit the roof apex. It is covered in brick paper and stuck to the back edge of the roof. The chimney pots are three large wooden beads painted with terracotta-coloured paint and stuck to the top of the chimney stack.

Front The front can be hinged in place at this stage, using three 1in hinges fixed in the same way as the door hinges but using screws instead of pins. You might prefer to wait until the interior has been decorated.

Finishing The exterior finishes can be added now or later. The brass door handle and numbers come from a dolls'-house shop. Alternative handles are suggested in Chapter 2, and the numerals could be cut from thin metal sheet or heavy-gauge aluminium foil. The keyhole is a brass eyelet flattened with a hammer and pushed into a hole drilled in the door.

The doorstep is a small block of obeche wood, cut to exactly

the same width as the doorway and covered in brick paper. It is wedged into place and glued to each side of the door frame. The porch is also made of obeche wood, then stuck to brackets cut from moulding, painted and stuck to the wall.

The left side wall of the house is decorated with a Victorian poster advertising marmalade, cut from a magazine and stuck on with wallpaper paste.

The first-floor window boxes are made of ¹⁄₁₆in thick obeche wood (see Chapter 5 for instructions for making boxes) and the flowers are plastic with a little lichen for greenery.

INTERIOR

We chose to decorate this house in light pretty colours rather

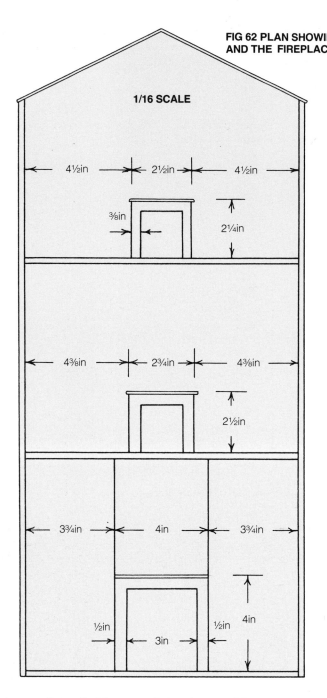

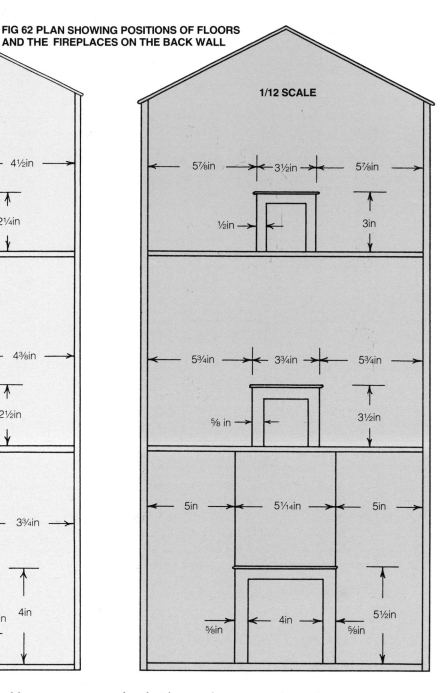

FIG 62 PLAN SHOWING POSITIONS OF FLOORS AND THE FIREPLACES ON THE BACK WALL

than traditionally Victorian dark colours and heavy patterns, and the kitchen is painted magnolia rather than a Victorian green or cream and brown which we felt would look rather gloomy.

Consult Chapter 3 for ideas, sources and detailed instructions for painting, papering and floor-coverings. As the house is small, the colour schemes in each room should harmonise so, unless you particularly want strict period accuracy, we recommend small patterns, and only two or three light colours, which also make a better background for the furnishings.

Before you begin decorating, check for tiny gaps, such as between cornice ledges and ceilings, or floors and walls. These gaps should be filled with Polyfilla – rub it in with the finger, and remove any surplus with a damp cloth. When the Polyfilla is quite dry, paint the ceilings. (The attic ceiling should be lined with paper first to cover the masking tape under the ridge and the slate paper at the front edge – bring the paper down an inch or two onto the side and back walls to cover any gaps under the roof.) Use magnolia-coloured emulsion which gives a softer effect than white, and include the cornices as part of the ceiling, so that they look like painted plaster. You will need two coats of emulsion to cover.

When the ceilings are dry, paper the walls, starting with the back wall. Even if you plan to paint the rooms, lining them with paper first will give a better finish. Divide the inside of the front into three sections and paint or paper each one to match the corresponding room. If you wish to put in skirting boards or picture rails, paint or stain them first, then stick them in place at this stage. Cut the floor papers to fit and apply with wallpaper paste.

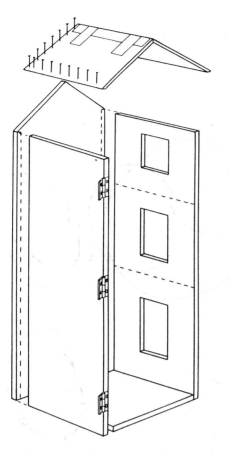

Fig 63 Assembling the Victorian town house

same lace stuck to thin wood-strip over the bottom half of the windows, and cream-linen roller blinds are hung from tiny eye-screws at the top of the windows.

Fireplaces The pattern given (Fig 64) is for the parlour fireplace. It is made from square wooden beading, with a mantelshelf of obeche wood. The brackets which hold the mantelshelf are pieces of moulding.

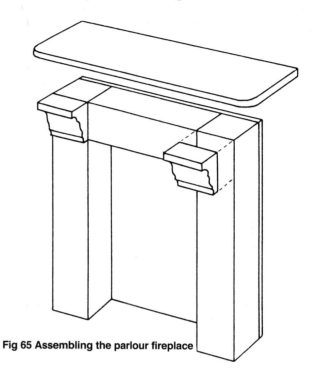

Fig 65 Assembling the parlour fireplace

Curtains The bedroom and parlour curtains are made from wide lace edging, hung from thin wood-strip mounted on wooden blocks stuck to the wall. The pelmets are fringed upholstery braid, stuck to wood blocks above the windows. Similar curtains and pelmets are hung at the front windows in the same way. The kitchen curtains are small pieces of the

FIG 64 PATTERN FOR THE PARLOUR FIREPLACE

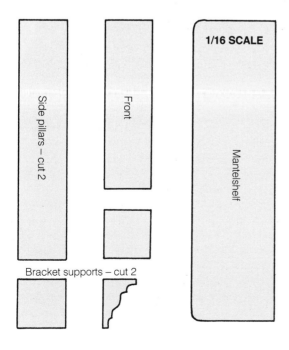

Side pillars – cut 2

Front

1/16 SCALE

Mantelshelf

Bracket supports – cut 2

Side pillars – cut 2

Front

1/12 SCALE

Mantelshelf

Bracket supports – cut 2

Interior of the Victorian town house, showing the inside-front decorated to correspond with the rooms

Cut the two uprights, the horizontal piece, the two brackets and the mantelshelf and assemble the pieces, sticking them to a backing of thin cardboard and to each other (Fig 65). When the glue is thoroughly dry, cut away the surplus cardboard from the outside using a sharp craft knife and sand the fireplace smooth. Stain or paint – using gloss enamel paint over an undercoat of matt enamel paint and leave to dry. Line the cardboard-back of the fireplace opening with brick paper.

When the fireplace is assembled, glue the cardboard backing to the wall, holding it in place until firmly stuck. The bedroom fireplace is made in the same way, a little narrower and lower.

The kitchen fireplace is made from ¹⁄₁₆in thick obeche wood, stained rosewood colour. Paper the opening, back, sides, and floor with brick paper. Cut two uprights and a crosspiece from obeche wood, stain them and stick around the opening. Cut two brackets from the cornice moulding, stain, and stick them to the front top edges of the side pieces. Cut and stain an obeche-wood mantelshelf, and stick it to the

76

The Victorian bedroom, showing the half-tester bed with pink silk bedspread and curtains

brackets. (If you plan to use the built-in dresser in the kitchen alcove, make sure the mantelshelf does not project into the alcove.)

FIXTURES AND FITTINGS

We have used simple inexpensive fire grates and fenders made from white metal kits in the bedroom and parlour. The empty grate in the bedroom is filled with a folded paper fan, and a fire of tiny pieces of coal, wood and paper is laid in the parlour grate. The range in our kitchen is a novelty pencil sharpener but ranges can be bought as white metal kits or ready-made from the specialist shops.

The kitchen sink is an inexpensive glazed pottery one (Bryntor) which comes complete with brick piers and a wooden draining board and is available from most dolls'-house shops in several sizes. The taps and waste pipe are simple white metal versions though you may prefer the more expensive brass variety.

See Chapter 4 for information on finishing white metal kits and other ideas for fixtures and fittings.

THE BEDROOM FURNITURE

The patterns for the furniture are drawn actual size, so that they can be traced from the book. Read the detailed instructions in Chapter 5 before beginning, and refer to them when necessary.

The chest of drawers (Fig 66) This is made of ⅛in thick obeche wood, stained mahogany, and the handles are brass gimp pins.

Draw the pattern pieces onto the wood, ensuring that the grain lines are consistent, the measurements and right-angles precise. Cut the pieces with a razor-toothed saw and chamfer the edges of the top and base pieces. Sand all parts with fine abrasive paper and stain them. Assemble the shell by sticking the shelves to the back, then glueing the sides in place, lining them up with the front edges of the shelves. Stick the top and the base pieces in place, and then the feet, set slightly back from the edges. Check that the drawer fronts fit snugly into the drawer spaces. Cut the bottom and sides of the drawers from unstained wood and assemble the drawers to fit the drawer space.

Sand the shell and the drawer fronts gently with fine abrasive paper and apply a coat of amateur French polish. Allow this to dry thoroughly, then gently sand again. Apply several coats of wax polish, well-buffed between each coat. Mark the positions of the drawer handles and drill holes with a ¹⁄₁₆in drill. Cut the shanks of the gimp pins to ³⁄₁₆in long and push them into the holes – secure with a dab of glue over the pinhole on the inside of the drawer.

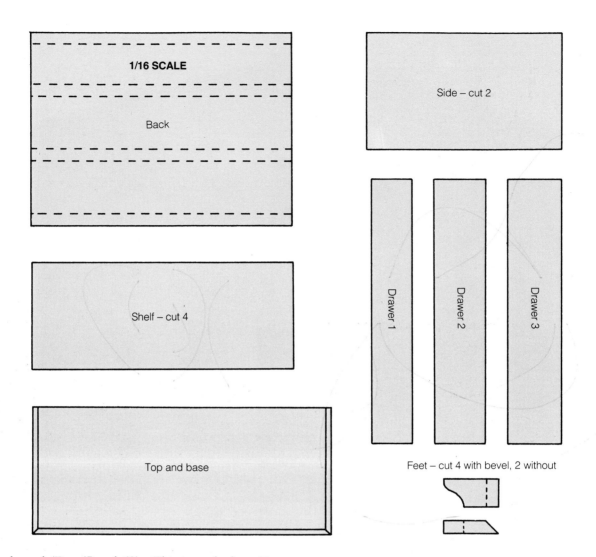

1/16 SCALE

Back

Shelf – cut 4

Top and base

Side – cut 2

Drawer 1

Drawer 2

Drawer 3

Feet – cut 4 with bevel, 2 without

The washstand (Figs 67 and 68) This is made from ³⁄₃₂in obeche wood, with legs of square beading, stained mahogany. Draw the pieces onto the wood and cut them with a razor-toothed saw. Sand the legs with fine sandpaper wrapped around a small wood block, tapering them towards the bottom. Sand all the pieces with fine abrasive paper and stain them.

Stick the back and side pieces to the top, matching the corners carefully. Stick one frieze piece between the two front legs, slightly recessed, and the other between the two back legs, again slightly recessed. Stick the two side-frieze pieces between the back and front legs, also slightly recessed. If necessary, support the legs in place while the glue dries. Stick the assembled legs under the top, so that the front overhangs.

When the glue is thoroughly dry, sand the washstand carefully until perfectly smooth, apply one coat of amateur French polish and sand again. Apply several coats of wax polish and buff well between each coat.

The half-tester bed (Figs 69 and 70) The half-tester bed is made from ⅛in thick obeche wood and square beading, stained walnut. The bedcover and curtains are rose-pink silk.

Draw the pieces onto the wood, ensuring that the measurements and right-angles are precise. Cut the pieces with a razor-toothed saw, taking particular care to cut the two pairs of

FIG 66 PATTERN FOR THE CHEST OF DRAWERS

bedposts of equal length with perfectly square ends. Whittle the knobs on the bottom bedposts with a craft knife, and sandpaper smooth. Sand all pieces with fine abrasive paper and stain them.

Stick the side rails to the base. Stick the headboard to the top edge of the base and the footboard to the bottom edge. Glue the bedposts into the corners between the head and footboards and the side. Ensure that the bedposts stand square, supporting them if necessary until the glue is dry. Stick the canopy (tester) to the top of the headboard and posts.

Cut a piece of thin cardboard the same size as the headboard and cover it with fabric, glueing the raw edges firmly on the underside of the card. Glue the back of the covered card and stick it to the headboard (not the bedposts). Cut and hem the bed curtains. Gather the top edges and stick them to the sides of the tester and glue the sides of the curtains to the bedposts if they do not hang well. Cut, hem and gather the frill and glue it around the sides and front of the tester, over the curtains. Make small ties from embroidery silk or ribbon and tie the curtains back to the bedposts.

Bedclothes Make a mattress (using the bed base as a pattern), two pillows, sheets and a blanket.

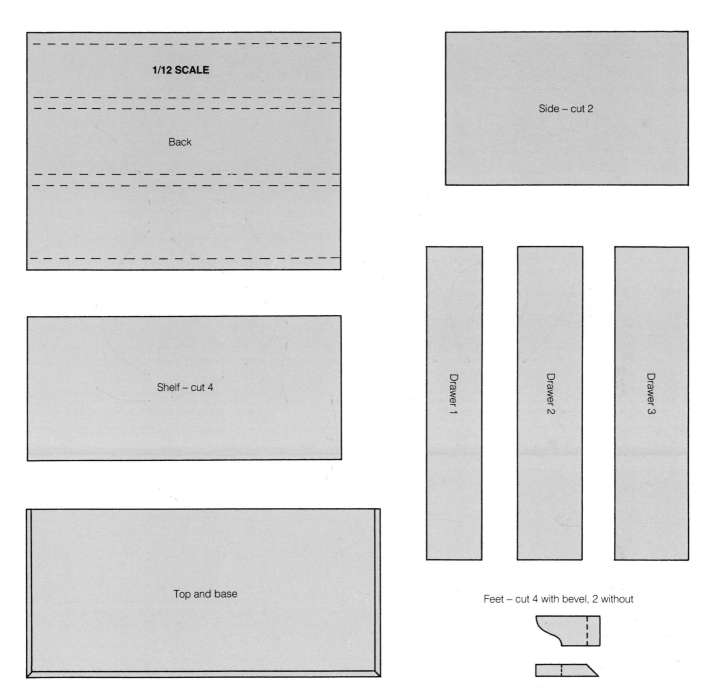

1/12 SCALE

Back

Side – cut 2

Shelf – cut 4

Drawer 1

Drawer 2

Drawer 3

Top and base

Feet – cut 4 with bevel, 2 without

Cut a bedspread ½in wider and 1in longer than the bed (base), for seam allowances. Cut the frill in three pieces, two sides and the bottom, to allow for the bedposts. Hem and gather the frills and sew them to the bedspread. Line the bedspread with a fine fabric, oversewn in place under the frill and slipstitched along the top edge. Press carefully. Put the bedspread onto the bed and push pins through each side into the mattress to hold the frills in place until they hang properly.

The nursing chair (Fig 71) This is made of cardboard, padded with foam and covered with printed cotton.

Cut the cardboard back. Cut the foam and cover ½in larger all-round than the pattern to allow for seams. Stick the foam padding to the cardboard, rolling the edges over to the back. Sew the cover, turn through and slip onto the padded cardboard. Pulling the cover taut, slip-stitch the bottom edge

closed. Cut the round seat from balsa block. Pad and cover the seat. Curve the back of the chair around the seat and stick in place, holding the pieces together with pins until the glue is dry. A small piece of upholstery braid is used to finish the bottom edge of the chair. Four small wooden beads can be glued to the underside for feet and a loose cushion, made in the same fabric, tucked into the back of the chair.

The bedside table This is made from a chess piece with the top sawn off and sanded flat, and a circle of obeche wood for the table top.

Use a cut-down chess piece, or any similar piece of turned wood, for a pedestal. If it is varnished, remove the varnish with paintstripper first. From ⅛in obeche wood, cut a circle 1½in in diameter, and sand with fine sandpaper. Stain both pieces, then stick the pedestal to the underside of the top,

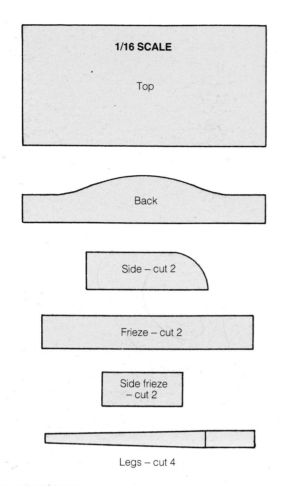

1/16 SCALE

Top

Back

Side – cut 2

Frieze – cut 2

Side frieze – cut 2

Legs – cut 4

FIG 67 PATTERN FOR THE WASHSTAND

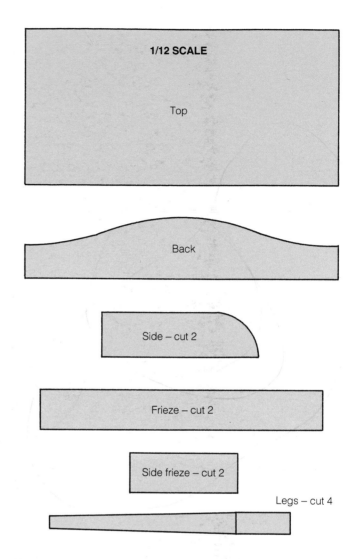

1/12 SCALE

Top

Back

Side – cut 2

Frieze – cut 2

Side frieze – cut 2

Legs – cut 4

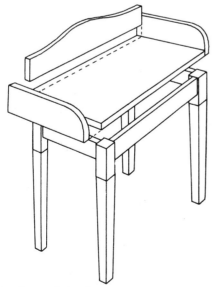

Fig 68 Assembling the washstand

taking care to centre it exactly. (We used button polish to stain the top, as the chess piece was this colour.) Finish the table with a coat of varnish or wax polish. It can be covered with a circular lace cloth.

THE PARLOUR FURNITURE
The bookcase (Figs 72 and 73)   This is made of ⅛in obeche wood, stained mahogany. The glass panels in the doors are ¹⁄₁₆in perspex.

Draw the pattern pieces onto the wood, ensuring that the grain lines are consistent, the measurements and the right-angles correct. Cut the pieces with a razor-toothed saw. Chamfer the underside front and side edges of the top piece. Stick the two base pieces together, and chamfer the top side and front edges. Sand all the pieces with fine abrasive paper and stain them. (At this stage, we painted the inside of the back piece matt dark green.)

Assemble the shell by sticking one side to the back, then sticking the shelves to this side and back. (The shelves are not as deep as the sides, to allow for the doors.) Stick the other side in place, then glue the assembled shelf unit to the base. Do not fix the top in place yet.

The door frames are made by cutting rabbetting in each piece using a craft knife and steel ruler, and making up the frames with mitred corners. If you cut a cardboard template the exact size of the door, and use this as a guide when cutting and mitring, building the frame on the cardboard template, this fiddly process becomes less difficult. When the frames are complete, cut the perspex to fit and put it into the frames with a little glue around the edges. Use brass pins with the shanks cut short for cupboard-door handles. Drill a tiny hole into the

The Victorian parlour – with piano for musical evenings

door frames, and glue the pins in place. Bore holes with a dressmaker's pin into the bottom and top edges of the doors, and the base and the top to receive the pin hinges. If necessary, sand the hinged door edges slightly round with fine abrasive paper to allow the doors to swing open freely. When the pin hinges are properly aligned, glue the top in place. Sand the bookcase, apply one coat of amateur French polish, sand again and apply several coats of wax polish, well-buffed between coats.

The pedestal table (Figs 74 and 75) This is made of ³⁄₃₂in obeche wood for the top, ⅛in for the feet, with a pedestal of dowelling. It is stained walnut.

Draw the pattern pieces onto the wood, using a compass to ensure accurate circles and, with the point, marking the centre on the underside of the smaller top piece. Cut a hole to accommodate the dowelling pedestal. Sand the pieces with fine abrasive paper and stain them.

Glue the smaller top to the underside of the larger top, centring it carefully. Glue the three feet to the bottom of the pedestal, ensuring that they are evenly spaced and that the pedestal stands upright. Glue the top end of the pedestal into the top, leaving upside-down until the glue is completely dry.

Sand the table with fine abrasive paper and apply one coat of amateur French polish. Sand again and apply several coats of wax polish, building up a good finish, especially if you do not intend to cover with a tablecloth.

The chairs (see Fig 41) Full instructions and patterns for these chairs (and other alternatives) are given in Chapter 5. For this parlour they are made of obeche wood, stained walnut, and finished with wax polish. The seat pads are covered in dark-green silk.

It is essential when making these chairs to cut the two side pieces with the grain of the wood running vertically, and to handle them carefully until they are fully assembled as the pieces are fragile.

The sofa (Fig 76) This is made of cardboard, padded with foam, and covered with printed cotton.

Cut the cardboard back from the pattern and score the fold lines. Cut the foam and covers ½in larger than the pattern to allow for seams. Stick the foam padding to the cardboard, rolling the edges over to the back (use a slightly thicker foam for an overstuffed effect). Stitch the cover, clip the curves, turn through and slip it over the padded cardboard. Pulling the cover taut, slipstitch the bottom edges closed.

Cut the seat from a block of balsa wood, pad with foam and cover with fabric. Fold the arms forward, and fit the back around the seat. Stick the back and arms to the seat and hold

FIG 69 PATTERN FOR THE HALF-TESTER BED

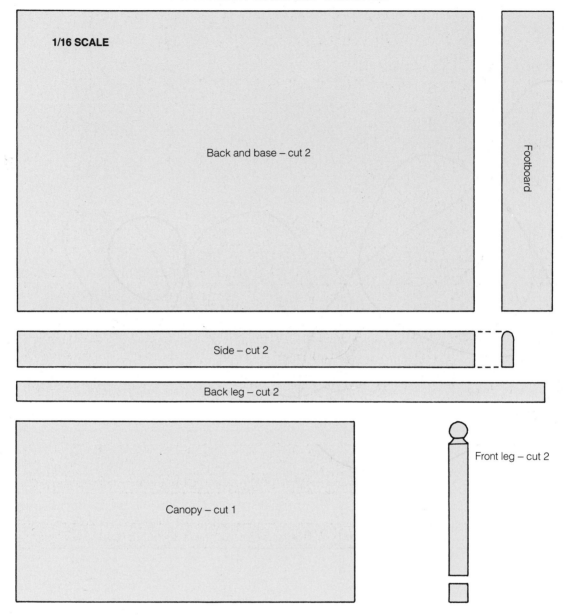

1/16 SCALE

Back and base – cut 2

Footboard

Side – cut 2

Back leg – cut 2

Canopy – cut 1

Front leg – cut 2

in place with pins until the glue dries. Stick four round wooden beads to the underside for feet, and make several loose cushions to tuck along the back of the sofa. An antimacassar of broderie anglaise or lace adds the finishing touch.

Piano   The piano shown in the photographs is an inexpensive imported miniature (Dijon) available from most dolls'-house shops. We have used the stool which comes with the piano as a small table in the bedroom. If you prefer, the wing chair described below and shown in the Tudor cottage can be made instead and the two small chairs used as dining chairs with the pedestal table.

The wing chair (Fig 77)   This is made of cardboard, padded with foam and covered with fabric.

Cut the cardboard back for the chair from the pattern and score the fold lines. Cut the padding and fabric ½in larger all-round than the pattern to allow for seams. Glue the foam to

the cardboard, rolling the edges over to the back. Stitch the cover, clip the curves and turn through. Slip the cover over the padded cardboard, pulling it taut, and slipstitch the bottom edges closed.

Cut the seat from a balsa block, pad with foam and cover with fabric. Fold the sides of the chair forward and fit the seat in place. Glue the seat to the back and sides of the chair, holding it in place with pins until the glue dries. Stick four square wooden beads to the underside for feet, and cut a scrap of lace or broderie anglaise for an antimacassar.

The wine table   The wine table is a black chess piece with a circular top 1½in in diameter cut from ⅛in obeche wood, stained mahogany. The top is cut, sanded, stained, and glued to the chess-piece pedestal. The table is varnished with one coat of polyurethane varnish.

(Any similar piece of turned wood can be used for the pedestal. If such a piece is unavailable, the pattern given for

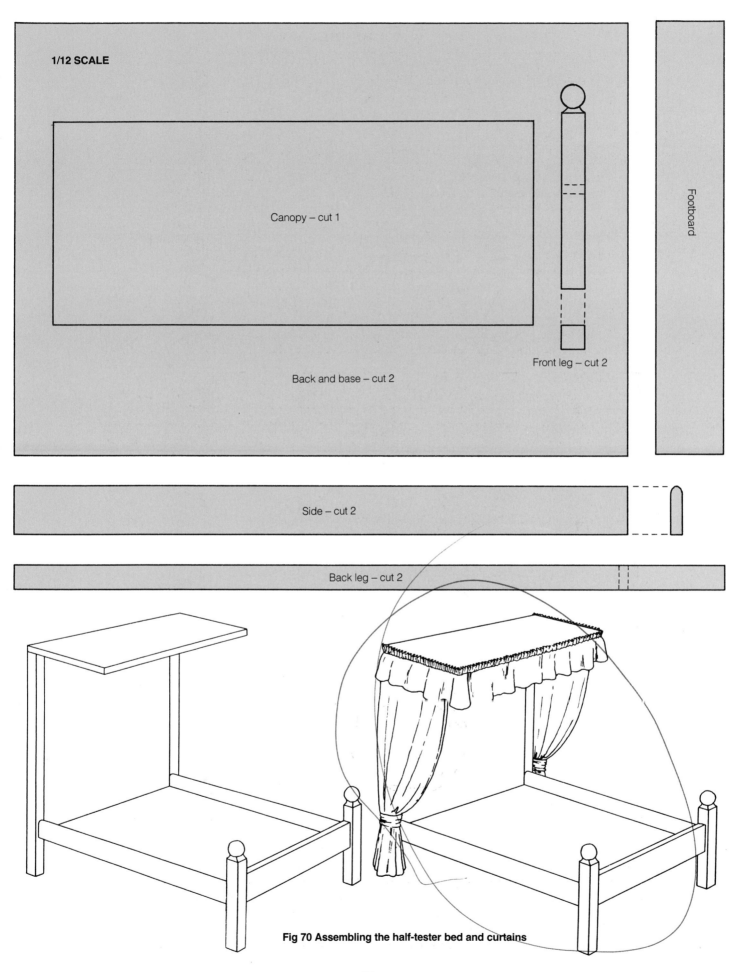

1/12 SCALE

Canopy – cut 1

Back and base – cut 2

Footboard

Front leg – cut 2

Side – cut 2

Back leg – cut 2

Fig 70 Assembling the half-tester bed and curtains

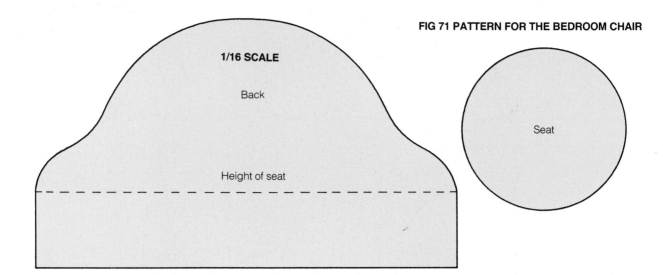

1/16 SCALE

Back

Height of seat

FIG 71 PATTERN FOR THE BEDROOM CHAIR

Seat

The Victorian kitchen, a light and airy workplace for the cook

the pedestal table could be used with the dowelling cut to 2in long.)

The footstool This is made from a piece of cotton reel padded with foam and covered with beige silk.

Cut a ½in piece from one end of a cotton reel with a razor-toothed saw (or use a circle of balsa wood or cork). Cut a circle of fabric 3in in diameter. Glue a little padding to the top of the cotton reel. Run a gathering thread around the edge of the fabric circle and draw it over the padded cotton reel, with the thread under the base. Pull the gathers as tightly as possible, distributing them evenly, so that the cover is taut. Fasten off the thread and trim the excess fabric. Cut a circle of felt and glue it to the underside of the stool to cover the raw edges.

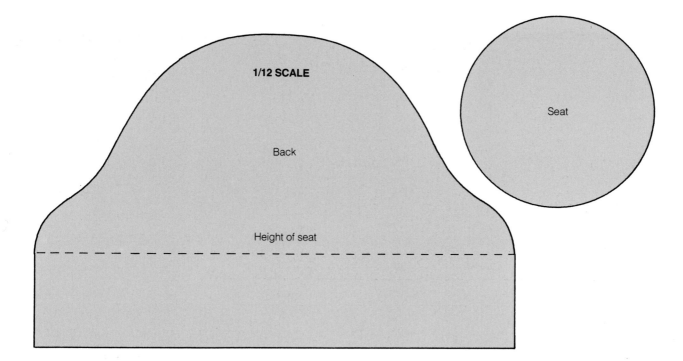

1/12 SCALE

Back

Height of seat

Seat

FIG 72 PATTERN FOR THE GLASS-FRONTED BOOKCASE

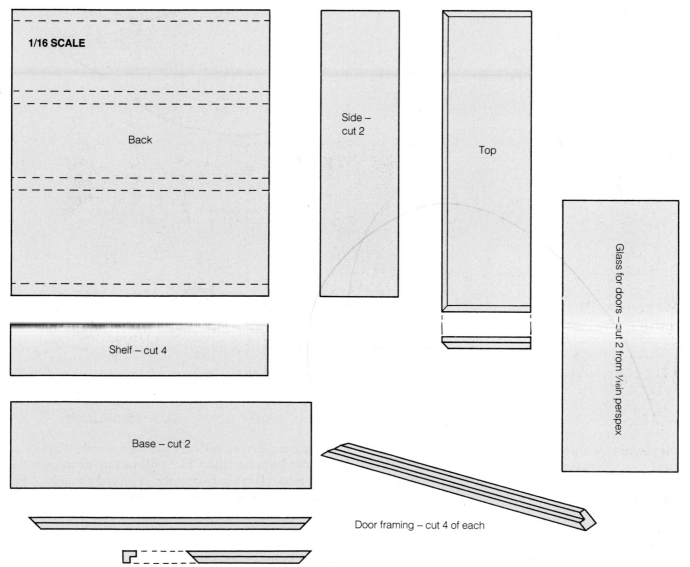

1/16 SCALE

Back

Side – cut 2

Top

Glass for doors – cut 2 from 1/16in perspex

Shelf – cut 4

Base – cut 2

Door framing – cut 4 of each

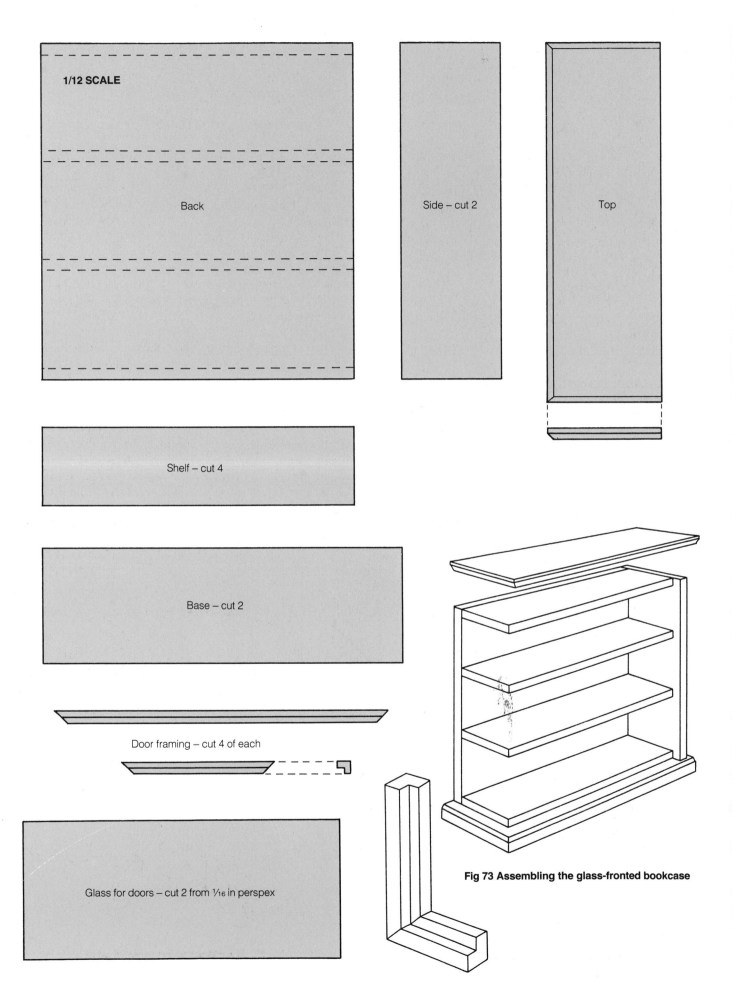

1/12 SCALE

Back

Side – cut 2

Top

Shelf – cut 4

Base – cut 2

Door framing – cut 4 of each

Glass for doors – cut 2 from 1/16 in perspex

Fig 73 Assembling the glass-fronted bookcase

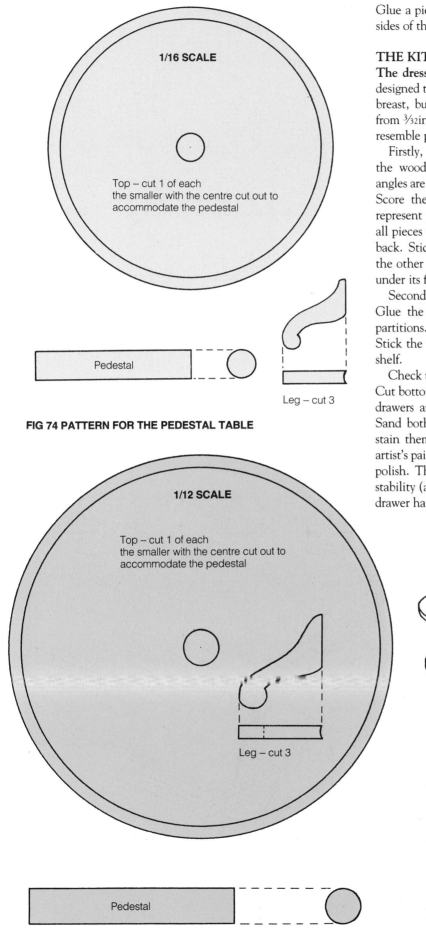

1/16 SCALE

Top – cut 1 of each
the smaller with the centre cut out to
accommodate the pedestal

Pedestal

Leg – cut 3

FIG 74 PATTERN FOR THE PEDESTAL TABLE

1/12 SCALE

Top – cut 1 of each
the smaller with the centre cut out to
accommodate the pedestal

Leg – cut 3

Pedestal

Glue a piece of narrow upholstery braid or ribbon around the sides of the stool to trim.

THE KITCHEN FURNITURE

The dresser (Figs 78, 79 and 80)   The kitchen dresser was designed to fit into the alcove on the right side of the chimney breast, but it could equally well be free-standing. It is made from ³⁄₃₂in thick obeche wood, coloured with button polish to resemble pine.

Firstly, assemble the top unit. Draw the pattern pieces onto the wood, ensuring that the measurements and the right-angles are precise. Cut out the pieces with a razor-toothed saw. Score the lines on the back piece with a scissor blade to represent planking. Chamfer the front edge of the top. Sand all pieces with fine abrasive paper. Glue one side piece to the back. Stick the shelves to the side and back, and then stick the other side in place. Glue the top in place, then the frieze under its front edge.

Secondly, the lower unit. Glue one side piece to the back. Glue the drawer shelf in place, then the upper and lower partitions. Glue in the bottom shelf, then the other side piece. Stick the top in place, then the frieze strips under the drawer shelf.

Check that the draw fronts fit snugly into the drawer spaces. Cut bottom, back and side pieces from unstained wood for the drawers and assemble the drawers to fit the drawer spaces. Sand both units of the dresser with fine abrasive paper and stain them with a coat of button polish painted on with an artist's paintbrush. Sand both units, and polish them with wax polish. The top unit can be stuck to the base unit for extra stability (a good idea if the dresser is to be free-standing). Add drawer handles – we used small brass knobs.

Fig 75 Assembling the pedestal table

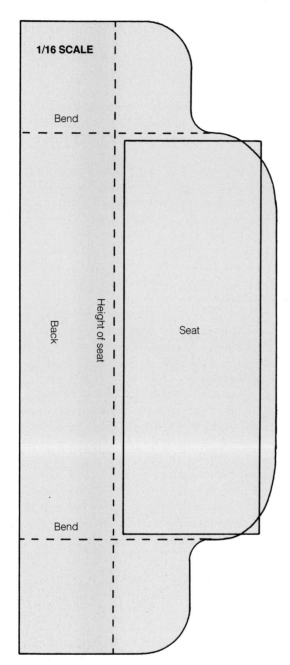

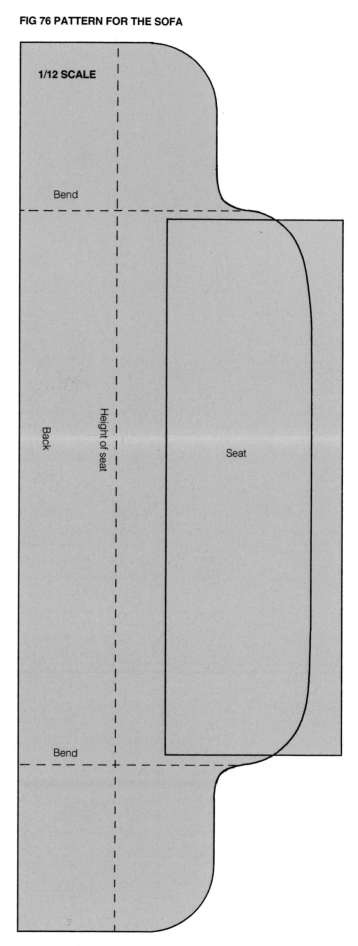

FIG 76 PATTERN FOR THE SOFA

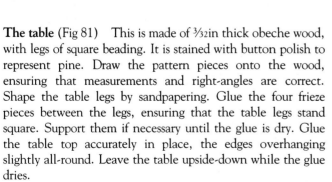

The table (Fig 81)   This is made of ³⁄₃₂in thick obeche wood, with legs of square beading. It is stained with button polish to represent pine. Draw the pattern pieces onto the wood, ensuring that measurements and right-angles are correct. Shape the table legs by sandpapering. Glue the four frieze pieces between the legs, ensuring that the table legs stand square. Support them if necessary until the glue is dry. Glue the table top accurately in place, the edges overhanging slightly all-round. Leave the table upside-down while the glue dries.

Sand the table with fine abrasive paper, and stain it with a coat of button polish, painted on with an artist's paintbrush. Sand again, and polish with wax polish.

Kitchen chairs (see Fig 42)   Full instructions and patterns for these chairs (and others) are given in Chapter 5.

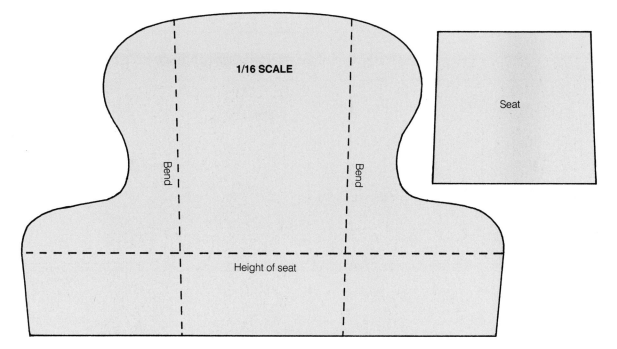

1/16 SCALE

Bend

Bend

Seat

Height of seat

FIG 77 PATTERN FOR THE WING CHAIR

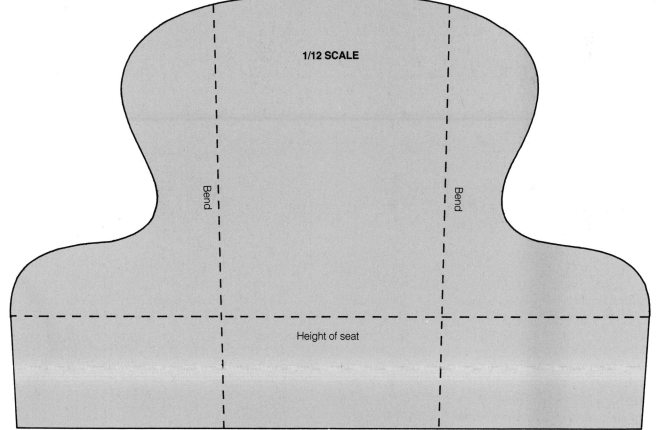

1/12 SCALE

Bend

Bend

Height of seat

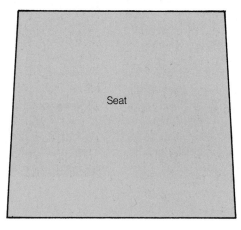

Seat

FIG 78 PATTERN FOR THE KITCHEN DRESSER (TOP UNIT)

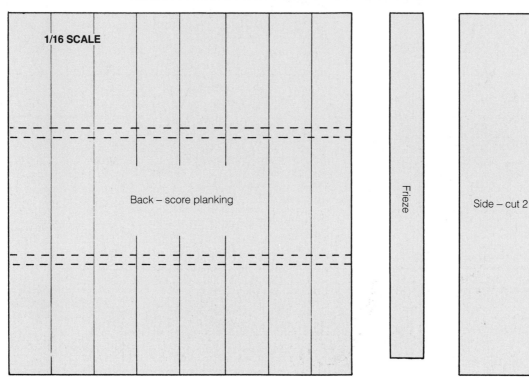

1/16 SCALE

Back – score planking

Frieze

Side – cut 2

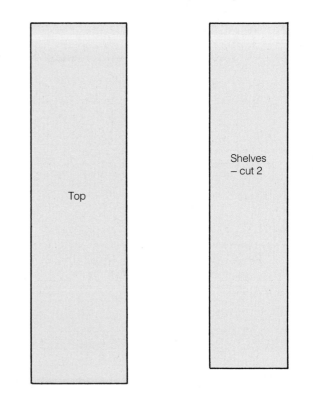

Top

Shelves – cut 2

The chairs in the kitchen are made of square beading with obeche-wood seats. They are stained with button polish to pine colour. Square loose cushions are held in place with thread ties.

Wall shelves (Fig 82)   These are made of ³⁄₃₂in thick obeche wood, stained light oak.

Draw the pieces onto the wood and cut them out with a razor-toothed saw and a fretsaw. Sand the pieces with fine abrasive paper and stain them. Stick one side to the back, then stick the shelves to the back and side. Stick the other side in place. Sand the shelves, and apply one coat of amateur French polish to the sides and the shelves. Sand again, and wax polish the sides and shelves. Glue the shelf unit to the wall, or fix it with double-sided tape or small pieces of BluTac.

Alcove shelf   The shelf in the alcove above the sink is made from ³⁄₃₂in thick obeche wood, the same width and depth as the alcove. Cut the shelf and sand it. Cut two brackets from picture-frame moulding or triangular pieces of obeche wood. Stain the shelf and the brackets (we used light oak) and sand it again. Stick the brackets under the shelf, lining up the back edges, and glue brackets and shelf to the wall.

Stool   The three-legged stool has a ⅛in obeche-wood top with fine-dowelling legs. The top is a circle 1–1⅜in in diameter. Three evenly spaced holes are drilled at a slight outward angle in the under-side of the seat. The seat and three 1–1¼in lengths of dowelling are sanded and stained light oak. The legs are glued into the holes. When the glue is dry, the stool is finely sanded and left unpolished.

Cupboard   The cupboard is made from the dresser-base pattern, with or without drawers as you prefer and with pin-hinged doors.

ACCESSORIES

The bedroom rug is a piece of tapestry fabric salvaged from a spectacles case, the edges sealed with Fraycheck and a small

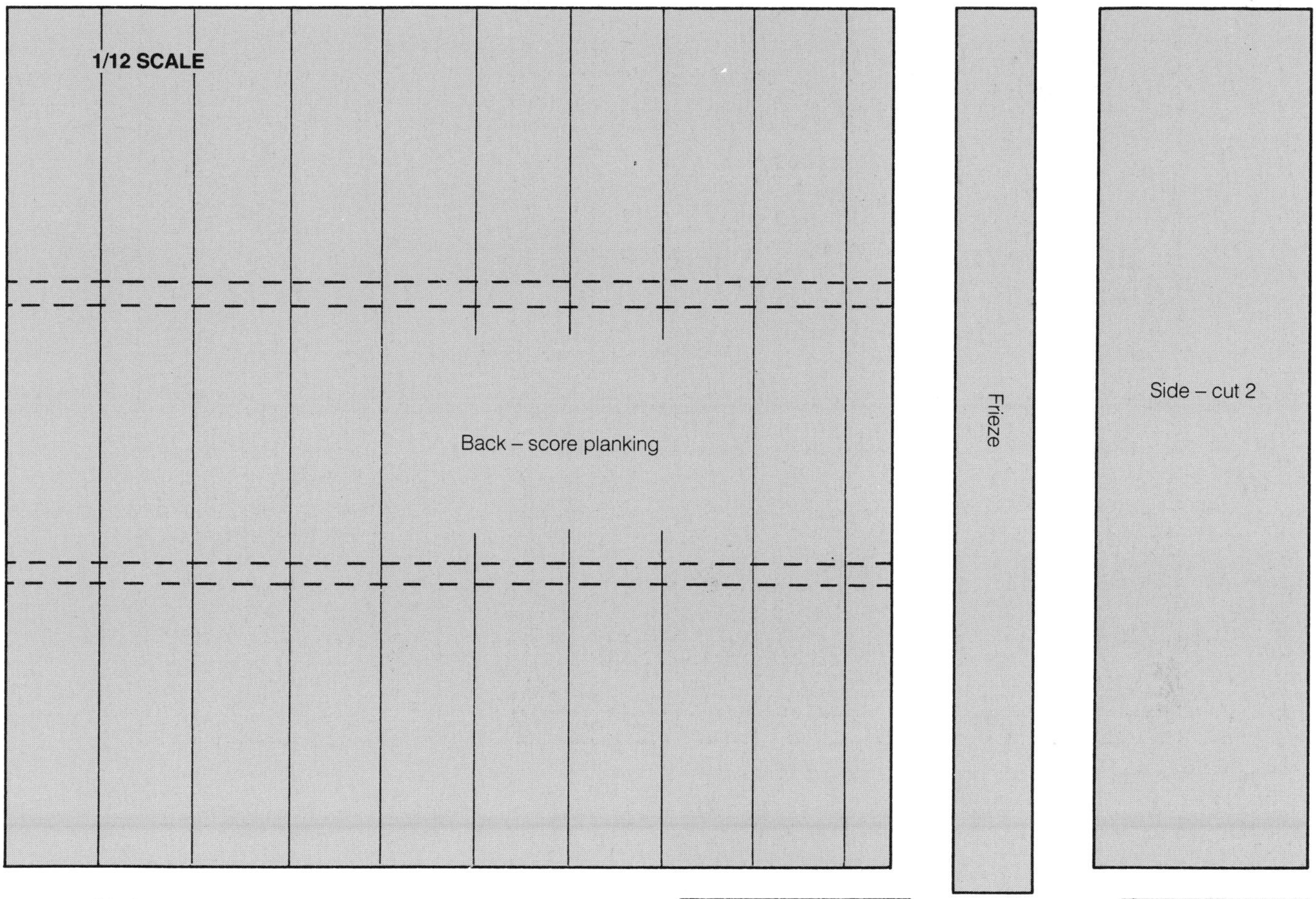

1/12 SCALE

Back – score planking

Frieze

Side – cut 2

Top

Shelves – cut 2

fringe added at each end. The rugs in the parlour (from Blackwells) and the kitchen are both commercial dolls'-house rugs.

The lights are inexpensive plastic fittings (Lundby) available from toyshops.

Many of the accessories are simple bead and button items and made or 'found' oddments as described in Chapter 6, including plastic saucepans painted with copper enamel, magazine cut-out pictures framed with woodstrip, and a marble 'crystal ball'. The remainder are inexpensive imported pieces (Dijon) such as the swing mirror in the bedroom and the wall shelves in the sitting room, and British accessories, chosen from the cheaper ranges – all of which are available from dolls'-house shops.

VARIATIONS

Although the tall, narrow design of this house is typical of a Victorian town house, the design can be adapted to other periods (Fig 83).

For example, with casement windows rather than sashes and an exterior of brick and timbering, the basic design could be transformed into a Tudor merchant's house. The roof should be covered with red tiles, the woodwork stained oak colour, and a planked door fitted for the complete Tudor effect. Inside, the house could be whitewashed or panelled, with planked floors upstairs and stone flags downstairs. The ground floor might be the merchant's shop, with a living room above and a sleeping chamber in the attic. In such a house, large heavy furniture such as a refectory table, benches and a

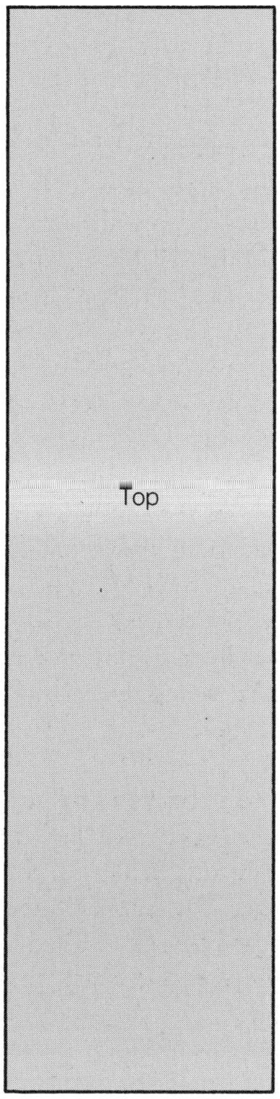

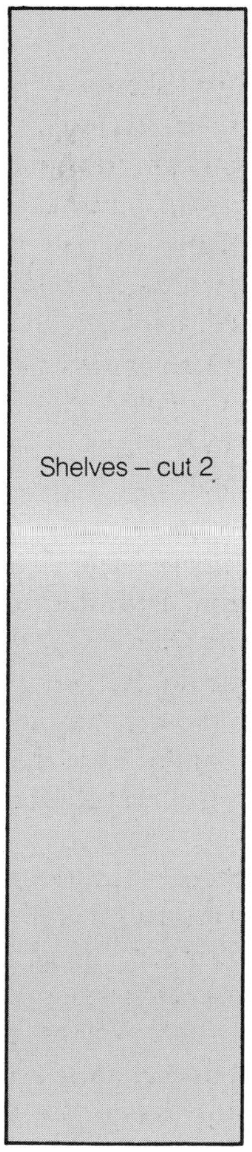

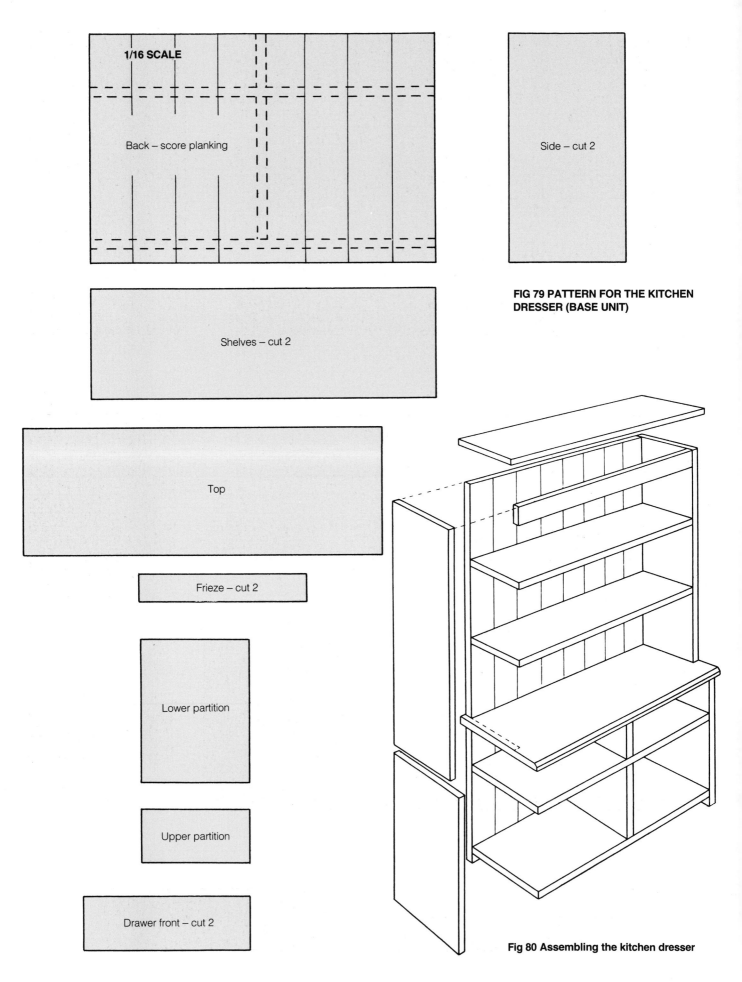

1/16 SCALE

Back – score planking

Side – cut 2

FIG 79 PATTERN FOR THE KITCHEN DRESSER (BASE UNIT)

Shelves – cut 2

Top

Frieze – cut 2

Lower partition

Upper partition

Drawer front – cut 2

Fig 80 Assembling the kitchen dresser

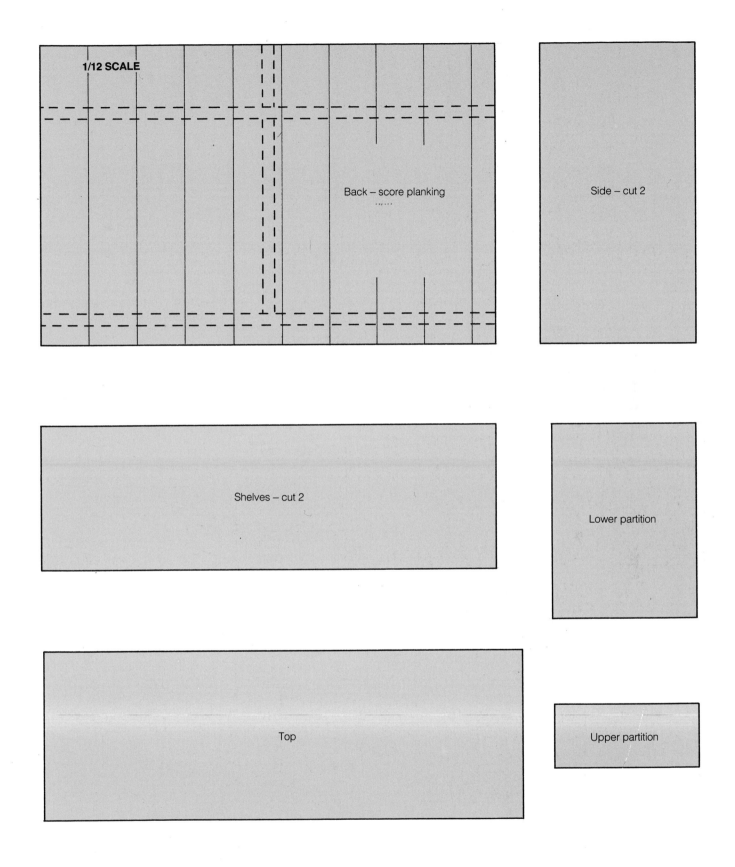

1/12 SCALE

Back – score planking

Side – cut 2

Shelves – cut 2

Lower partition

Top

Upper partition

Frieze – cut 2

Drawer front – cut 2

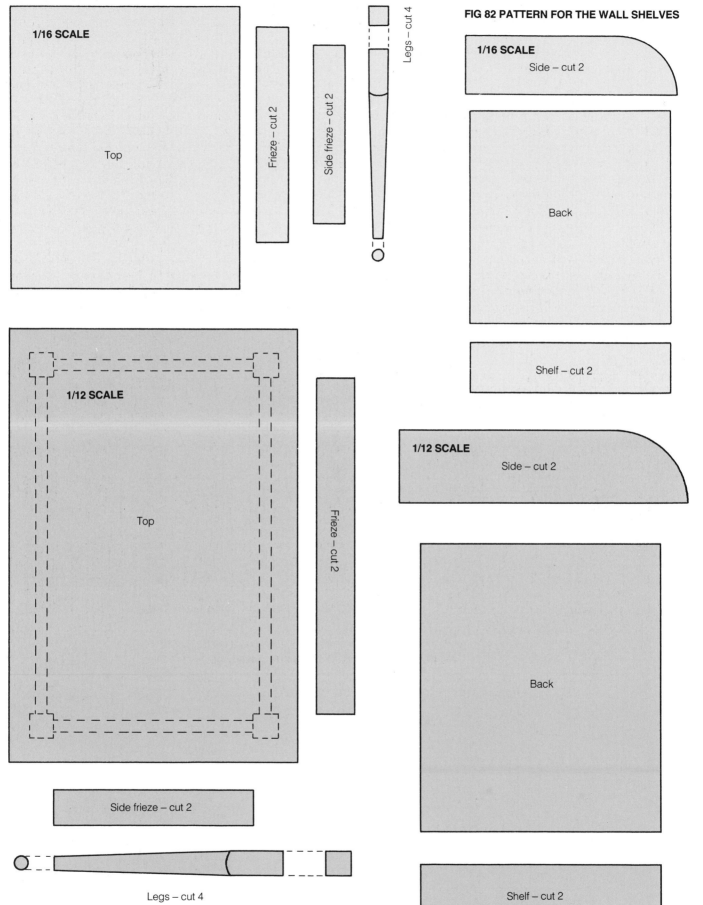

FIG 81 PATTERN FOR THE KITCHEN TABLE

1/16 SCALE

Top

Frieze – cut 2

Side frieze – cut 2

Legs – cut 4

1/12 SCALE

Top

Frieze – cut 2

Side frieze – cut 2

Legs – cut 4

FIG 82 PATTERN FOR THE WALL SHELVES

1/16 SCALE

Side – cut 2

Back

Shelf – cut 2

1/12 SCALE

Side – cut 2

Back

Shelf – cut 2

94

four-poster bed would be appropriate. Tudor details such as leaded windows, elaborate chimney pots and tapestry wallhangings will enhance the effect.

Alternatively, the Victorian house might be inhabited by a modern family and decorated in modern colours and styles. The outside might be colour washed, perhaps cream or blue, with white paintwork and a brightly coloured front door. Inside, the fireplaces might have been blocked up, with electric fires in front of them and an Aga cooker in the kitchen fireplace. The wallpapers would be modern and the furniture in the latest style. The kitchen would have fitted units and vinyl flooring. Upstairs, the modern sitting room could have a fitted carpet, wall units and a television. The bedroom would have a divan bed and built-in cupboards.

Two of these houses, fixed side-by-side, would make a large dolls' house with six rooms. Cut the side-window holes full length, to make doorways (on the opposite side in the second house) to give access from one part of the house to the other. The door on the front of the second house should be replaced with a window, and the front hinged to open on the right side rather than the left. The two houses could be made separately, then glued and screwed together before decorating the exterior.

You might fit a staircase into one half of the double-fronted house, making smaller rooms in the remaining space. Or a small building could be constructed, to house the staircase, the same height and depth as the houses with about a six inch frontage. This could have a flat roof, and doorholes on each floor, to line-up with the doorholes in the two wings. Sandwiched between the two wings, and glued and screwed in place before the house is decorated, this staircase section would have its own front panel, either hinged to one side or made to lift off completely. This large house, with its central hall and staircase and two gabled wings, would make a typical large Victorian house, and provide a lot of space and scope for decorating and furnishing.

The basic Victorian-town-house design is also a good choice if you want to make a pair of semi-detached houses. It might be amusing to decorate and furnish one in the style of the 1890s and next-door in the style of the 1990s.

Fig 83 Variations on the Victorian town house

11 THE TUDOR COTTAGE

The Tudor cottage is larger and a little more complex than the Victorian town house but still fairly simple to build. The front opens in two pieces to show four rooms, and the hinged roof opens to show an attic which can be used for storage or decorated as a room. The interior layout is simple and typical of period cottages, with two larger and two smaller rooms and a central staircase from the kitchen which emerges behind a small partition wall in the bedroom – common practice where space could not be wasted on halls and landings. There is a door between the two bedrooms and another between the kitchen and parlour, a trapdoor to the attic, and each room has a chimney breast and fireplace. The rooms are not large and the beamed ceilings are fairly low which, with the small-paned casement windows, gives the cottage a cosy atmosphere.

The cottage is decorated and furnished to represent a home of the early twentieth century so the exterior has mellowed brick and weathered roof tiles, and the old timbers are sagging just a little. Inside, the woodwork is dark stained and the wallpapers and furnishings are in subdued colours. Colour is important when you are planning an 'old' house, natural colours in subdued shades and soft dark colours give the right mellow effect – bright primary colours should be avoided and pastel colours, though they are suitable for Georgian or Regency houses, are not appropriate for this period. We have used dolls'-house brick paper with wood veneer timbering for the exterior and lifesize wallpapers with tiny patterns for the interior. The roof tiles are made of cardboard. There are no cornices and the skirting boards and architraves are simply made of wood strip, but if you prefer a more sophisticated effect, commercial mouldings could be used for skirting and door and window frames. A commercial staircase with banisters and handrail could be used if you prefer not to make your own but it will need careful measuring and cutting to fit.

The furniture patterns are for simple 'rustic' pieces which can be made in obeche or bass wood and stained to represent oak or pine. As an alternative, you might like to try painting a few pieces of furniture in subtle 'country' shades of dull blue, green or rust acrylic paint and lightly sanding edges where wear would naturally occur to 'age' the piece. This finish is particularly effective on pieces which would most likely have been painted such as dressers or chairs.

The house plans and furniture patterns in this chapter are all given in both 1/16 scale and 1/12 scale so you can choose whichever you prefer. You may find it helpful to read Chapter 2 before beginning and refer to it as necessary.

Note: Where patterns refer to 3/32in or 1/8in thick wood, the first measurement is for 1/16 scale and the second for 1/12 scale – where only one measurement is given, it applies to both scales.

MATERIALS

In 1/16 scale:
  1/4in plywood for the house
  1/8in plywood for the roof and half-landing
  4 × 1 1/8in balsa block for kitchen chimney breast
  3 × 3/4in balsa blocks for parlour and bedroom chimney breasts
  1/2in triangular beading for the stairs
  3/32in obeche wood for stairs skirting

In 1/12 scale:
  3/8in plywood for the house
  1/8in plywood for the roof and half-landing
  5 1/2 × 1 1/2in balsa block for kitchen chimney breast
  4 × 1in balsa blocks for parlour and bedroom chimney breasts
  3/4in triangular beading for the stairs
  1/8in obeche wood for stairs skirting

In either scale:
  thin posterboard or card for the roof tiles
  commercial moulding or picture framing for bargeboards
  1/8in obeche or bass wood for the doors
  narrow wood strips for door and window frames and glazing bars
  1/16in perspex for the windows
  1/2in square beading for the ridgepole
  six 1in hinges for the roof and fronts
  six 3/8in hinges for the doors
  woodwork glue, veneer pins, masking tape

CUTTING

Draw all the pattern pieces onto the plywood, using a sharp pencil and ruler. Ensure that all measurements and right-angles are precise. Label each piece in pencil to avoid confusion when assembling. Cut out door and window holes, stairwell and trapdoor opening. Sand all edges and tape the pieces together with masking tape to check that they fit properly. Make any necessary adjustments.

ASSEMBLY

Glue and pin one side onto the base (Fig 88). Glue and pin the back and second side onto the base and to each other. Glue and pin the top ceiling onto the side and back walls. Mark the positions of floor and partition walls on the inside and outside of the base, back, sides and ceiling in pencil. Cross-halve the floor and partition walls and fit in place. Glue

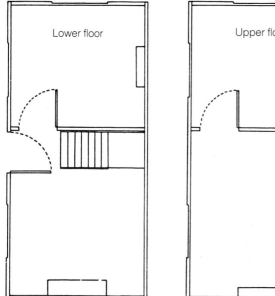

Lower floor

Upper floor

Exterior of the Tudor cottage, mellow brick and timber, and red roof tiles, shown with a small garden

and pin in place, through the back and sides, the base and top ceiling, (see Chapter 2 for instructions on cross-halving). Cut and fit the small partition wall but do not fix in place yet.

Stairs The stairs are made of triangular beading on a backing of ⅛in obeche wood. The half landing and the skirting are obeche. (Our staircase is stained dark oak.)

Draw the pattern pieces for the landing, skirting boards and backing for both flights onto the wood, ensuring that the measurements and angles are precise (Fig 89). Cut the pieces with a razor-toothed saw, sand them with fine abrasive paper and stain. Cut thirteen steps from triangular beading, ensuring that each step is exactly the same width as the backing. Sand the steps and stain them. Cut a fourteenth step from triangular

Fig 84 Floor plans for the Tudor cottage

FIGS 85, 86 AND 87 PLANS FOR THE TUDOR COTTAGE

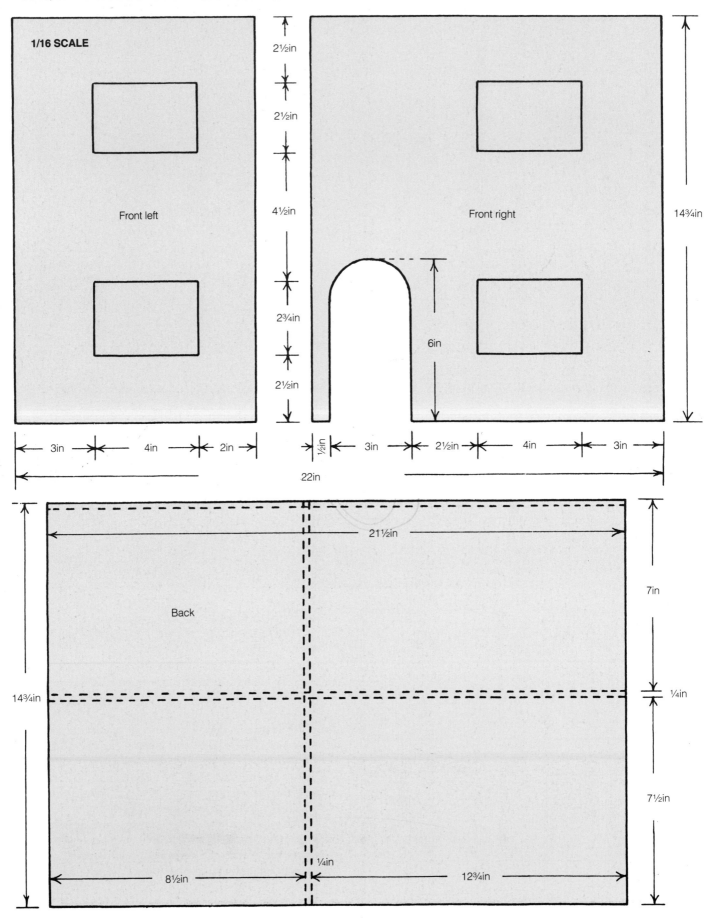

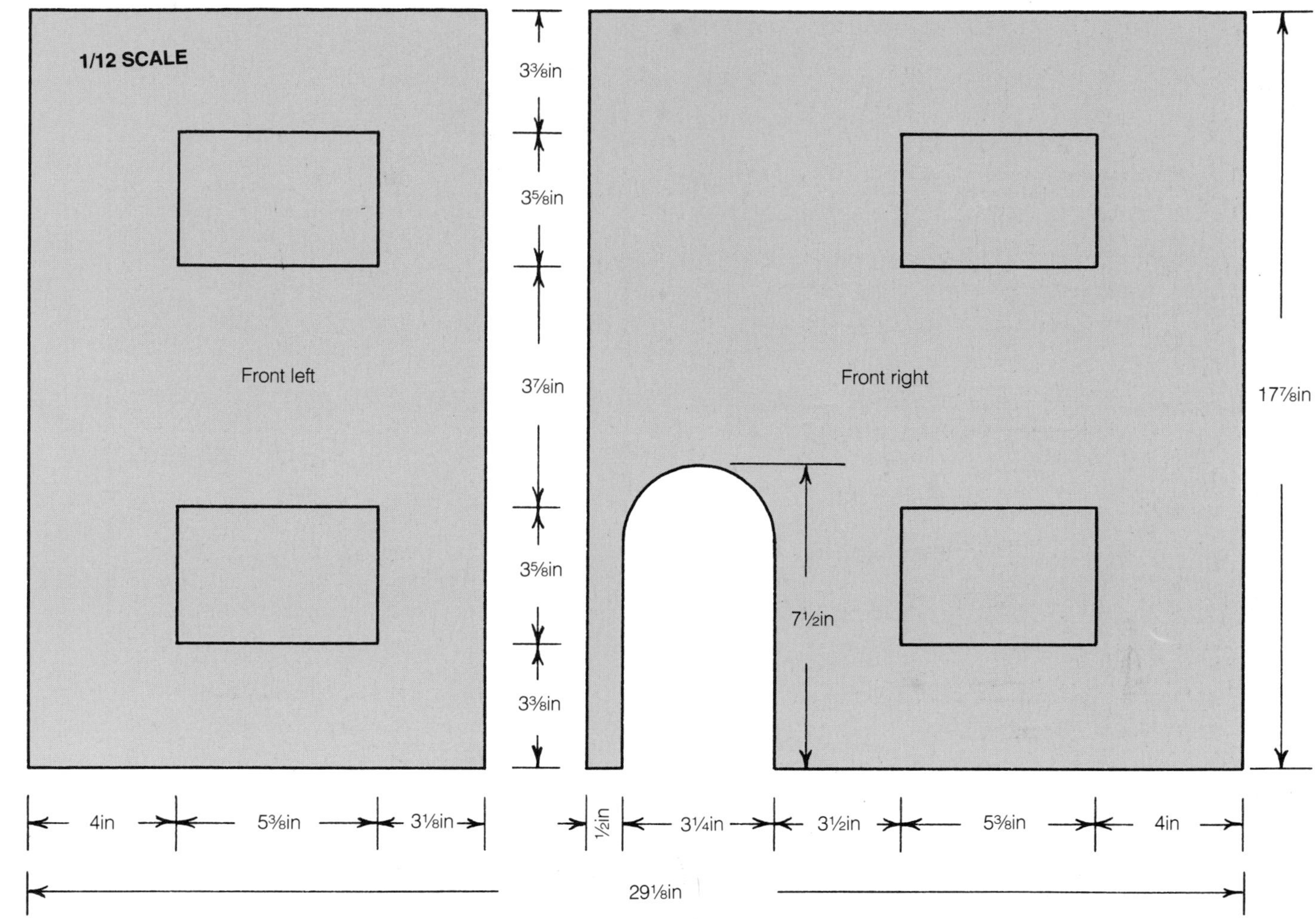

1/12 SCALE
Front left
Front right
3⅜in
3⅝in
3⅞in
3⅝in
3⅜in
17⅞in
7½in
4in
5⅜in
3⅛in
½in
3¼in
3½in
5⅜in
4in
29⅛in

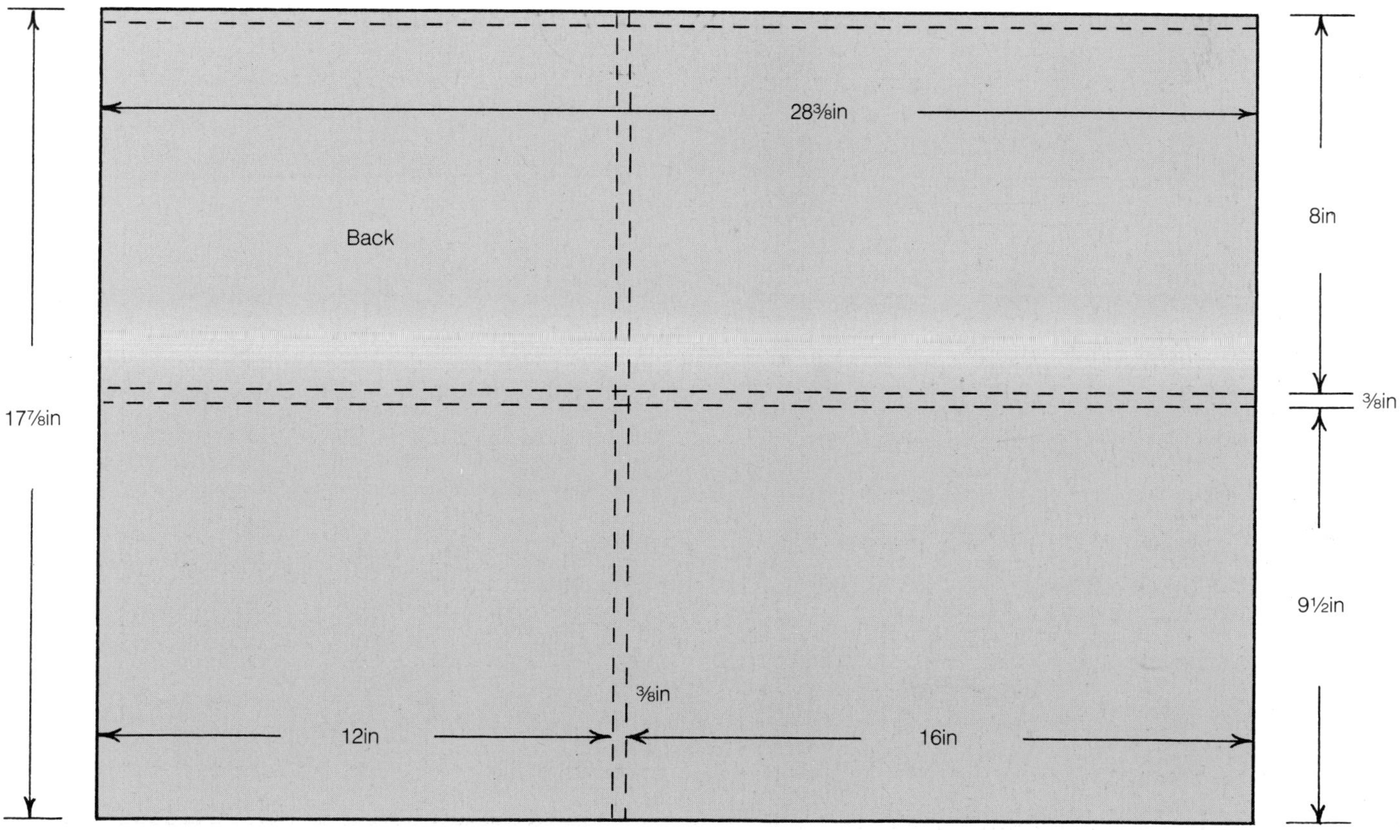

28⅜in
Back
17⅞in
8in
⅜in
9½in
⅜in
12in
16in

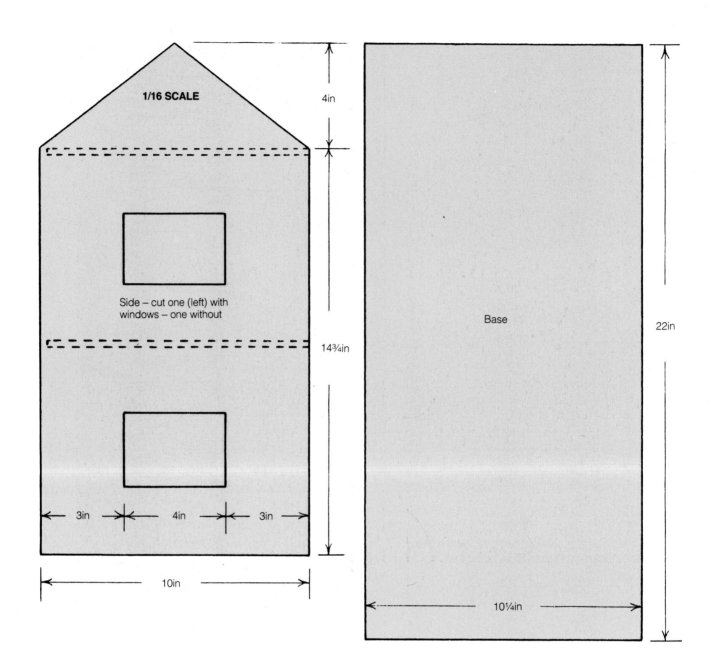

1/16 SCALE

4in

14¾in

Side – cut one (left) with
windows – one without

3in   4in   3in

10in

Base

22in

10¼in

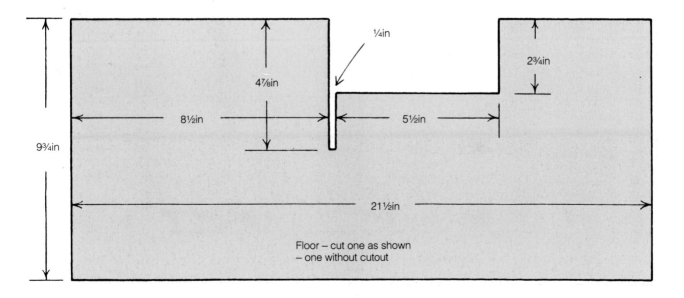

¼in

4⅞in

2¾in

8½in   5½in

9¾in

21½in

Floor – cut one as shown
– one without cutout

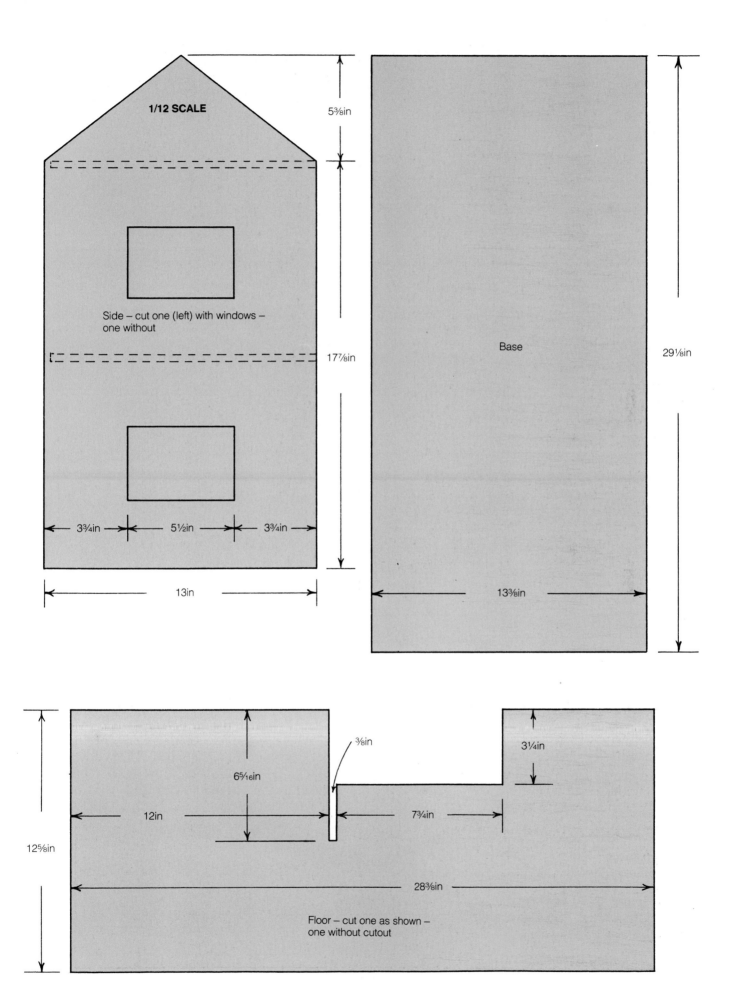

1/12 SCALE

Side – cut one (left) with windows –
one without

5⅜in

17⅞in

3¾in   5½in   3¾in

13in

Base

29⅛in

13⅜in

⅜in

6⁵⁄₁₆in

3¼in

12in   7¾in

12⅝in

28⅜in

Floor – cut one as shown –
one without cutout

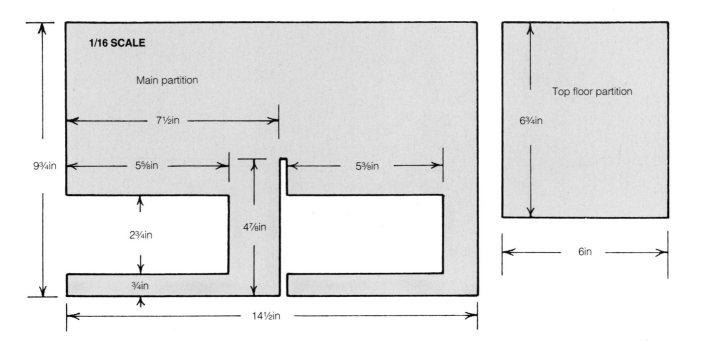

1/16 SCALE

Main partition

7½in

9¾in

5⅝in

5⅜in

2¾in

4⅞in

¾in

14½in

Top floor partition

6¾in

6in

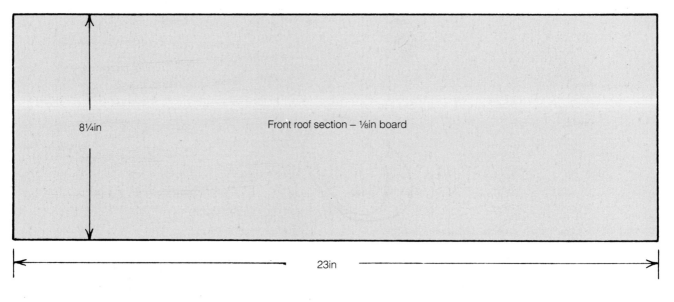

8¼in

Front roof section – ⅛in board

23in

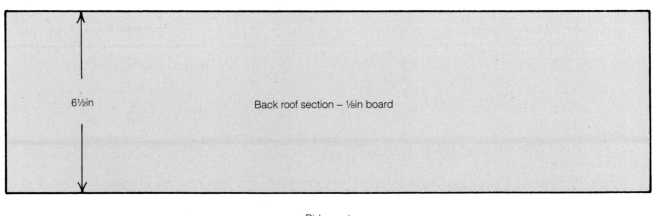

6½in

Back roof section – ⅛in board

Ridge pole

21½in

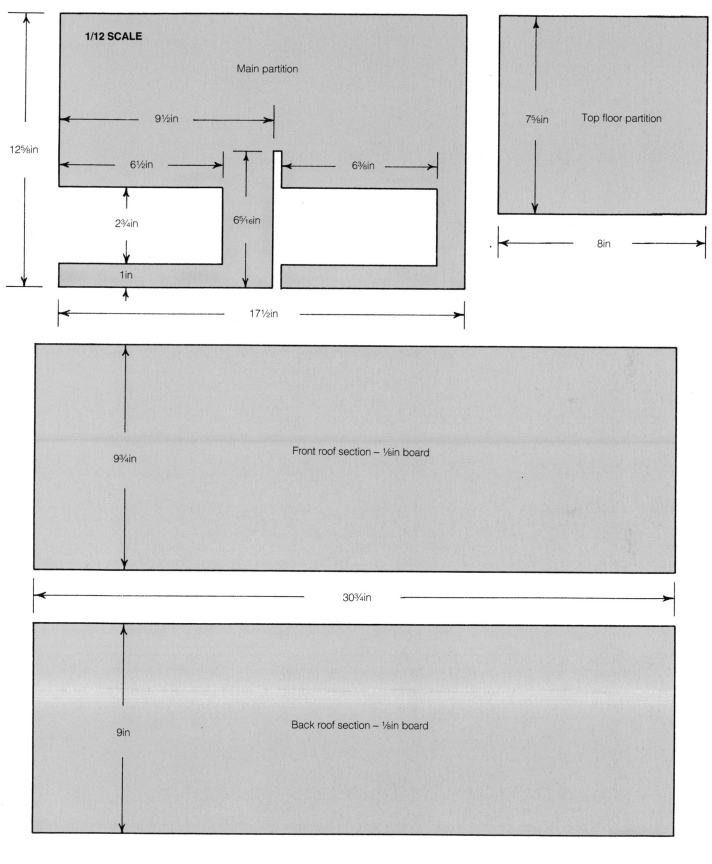

1/12 SCALE

Main partition

9½in

12⅝in

6½in

6⅜in

2¾in

6⁵⁄₁₆in

1in

17½in

7⅝in   Top floor partition

8in

Front roof section – ⅛in board

9¾in

30¾in

Back roof section – ⅛in board

9in

Ridge pole

28⅜in

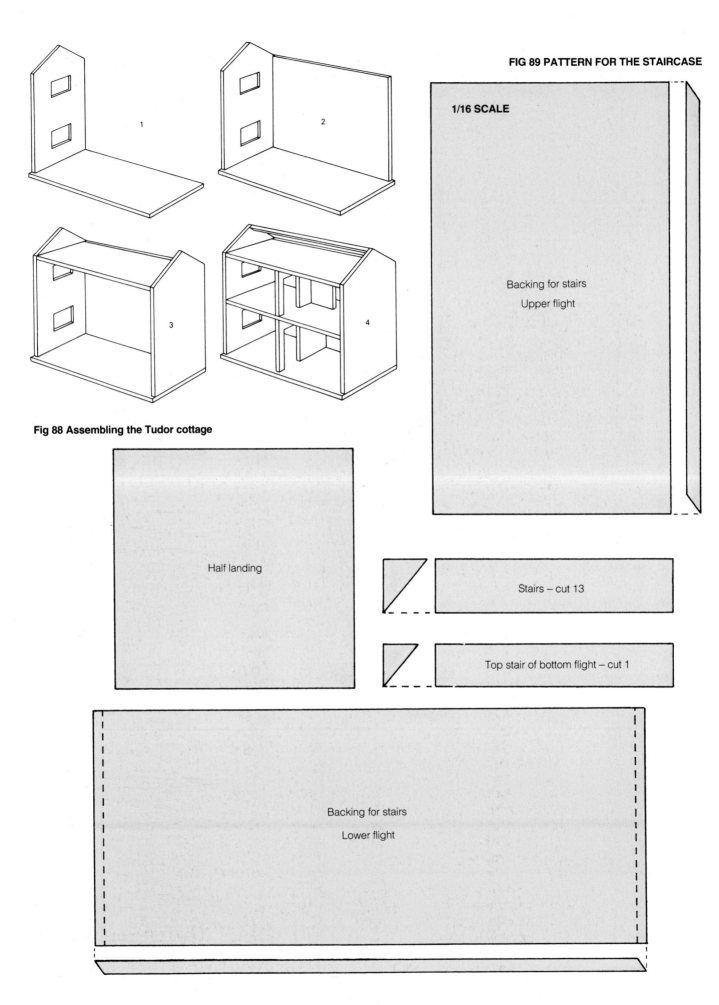

FIG 89 PATTERN FOR THE STAIRCASE

1

2

3

4

1/16 SCALE

Backing for stairs

Upper flight

Fig 88 Assembling the Tudor cottage

Half landing

Stairs – cut 13

Top stair of bottom flight – cut 1

Backing for stairs

Lower flight

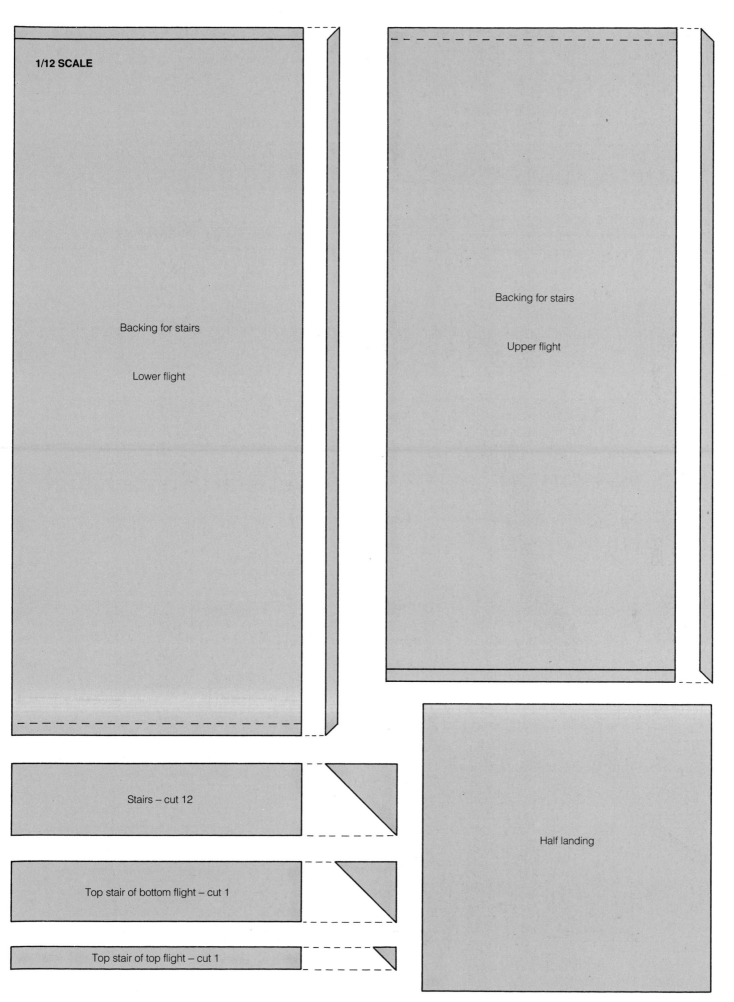

1/12 SCALE

Backing for stairs

Lower flight

Backing for stairs

Upper flight

Stairs – cut 12

Top stair of bottom flight – cut 1

Top stair of top flight – cut 1

Half landing

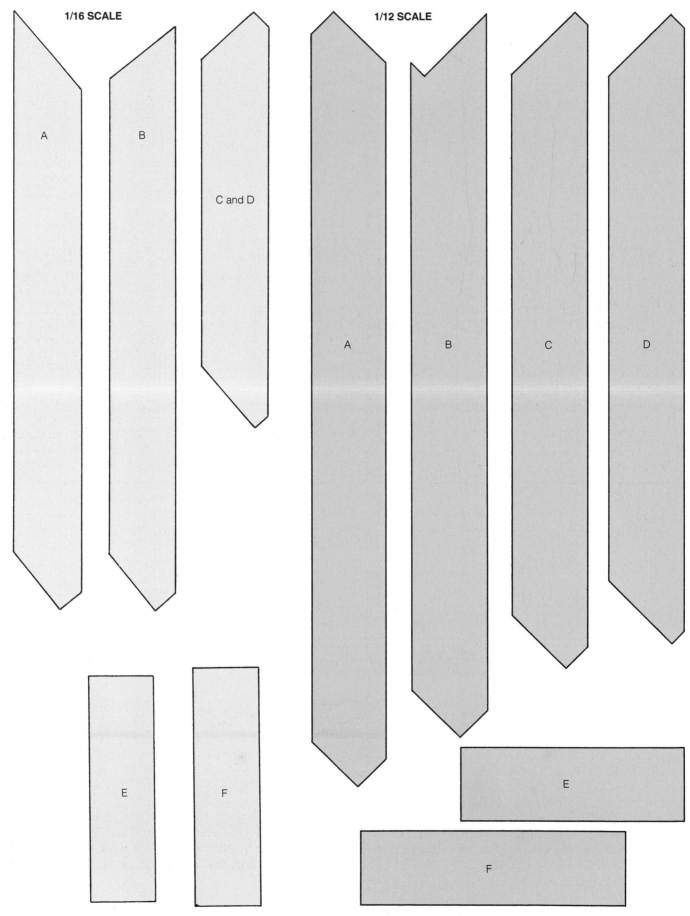

1/16 SCALE

A

B

C and D

E

F

FIG 90 ASSEMBLY AND PATTERN FOR THE STAIRCASE SKIRTING BOARDS

1/12 SCALE

A

B

C

D

E

F

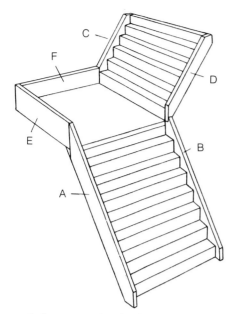

beading, and plane one side of it down to fit the pattern for the top stair of the bottom flight. Sand and stain as the others.

To assemble the staircase, begin with the bottom flight. Glue the stairs to the backing, beginning with the bottom step, and butting each step tightly against the next so that the top step fits where the chamfered edge of the backing begins.

Make the top flight in the same way, but starting with the top step, and ending with the bottom step against the chamfered edge of the backing. Glue this edge of the top flight to the edge of the half landing. This is temporarily a weak joint, so allow it to dry thoroughly before you proceed. Glue the top step of the bottom flight under the half landing. Glue the skirting boards in place on the outsides of each flight and the half landing as shown in the pattern (Fig 90), ensuring that the joints match correctly. Do not fix the staircase in place until the house has been decorated.

Chimney breasts   Cut the chimney breasts to fit each room from balsa-wood block. Cut out the fireplace opening and glue the chimney breasts to the wall in each room, lining them up carefully, one above the other.

Doors   Cut, stain and assemble the two planked interior doors and hang them in the doorways with hinges recessed into the door and the doorway (or cloth hinges). We used large loops from hook and loop fastenings for door handles, painted with black enamel paint and stuck to the doors with super-glue.

EXTERIOR

Paper the exterior and the fronts. We chose red-brick paper, but a white woodchip wall-paper looks like whitewashed plaster or you might prefer to paint the exterior (consult Chapter 3 for ideas). Paper the house, lapping the paper around the edges onto the walls inside. Cut strips about 1½in wide to paper over the front edges of the floors and partition walls, lapping the paper onto the floors, ceilings and into the rooms. Paper the fronts, lapping the paper round all sides and through the door and window holes. Make sure that the paper is straight and line up the bricks at the centre-front join. Do not stick the timbering in place at this stage.

Windows   When the paper is thoroughly dry, you can fix all the windows in place. Stain the lengths of wood-strip before cutting – we used walnut stain, but dark oak or rosewood would also be suitable. Make a frame for each window from wood-strip, mitred at each corner, and stick to the inside front edge of the window hole. Cut the perspex and fix in place. Make a similar frame on the inside back edge of each window to hold the perspex in place. The glazing bars are stuck to the window, both inside and out. Firstly, divide each window down the centre to make two casements, and make a frame for each half, mitred at the corners. The vertical bars are stuck in place first, then the horizontal bars are cut to fit and stuck in place. Although time consuming, glazing bars on both sides of the window are very realistic, and worth the effort. The handles on the windows are large loops from hook and loop fastenings, pulled open with pliers, painted black and stuck to the window frame at the centre with super-glue.

Front door   Cut and assemble the planked front door from obeche wood, sand, paint or stain it on both sides. Hang the door from hinges on the right-hand side, recessed into the wood. These hinges are too small to fix with screws so we use fine pins. To avoid splitting the wood, mark the holes through the hinges onto the door and use a fine drill or dressmaker's pin to drill the holes. Use super-glue to hold both the hinges and the pins. Repeat this process to hinge the door to the doorway, recessing the hinges into the door frame and holding them with super-glue and pins. (Before hanging the door, the doorway can be faced with fine wood-strip – stained, then steamed over a kettle until it is pliable. The arched top of the door frame is formed by taping the wood-strip around a jam jar until it is dry. The strip is then glued into the doorway and the door is cut to fit.)

Roof   The ridgepole is fitted between the tops of the gable-end walls, and screwed in place. The back-roof section is glued and pinned to the top of the gable-end walls and the ridgepole, with an overhang at each side. The front-roof section is hinged to the ridgepole, with an overhang at each side and the bottom edge (full instructions are given in Chapter 2).

The roof tiles are cut from strips of thin cardboard and stuck to each side of the roof in overlapping layers. The tiles are then painted a dark brownish red to represent old clay roof tiles. The bargeboards are cut from moulding, stained and stuck to the underside of the gable ends of the roof, with the apex join mitred to fit.

This house does not have chimneys, but chimneys can be cut from balsa block, covered in brick paper and stuck to the back roof above the chimney breasts. Clay or bead chimney pots should be stuck to the chimneys – one pot for each room.

Fronts   The fronts can be hinged in place at this stage, using two 1in hinges at each side, fixed in the same way as the door hinges but using super-glue and screws rather than pins. You might prefer to leave this until the interior has been decorated. The timbering effect and the front porch are fitted after the fronts have been fixed onto the house.

Timbering   Mark lightly in pencil on the front and sides of the house where the timbers are to go, ensuring that the horizontal beams line up (Fig 91).

Using any thin wood-veneer sheets (available from art and craft shops), stained to the appropriate colour, cut strips, roughly ½in wide for the main beams and ⅜in wide for the smaller beams. Cut the strips with scissors so that they are not too straight and even. Stick the veneer strips in place using UHU or similar glue. The large horizontal beams are fixed first, and the vertical beams cut to fit around them.

Porch   The gabled porch is made from ⅛in thick obeche wood (Fig 92). Cut the roof pieces, chamfer the top edges, stick them together and then stick the porch roof to the house, above the front door. Cut brackets from ¼in thick wood with a fretsaw, stain and stick in place either side of the door, under the porch. Cut the bargeboards from square beading, stain and

stick to the underside front edges of the porch roof, with the apex join mitred to fit. The porch-roof tiles are made from painted cardboard as for the roof, with a narrow strip of card folded down the middle to cover the ridge.

Finishing   The plaque or datestone above the front door is modelled in Das. This is rolled flat about ⅛in thick, and a rectangle cut with a knife. The name of the house and the date are incised with a pointed instrument. When the plaque is dry, it is stuck to the front of the house with UHU.

The metal door furniture we used for this house came from a specialist dolls'-house shop but similar elaborate hinges could be cut from thin metal sheet or cardboard, painted black and stuck in place. The door knocker could be made from a broken ear-ring and small brass or plastic ring, and the door knob from a map pin.

You might wish to add window boxes or a creeper climbing over the front porch (see Chapter 7), a porch lantern or a letterbox. If you have used white woodchip wallpaper instead

Interior of the Tudor cottage, showing the tenants 'at home'

of brick paper, you might like to give it the effect of pargetting by painting a shadowy design in the plaster panels between the timbers. Grey poster paint and a fine artist's paintbrush will do this efficiently, and choose simple patterns, birds, stylised flowers, etc, for the pargetting designs.

Tie-rods were often used on old houses when the brick walls started to lean outwards or bulge. A tie-rod runs through the house (usually from gable to gable) and is held with tie-plates on the outside walls. The tie-plates can be decorative, often an S or X shape in wrought iron. Dolls'-house tie-plates can be made from thin metal, cut to shape and painted matt black. They can be stuck to the wall, and look more realistic if a nut or washer is stuck to the centre to represent the end of the tie-rod.

INTERIOR
The wallpapers we used are ordinary household wallpapers with small designs, and the kitchen is painted with two coats

Fig 91 Design for the timbering on front and sides

FIG 92 PATTERN AND ASSEMBLY FOR THE GABLE PORCH

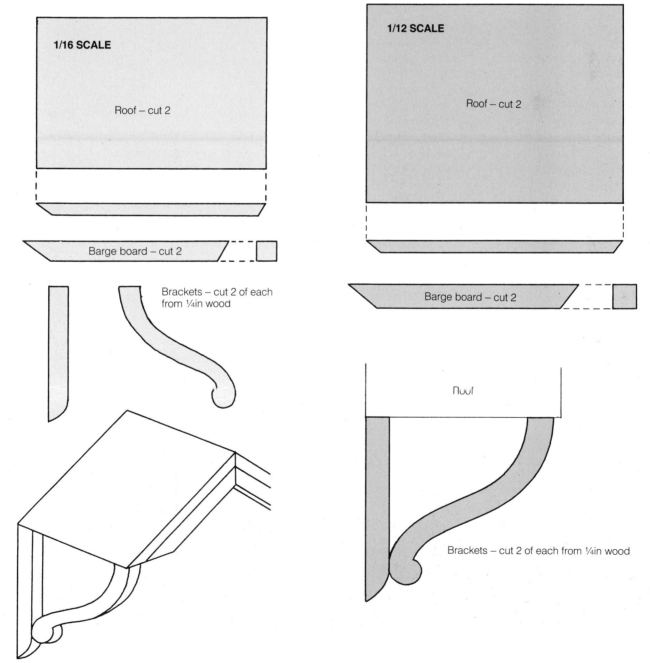

of magnolia emulsion paint. Green, brown and cream are the only colours used for the walls in this house, so that the general effect is harmonious and subdued. All three papers are very similar to late-Victorian wallpaper patterns, especially the striped design, and all have the right 'cottagey' feel about them. The rich flocked and gilded papers which were fashionable in opulent houses would look out of place in a cottage.

Before you begin decorating, fill any small gaps with Polyfilla rubbed with a finger, and wipe off any surplus filler with a damp cloth. When the Polyfilla is dry, begin by painting the ceilings. These can be papered with lining paper first but in a cottage a slightly rough texture is appropriate. Use household emulsion paint for the ceilings, two or three coats as necessary. Magnolia gives a softer effect than white, which would be too garish for this sort of house.

When the ceilings are dry, paper the rooms (except the right-hand bedroom). Even if you plan to paint the walls, lining them with paper first will give a better finish. Start with the back wall of each room (*see* Chapter 3). When the paste is thoroughly dry, paint the kitchen with two coats of emulsion paint, continuing the paint up into that part of the bedroom which will be behind the partition wall above the stairs. When the paint is dry, glue and pin this partition wall in place, before wallpapering the bedroom. The insides of the fronts can be papered to match the rooms or in a harmonising colour.

The kitchen floor is papered with the same red-brick we used for the outside of the house, but stone flags would look equally good. The parlour and bedroom floors are covered with plain-brown wrapping paper.

When the walls and floors are papered, cut, stain and fix the door and window frames made from fine wood-strip and the skirting boards made from ½in wide strips of ¹⁄₁₆in thick obeche wood.

The staircase, stained and carpeted, is then glued into place in the kitchen, followed by the banister rail, if required.

Fireplace surrounds (Figs 93 and 94) The fireplace surrounds in the bedrooms are cut from the pattern given, using ³⁄₃₂in thick obeche wood. Assemble, paint with ivory enamel paint, and use varnished paper tiles for decoration. Glue the surrounds in place over the fireplace openings on the chimney breasts. The grates are pieces of thin metal, curved and glued into the fireplace openings.

The parlour fireplace surround (Figs 95 and 96) is cut from obeche wood and stained walnut. The brackets which support the mantelshelf are cut from picture-frame moulding, and the rope-twist decoration is cut from a piece of fancy wood moulding. The sides and back of the opening are papered with brick paper. Full instructions for making the grate and fireback are given in Chapter 4.

The mantelshelf above the kitchen fireplace is cut from ⅛in thick obeche wood, stained and mounted on picture-frame-moulding brackets stuck to the wall. The kitchen stove, made from a Colman's-mustard tin, is fully described in Chapter 6.

Ceiling beams The ceiling beams in this cottage run from back to front. They are made from lengths of wood ½in wide and ¼in deep. Each beam is cut to fit, 'aged' with a hammer,

then stained walnut and stuck to the ceiling with UHU glue. These beams are not essential, but they give a period effect, and are simple to fix. Smaller beams about ¼in square could be glued to the ceiling instead, evenly spaced about 2in apart.

Attic The attic in our cottage is used as storage space rather than a room. The under-side of the roof is painted with magnolia emulsion paint, the gable walls are papered with red-brick paper, and the floor with brown wrapping paper. This

FIG 93 PATTERN FOR THE BEDROOM FIREPLACE

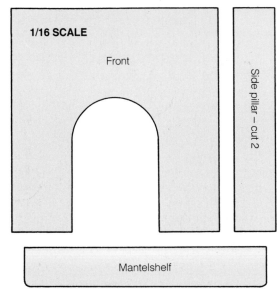

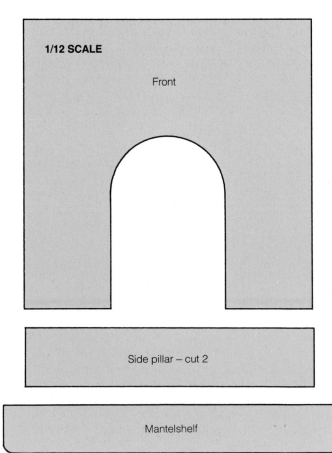

110

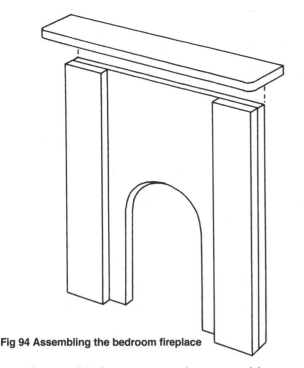

Fig 94 Assembling the bedroom fireplace

provides a useful place to put surplus pieces of furniture and junk, as in real houses. It can also be a convenient place, if the house is to be wired, for the wiring connections, batteries or transformer. The trapdoor is made of wood scrap, scored to represent planking. Glue a frame of wood strip to the bedroom ceiling around the trapdoor opening to overlap the edges by approximately ⅛in and form a ledge on which the trapdoor will rest. Glue a similar frame of woodstrip to the attic floor – but not overlapping the edge. Cut the trapdoor to fit snugly into the opening, sand the edges and score planking on both sides with a pointed tool (scissors' blade or similar). Add small knobs or pins on both sides as handles.

We fitted a low wall along the back of the attic, cut from 1in wide triangular beading, covered with brick paper, glued and pushed into place under the eaves. This provides additional support for the back roof and ensures that there is no gap showing under the roof. We made a chimney breast of balsa block, with the top edge angled to follow the gable wall, covered in brick paper and glued in place to line up with the chimney breasts in the rooms below.

When the roof is open it can be supported on posts of dowelling or brass rod – or it you prefer, posts of ½in square wood can be hinged to the floor to fold down when the roof is closed.

Curtains   There are lace curtains at each window, made from wide cream cotton lace edging. White lace can be dyed to the appropriate colour by soaking in cold tea. The curtains are hung on fine woodstrip battens, glued to the top of the window frame. The printed cotton curtains in the bedroom and parlour are gathered onto brass rods (available from model shops or dolls'-house suppliers) hung from small eyes screwed into the wall at each side of the window. The lace curtains are permanently fixed, but the heavier curtains can be drawn open and closed. The windows on the front of the house can be hung with just lace curtains on woodstrip, or with two sets of curtains.

FIG 95 PATTERN FOR THE PARLOUR FIREPLACE

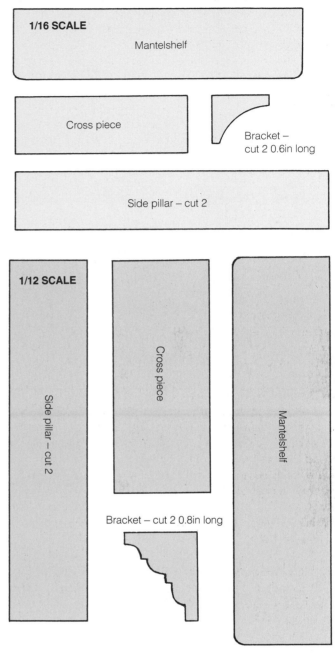

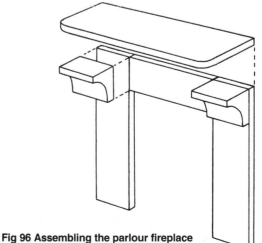

Fig 96 Assembling the parlour fireplace

111

Left-hand bedroom in the cottage – the dower chest contains the deeds of the house

FURNITURE FOR THE LEFT-HAND BEDROOM

The patterns for the furniture are drawn actual size, so that they can be traced from the book. Before beginning, read Chapter 5 and refer to it when necessary.

Chest of drawers (Fig 97) This is made of ³⁄₃₂in or ⅛in thick obeche wood, stained light oak. The handles were bought from a specialist shop, but brass gimp pins would be a good alternative.

Draw the pattern pieces onto the wood, ensuring that the grain lines are consistent, the measurements and right-angles are correct. Cut the pieces with a razor-toothed saw and chamfer the edges of the top and base pieces. Sand all the parts with fine abrasive paper and stain them.

Assemble the shell by sticking the shelves to the back, then sticking the sides in place, lining them up with the front edges of the shelves. Stick the top and base in place. Check that the drawer fronts fit snugly into the spaces. Cut the bottoms and sides of the drawers from unstained wood and assemble the drawers to fit the drawer spaces.

Sand the shell and the drawer fronts gently with fine abrasive paper and apply one coat of amateur French polish.

Allow this to dry thoroughly, then gently sand again. Apply several coats of wax polish, well-buffed between each coat. Mark the position of the drawer handles, and drill fine holes to take the shanks of the handles or gimp pins. (If you are using gimp pins cut the shanks to ³⁄₁₆in long.) Push the handles into the holes and fix with a small dab of glue over the pin hole on the inside of the drawer.

Double bed (Figs 98 and 99) This is made from ⅛in thick obeche wood, and square beading stained mahogany.

Draw the pieces onto the wood, ensuring that the measurements and right-angles are precise. Cut the pieces with a razor-toothed saw, taking particular care to cut the pairs of bedposts of equal lengths with perfectly square ends. Cut the top rails for the head and foot of the bed with a fretsaw.

Assemble the head and foot by glueing the upright stretchers between the top and bottom rails, and the bedposts onto each side. Ensure that the leg part of each post is exactly equal so that the bed will stand square. Glue the side rails to the base. Glue the head and foot onto the base so that the bedposts line up with the side rails. Ensure that the legs stand square, supporting them if necessary until the glue is dry. Sand the bed carefully with fine abrasive paper and apply one coat of amateur French polish with an artist's paintbrush. Sand again with very fine abrasive paper and apply several coats of wax polish, well-buffed between each coat.

Make a mattress using the bed base as a pattern, two pillows, sheets and a blanket. Cut a bedspread ½in wider and 1in longer than the bed, to give seam allowances. Hem the top and bottom edges. Cut two strips for the frilled sides; hem the bottom and side edges of each frill and gather the top edges. Sew them to either side of the bedspread. Put the bedspread onto the bed, and, if necessary, push pins through each side into the mattress to hold the frills in place until they hang properly. (We used the same printed cotton for the bedspread and curtains here, though any lightweight natural fabric could be used.)

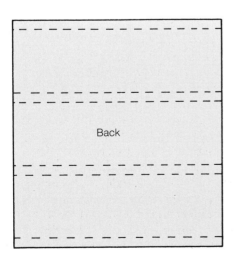

FIG 97 PATTERN FOR THE CHEST OF DRAWERS

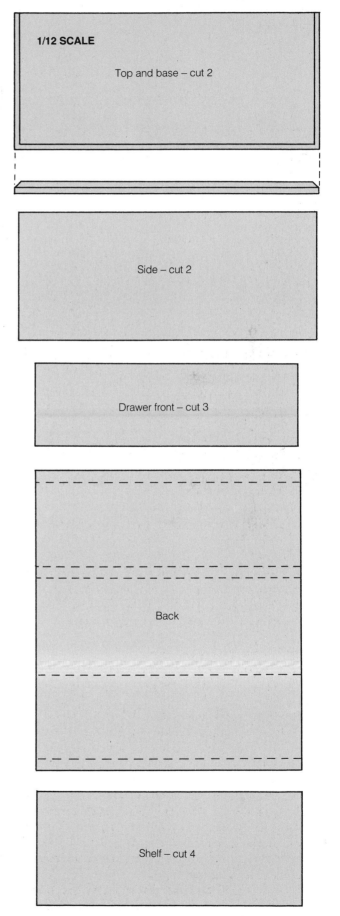

113

FIG 98 PATTERN FOR THE DOUBLE BED

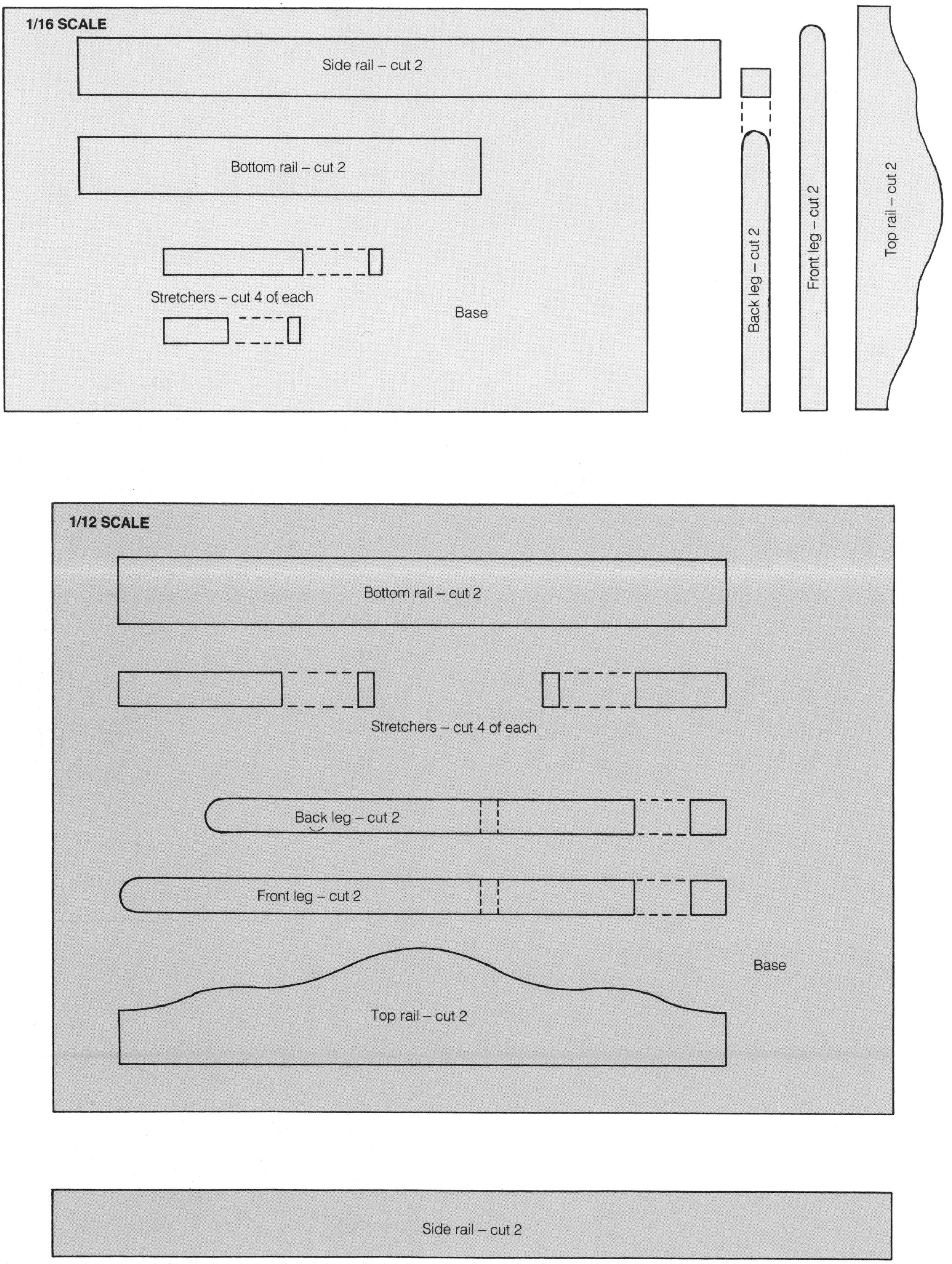

1/16 SCALE

Side rail – cut 2

Bottom rail – cut 2

Stretchers – cut 4 of each

Base

Back leg – cut 2

Front leg – cut 2

Top rail – cut 2

1/12 SCALE

Bottom rail – cut 2

Stretchers – cut 4 of each

Back leg – cut 2

Front leg – cut 2

Base

Top rail – cut 2

Side rail – cut 2

114

Fig 99 Assembling the double bed

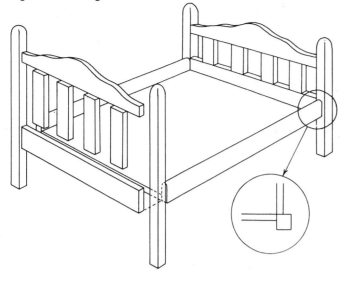

Washstand (Figs 100 and 101)   This is made of ³⁄₃₂in or ¹⁄₈in thick obeche wood, stained walnut. The towel rail is a fine wooden toothpick and the tiles are varnished paper.

Draw the pattern pieces onto the wood, ensuring that the measurements and right-angles are correct. Cut the pieces with a razor-toothed saw, the curved side pieces with a fretsaw.

FIG 100 PATTERN FOR THE WASHSTAND

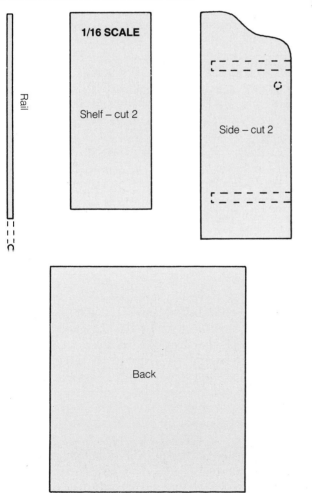

Rail

1/16 SCALE

Shelf – cut 2

Side – cut 2

Back

Sand the pieces with fine abrasive paper and stain them, including the wooden toothpick. Drill fine holes in the side pieces where indicated, to take the towel rail.

Glue one side piece to the back, then glue the two shelves to the side and back. Glue the other side in place. Push the toothpick into the holes drilled in the sides, trimming the ends if necessary so that they do not protrude.

Fig 101 Assembling the washstand

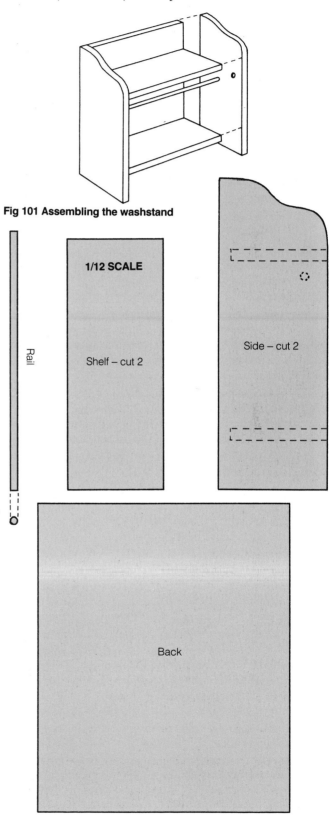

Rail

1/12 SCALE

Shelf – cut 2

Side – cut 2

Back

115

Right-hand bedroom in the cottage, showing trapdoor to the attic

Sand the washstand with fine abrasive paper and apply one coat of amateur French polish. Sand again with very fine abrasive paper and apply several coats of wax polish, buffing well between each coat. Cut the paper tiles (we used tiles cut from a magazine illustration) to fit the back and the top shelf and stick them in place with UHU or similar glue. A coat of varnish (colourless nail varnish works well) gives the tiles a more realistic effect. Cut a towel and hang it from the rail. The top shelf of the washstand holds a wash-bowl and jug, the bottom shelf a chamber pot.

Dower chest (Figs 102 and 103)   This is made of ⅛in thick obeche wood stained medium oak. The panelling is made with fine wood-strip.

Draw the pattern pieces onto the wood, ensuring that the measurements and right-angles are precise. Cut the pieces with a razor-toothed saw, sand with fine abrasive paper and stain them, including the wood-strip. The top edges of the lid should be chamfered slightly before staining if the chest is to look old.

Glue the front and back to the base, with the base inside. Glue the ends to the back, front and base, to form the box. The under-lid piece is glued to the underside of the lid, leaving a larger overhang at the front edge than the back to allow for the panelling. Make a frame of fine wood-strip on the front of the box, mitring the corners. Divide the panel into three equal sections with two small uprights of wood-strip, fitting exactly into the frame.

Sand the box and the lid carefully with fine abrasive paper. Apply one coat of amateur French polish to the outside of the box and the top of the lid. Sand again with fine abrasive paper and apply several coats of wax polish, well-buffed between coats.

The dower chest in this house holds the deeds of the house but it might contain folded linen or small treasures.

FURNITURE FOR THE RIGHT-HAND BEDROOM
Wardrobe (Figs 104 and 105)   This is made of ³⁄₃₂in or ⅛in thick obeche wood stained light oak. The handles on this piece were bought from a specialist shop, but brass gimp pins would be a good alternative. The rail inside is made of fine dowelling.

Draw the pattern pieces onto the wood, ensuring that the measurements and right-angles are precise. Score outlines of door panels on the door fronts with a sharp instrument, using a metal ruler as a guide. Cut the pieces, using a razor-toothed saw. Drill shallow holes on the insides of the side pieces, where marked, to hold the hanging rail. Glue the two base pieces together and press under a weight until the glue is dry. Chamfer the underside of the top piece at the front and sides. Sand all pieces with fine abrasive paper and stain them. Assemble the wardrobe by glueing one side to the back. Glue the inner top inside the back and side, and the base inside the back and side, as marked on the pattern. Glue the other side in place, fixing the rail into the holes. Pin hinge the doors into the base, then into the top (with the chamfered edge to the underside). Glue the top in place. Assemble the cornice with mitred corners and glue to the top, overhanging slightly. Glue the sides of the plinth to the bottom of the wardrobe sides and the front of the plinth to the front of the wardrobe below the doors.

Sand the wardrobe carefully with fine-grade abrasive paper and apply one coat of amateur French polish. Sand again with very fine abrasive paper and apply several coats of wax polish,

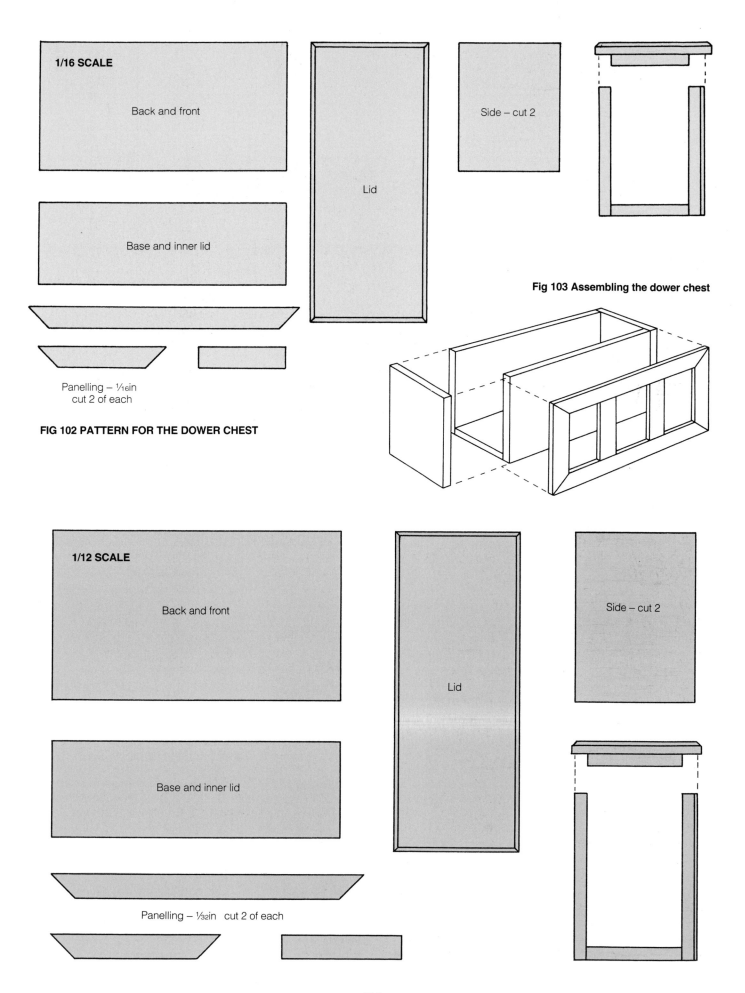

1/16 SCALE

Back and front

Base and inner lid

Lid

Side – cut 2

Panelling – 1/16in
cut 2 of each

FIG 102 PATTERN FOR THE DOWER CHEST

Fig 103 Assembling the dower chest

1/12 SCALE

Back and front

Base and inner lid

Lid

Side – cut 2

Panelling – 1/32in   cut 2 of each

117

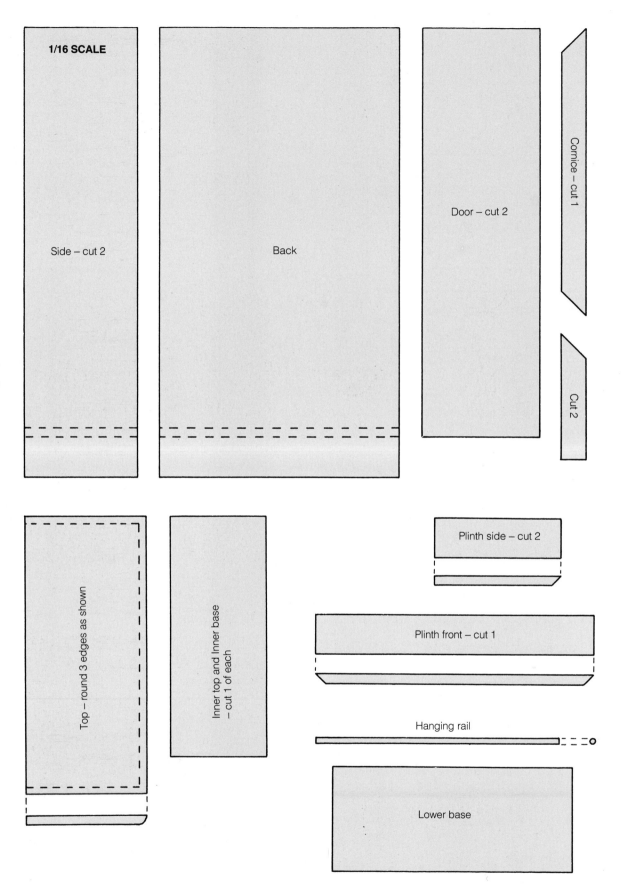

1/16 SCALE

Side – cut 2

Back

Door – cut 2

Cornice – cut 1

Cut 2

Top – round 3 edges as shown

Inner top and Inner base – cut 1 of each

Plinth side – cut 2

Plinth front – cut 1

Hanging rail

Lower base

FIG 104 PATTERN FOR THE WARDROBE

118

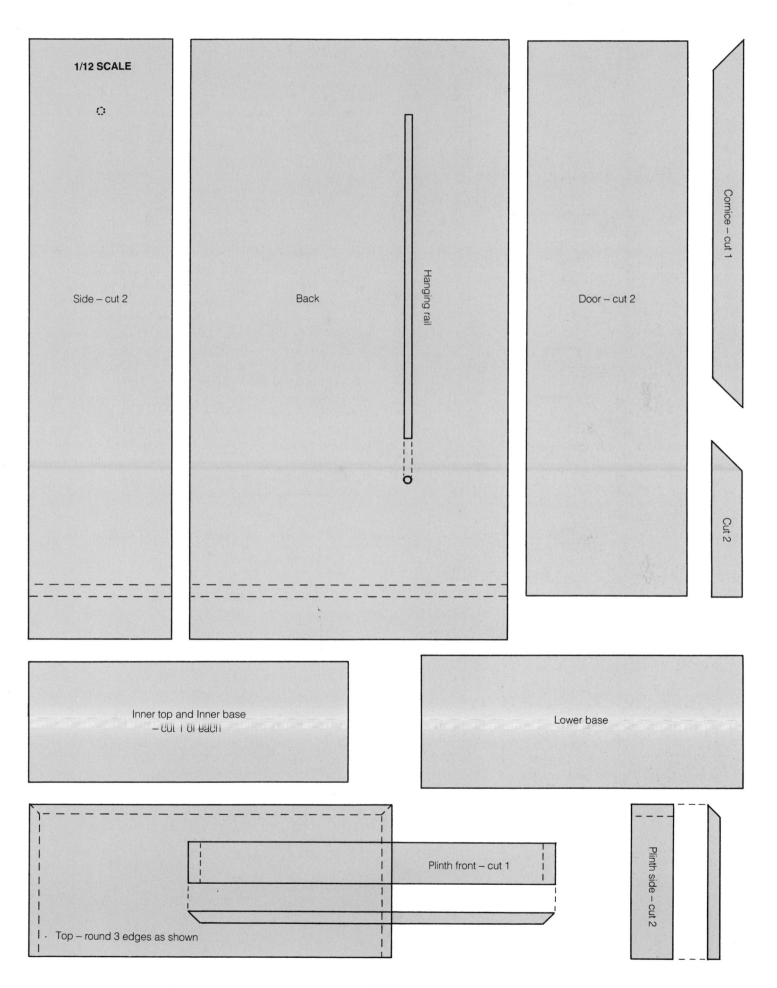

1/12 SCALE

Side – cut 2

Back

Hanging rail

Door – cut 2

Cornice – cut 1

Cut 2

Inner top and Inner base
– cut 1 of each

Lower base

Top – round 3 edges as shown

Plinth front – cut 1

Plinth side – cut 2

Fig 105 Assembling the wardrobe

well-buffed between coats. Mark the positions of the door handles and fix in place.

Single bed (Fig 106)   The bed is made from ⅛in thick obeche wood with square-beading posts, stained walnut.

Draw the pattern pieces onto the wood, ensuring that the measurements and right-angles are precise. Follow the instructions for cutting out and assembling the double bed on page 112.

Make a mattress using the bed base as a pattern, plus a pillow, sheets, a blanket and a bedspread.

Armchair (Fig 107)   This is made of cardboard, padded with foam and covered with printed cotton.

Cut the cardboard back for the chair from the pattern and score the fold lines. Cut the padding and the fabric cover ½in larger all-round than the pattern, to allow for seams. Glue the foam to the cardboard, rolling the excess foam to the back, and glueing the edges to the back of the cardboard. Stitch the cover, clip the corners and curves and then turn through to the right side. Slip the cover over the padded cardboard, pulling it taut, and slip-stitch the bottom edges closed.

Cut the seat from balsa block, pad with foam and cover with fabric. Fold the sides of the chair forward and fit the seat in place. Glue the seat to the back and sides of the chair, holding it in place with pins until the glue dries. Glue four square wooden beads to the underside for feet. Make a loose cushion in the same fabric for the seat, and a small cushion in toning fabric to tuck into the corner of the chair.

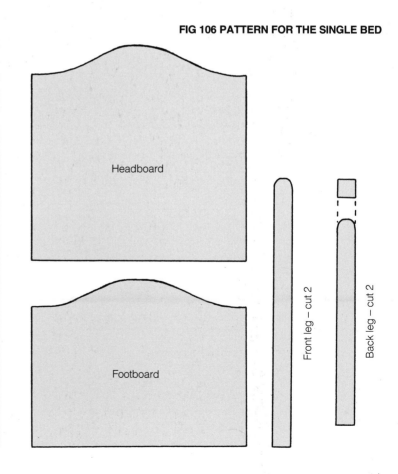

1/16 SCALE

Base

Side stretcher – cut 2

FIG 106 PATTERN FOR THE SINGLE BED

Headboard

Footboard

Front leg – cut 2

Back leg – cut 2

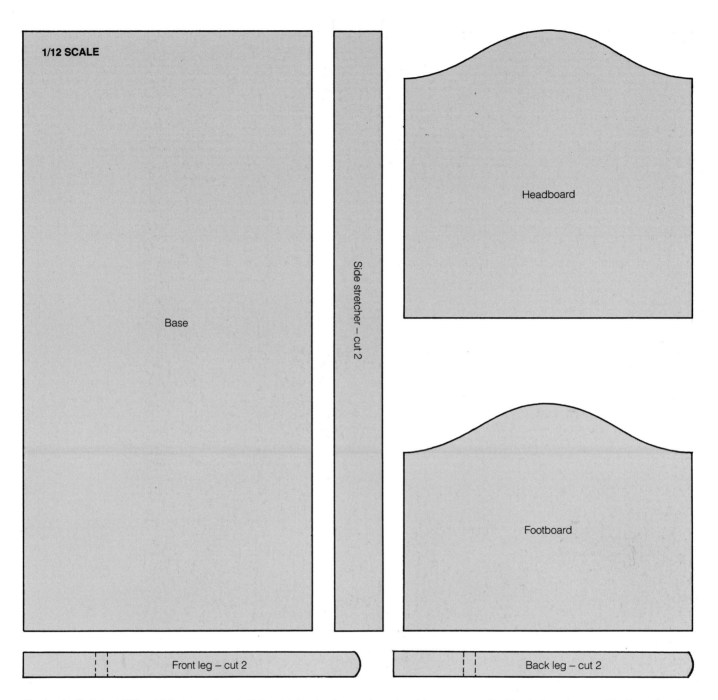

1/12 SCALE

Base

Side stretcher – cut 2

Headboard

Footboard

Front leg – cut 2

Back leg – cut 2

Book shelf (Fig 108) This is made of ³/₃₂in thick obeche wood, stained with button polish to pine colour.

Draw the pieces onto the wood, and cut them with a razor-toothed saw, and fretsaw for the curved side pieces. Sand the pieces carefully with fine abrasive paper.

Assemble the shelves by sticking one side to the back, then sticking the shelves to the back and side. Stick the other side in place. Sand the shelves with very fine abrasive paper and stain them with a coat of button polish, applied with an artist's paintbrush. Sand again, and polish with wax polish. The shelf is stuck to the wall with double-sided tape.

Small table (Figs 109 and 110) This is made ¹/₁₆in thick obeche wood with square beading for legs. It is stained walnut.

Draw the pattern pieces onto the wood, ensuring that the right-angles are precise, and the legs are exactly the same

length with square ends. Sand the pieces with fine abrasive paper and stain them. Glue the four frieze pieces to the underside of the table top to form a closed box. Glue the legs into the corners of this box, supporting them if necessary to keep them straight whilst the glue dries. Glue the notched corners of the shelf and fit it in place between the legs. Sand the table carefully with fine abrasive paper and apply one coat of amateur French polish. Sand again with very fine abrasive paper and apply several coats of wax polish, well-buffed between coats.

THE PARLOUR FURNITURE

Wing chairs (see Fig 77) These are made of cardboard, padded with foam and covered in printed cotton. Full instructions are given in Chapter 10.

Glue four wooden beads to the underside of the chair. Make

FIG 107 PATTERN FOR THE BEDROOM CHAIR

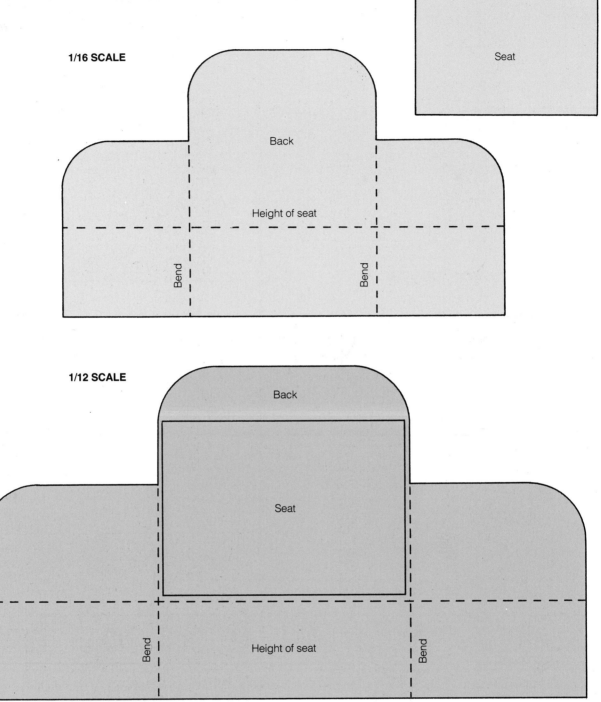

1/16 SCALE

Back

Seat

Height of seat

Bend

Bend

1/12 SCALE

Back

Seat

Height of seat

Bend

Bend

a cushion and, if required, an antimacassar of broderie anglaise. Splay the wings of the chair gently outwards, and place a cushion in the back of the chair.

Footstool   This is made of a ½in piece sawn from one end of a cotton reel. It is padded with foam and covered with brown velveteen.

Cut a ½in piece from one end of a cotton reel (or use a circle of balsa wood or cork) with a razor-toothed saw. Cut a circle of fabric 3in in diameter. Glue a little padding to the top of the cotton reel. Run a gathering thread around the edge of the fabric circle and draw it over the padded cotton reel with

the gathered edge under the base. Pull the gathers up as tightly as possible, distributing them evenly so that the cover is taut. Fasten off and trim the excess fabric. Cut a circle of felt and glue it to the underside to cover the raw edges. Glue a piece of narrow upholstery braid or ribbon around the sides of the stool to trim.

Shelf unit (Figs 111 and 112)   This is made of ³⁄₃₂in thick obeche wood, stained light oak.

Draw the pattern pieces onto the wood, ensuring that the measurements and right-angles are precise. Cut the straight-edged pieces with a razor-toothed saw, and the curved side

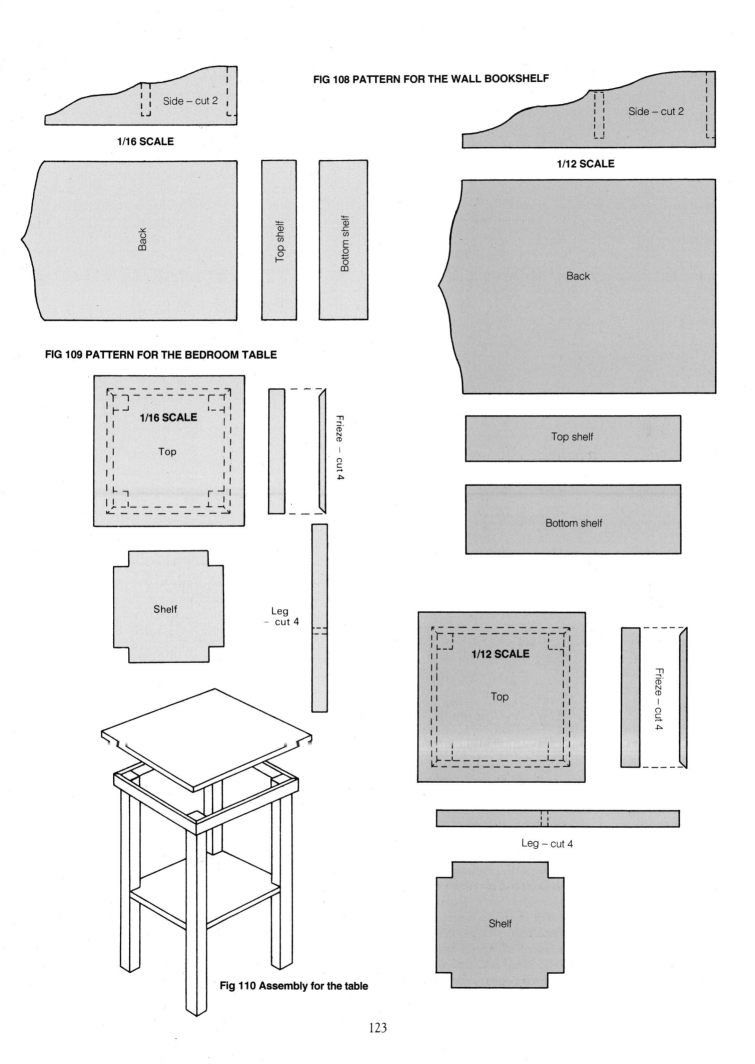

FIG 108 PATTERN FOR THE WALL BOOKSHELF

Side – cut 2

1/16 SCALE

Back

Top shelf

Bottom shelf

1/12 SCALE

Side – cut 2

Back

Top shelf

Bottom shelf

FIG 109 PATTERN FOR THE BEDROOM TABLE

1/16 SCALE

Top

Frieze – cut 4

Shelf

Leg – cut 4

1/12 SCALE

Top

Frieze – cut 4

Leg – cut 4

Shelf

Fig 110 Assembly for the table

123

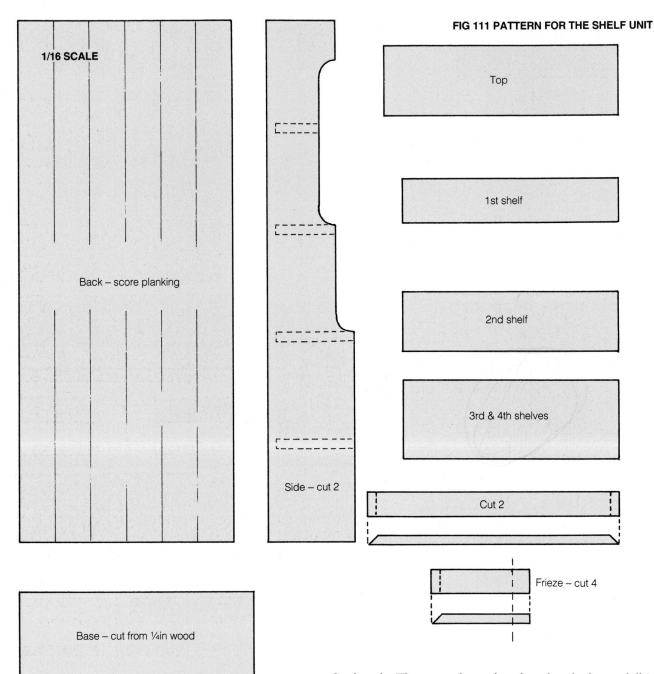

1/16 SCALE

Back – score planking

Side – cut 2

Base – cut from ¼in wood

FIG 111 PATTERN FOR THE SHELF UNIT

Top

1st shelf

2nd shelf

3rd & 4th shelves

Cut 2

Frieze – cut 4

pieces with a fretsaw. Sand the pieces with fine abrasive paper and stain them.

Assemble the shelf unit by glueing one side to the back, then the shelves to the back and side, then the other side to the back and shelves. Glue the shelves onto the base, lining them up carefully. Glue ¼in wide dolls'-house architrave moulding around the top and base, with mitred corners.

Sand the shelf unit carefully with fine abrasive paper and apply one coat of amateur French polish. Sand again with very fine abrasive paper and apply several coats of wax polish, buffing well between coats.

Sofa (see Fig 47)   The sofa is made of cardboard, padded with foam and covered with printed cotton. Full instructions are given in Chapter 5.

Cupboard   This particular cupboard was bought from a dolls'-house shop, but a similar cupboard could be made from the pattern for the wardrobe, reduced in height. Follow the directions given for the wardrobe, using ⅛in thick obeche wood and rosewood stain. In place of the wardrobe cornice, cut a flat top to overhang the front and sides slightly. Brass gimp pins would make suitable handles.

Sofa table (Fig 113)   This is made in ⅛in thick obeche wood, stained mahogany. Draw the pattern pieces onto the wood, ensuring that the two legs are exactly alike. Cut the top and the stretcher with a razor-toothed saw, the legs with a fretsaw, omitting cut-outs on the legs if you prefer. Sand the pieces carefully with fine abrasive paper and stain them. Glue the stretcher and the two legs in place to the underside of the top, positioning them carefully while the glue is wet and supporting them if necessary until the glue is dry. Sand the

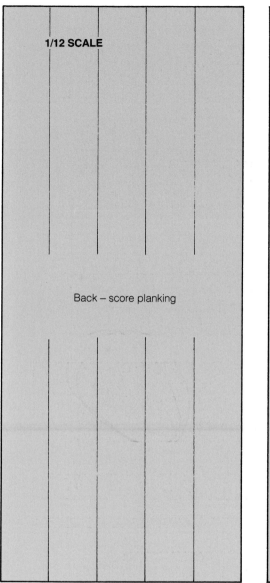

1/12 SCALE

Back – score planking

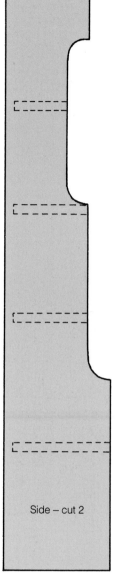

Side – cut 2

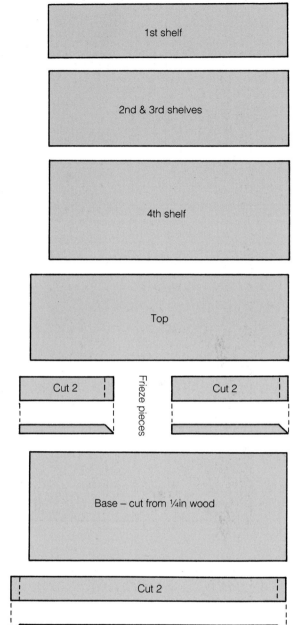

1st shelf

2nd & 3rd shelves

4th shelf

Top

Cut 2

Frieze pieces

Cut 2

Base – cut from ¼in wood

Cut 2

Fig 112 Assembling the shelf unit

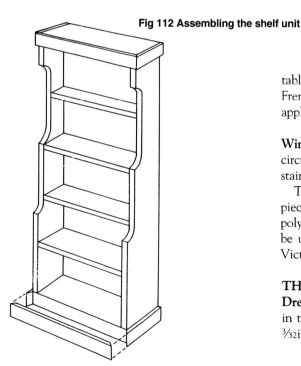

table with fine abrasive paper and apply one coat of amateur French polish. Sand again with very fine abrasive paper and apply several coats of wax polish, well-buffed between coats.

Wine table   This is made from a black chess piece, with a circular top 1½in diameter, cut from ⅛in thick obeche wood stained walnut.

The top is cut, sanded and stained, and glued to the chess-piece pedestal. The table top is varnished with one coat of polyurethane varnish. Any similar piece of turned wood could be used for the pedestal, or adapt the pedestal table in the Victorian town house.

THE KITCHEN FURNITURE

Dresser (Figs 114, 115 and 116)   The kitchen dresser is made in the traditional manner as two separate units. It is made of ³⁄₃₂in or ⅛in thick obeche wood, stained dark oak. The

125

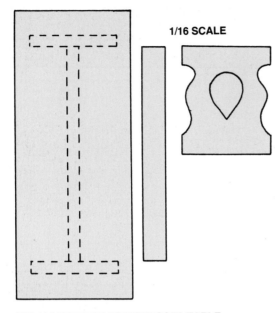

1/16 SCALE

FIG 113 PATTERN FOR THE SOFA TABLE

1/12 SCALE

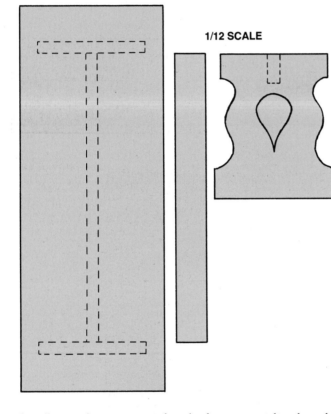

FIG 114 PATTERN FOR THE KITCHEN DRESSER (TOP UNIT)

1/16 SCALE

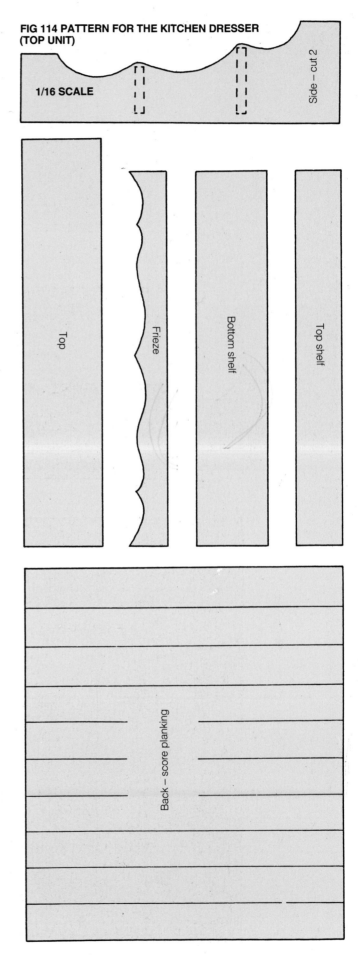

handles on this piece were bought from a specialist shop, but brass gimp pins or the loop part of hook and loop fasteners would make suitable alternatives.

Draw the pattern pieces onto the wood, ensuring that the measurements and right-angles are precise. Cut the straight-edged pieces with a razor-toothed saw, and the curved sides and frieze pieces with a fretsaw. Score the back pieces with a sharp instrument (eg scissor blade) to represent planking. Chamfer the top front and side edges of the base-unit top. Sand all the pieces with fine abrasive paper and stain them.

Firstly, the base unit; glue one side piece to the back. Glue the drawer shelf in place, then the drawer divider and the

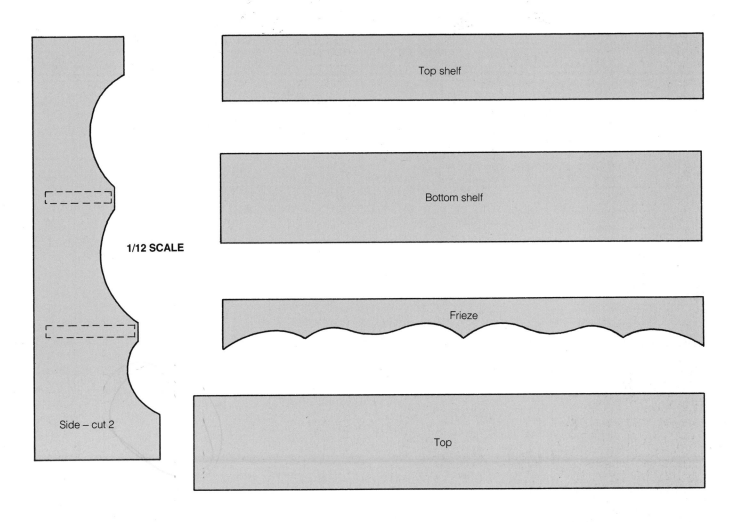

1/12 SCALE

Side – cut 2

Top shelf

Bottom shelf

Frieze

Top

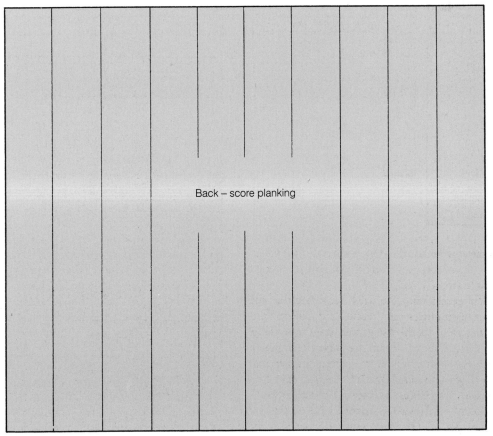

Back – score planking

The cottage parlour, simply but comfortably furnished

lower partition. Glue the bottom shelf then the other side piece. Stick the top in place, overhanging at the front and sides, then the small curved frieze pieces under the drawer shelf. Check that the drawer fronts fit snugly into the drawer spaces. Cut bottom, back and side pieces from unstained wood and assemble the drawers to fit into the spaces.

Secondly, the top unit: glue one side piece to the back. Stick the shelves to the side and back, then stick the other side in place. Glue the top in place, overhanging the front and sides, then the frieze under the top.

Sand the top and base units carefully with fine abrasive paper and apply one coat of amateur French polish. Sand again with very fine abrasive paper and apply several coats of wax polish, well-buffed between each coat. Mark the positions of the handles on the drawer fronts and fit the handles. If you prefer, the top unit can be glued to the base unit for extra stability.

Wooden wing chair (Figs 117 and 118)   This is made of ⅛in thick obeche wood, stained dark oak. Draw the pattern pieces onto the wood and cut them with a fretsaw. Sand the pieces with fine abrasive paper and stain them. Glue one side to the outer edge of the back. Glue the seat into the side and back, and the seatboard, at a backward-tilted angle, under the front of the seat. Glue the other side in place. Sand the chair with fine-grade abrasive paper and apply one coat of amateur French polish. Sand again with very fine abrasive paper and apply several coats of wax polish, buffing well between coats. Make a fabric cushion for the chair seat.
Note: This pattern can be used to make a settle by cutting the back, seat and seatboard pieces twice as wide. Assemble as the chair.

Refectory table (Figs 119 and 120)   This is made of ⅛in thick obeche wood, stained dark oak.

Draw the pattern pieces onto the wood, choosing wood with a good grain for the top. Cut the top and stretchers with a razor-toothed saw, and the legs with a fretsaw. Sand the

The cottage kitchen with a 'mustard tin' stove and traditional oak-stained furniture

pieces with fine-grade abrasive paper, rounding the corners and sides of the top. Stain the pieces. Glue the support stretchers to the underside of the top as marked on the pattern. Glue the legs inside the stretchers to the underside of the top. Glue the stretchers between the legs as shown on the pattern.

Sand the table with fine-grade abrasive paper and apply one coat of amateur French polish. Sand again with very fine abrasive paper and apply several coats of wax polish, well-buffed between each coat.

Benches (Figs 119 and 120)   The benches are made of ⅛in thick obeche wood stained dark oak. Draw the pattern pieces onto the wood and cut them with a razor-toothed saw. Sand the pieces with fine abrasive paper, rounding the sides and corners of the bench seat. Stain the pieces. Glue the legs to the underside of the seat, and the stretcher to the underside of the seat between the legs. Sand the bench with fine abrasive paper and apply one coat of amateur French polish. Sand again with very fine abrasive paper and polish with wax polish.

ACCESSORIES
The accessories in the Tudor cottage are mostly made or 'found' items as described in Chapter 6, supplemented with inexpensive miniatures from the commercial ranges available from toyshops and dolls'-house suppliers.

The bedroom rugs are pieces of Dralon furnishing velvet,

the edges sealed with Fraycheck or fringed, and felt with a pattern drawn with felt pens. The parlour carpet (Dijon) is from a specialist shop and the rug in the kitchen from a toyshop. The stair carpet is cut from a piece of furnishing fabric with a striped pattern – the edges sealed with Fraycheck.

The lights are inexpensive plastic fittings (Lundby) from a toyshop, installed with wires emerging through the back wall to connect with the transformer.

The mustard-tin stove, broom, mop, magazine cut-out pictures framed with woodstrip, plaited raffia baskets and bead and button ornaments are all homemade and the teddy bear is from a gift shop. The packages (Thames Valley), and washstand set are from a dolls'-house shop. The toyshop plastic saucepans are painted with copper enamel and the plastic tea-set is decorated with tiny transfers.

Patterns and instructions for making the simple bead and pipecleaner dolls can be found in Chapter 14.

The chair in the left-hand bedroom is from our book *Making Miniatures*, where you will also find further information on 'Tudor' building effects and a number of furniture patterns which would be suitable for a Tudor cottage in 1/12 scale (see Books).

VARIATIONS
When decorated with red-brick and timbering, this house is typically Tudor, but with different decorating schemes the basic design could be used to make other houses (Fig 121).

The proportions of the exterior make the design suitable for a small Queen-Anne house. The windows should be paned sashes rather than casements and the doors panelled rather

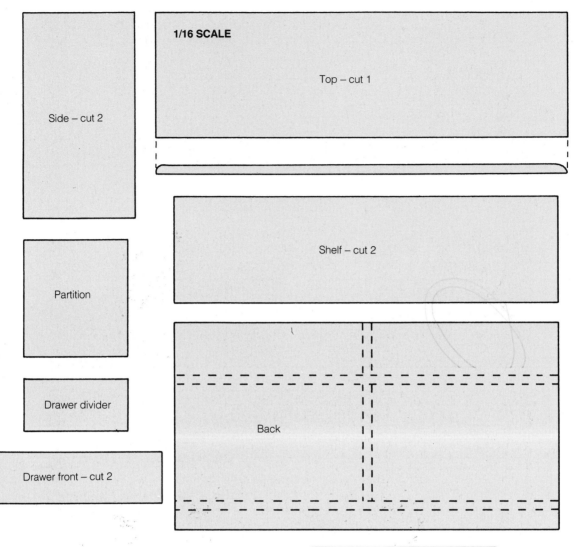

1/16 SCALE

Side – cut 2

Top – cut 1

Shelf – cut 2

Partition

Drawer divider

Back

Drawer front – cut 2

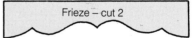

Frieze – cut 2

FIG 115 PATTERN FOR THE KITCHEN DRESSER (BASE UNIT)

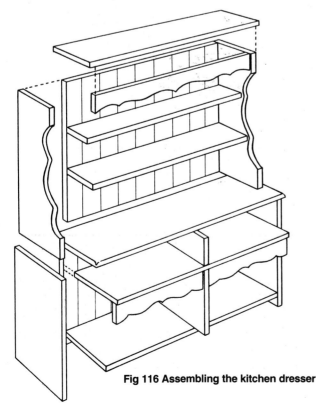

Fig 116 Assembling the kitchen dresser

than planked. The red-brick paper is suitable, but the paintwork should be cream, and typical features such as a pediment and fanlight over the front door should be added. Inside the house, the lower floor might be partitioned into two equal-sized rooms with a central hall and staircase. Upstairs, the bedrooms could be partitioned as for the Tudor house, or divided to correspond with the rooms below, the stairs emerging on a central landing. The interior decor would follow contemporary fashion, with pastel colours on the walls, polished wood floors and white or cream paintwork. Although modest in size, furnishings might include an elegant four-poster bed, with a dressing chest and mirror. The smaller bedroom might be a nursery, with a hooded cradle on rockers and a truckle bed for an older child. The parlour might be panelled in wood with a gilt-framed mirror above an elaborate marble fireplace, and a polished wood floor covered by a rug. The parlour furnishings could include a gate-legged table and several tall-backed chairs, a cabinet to store and display silver

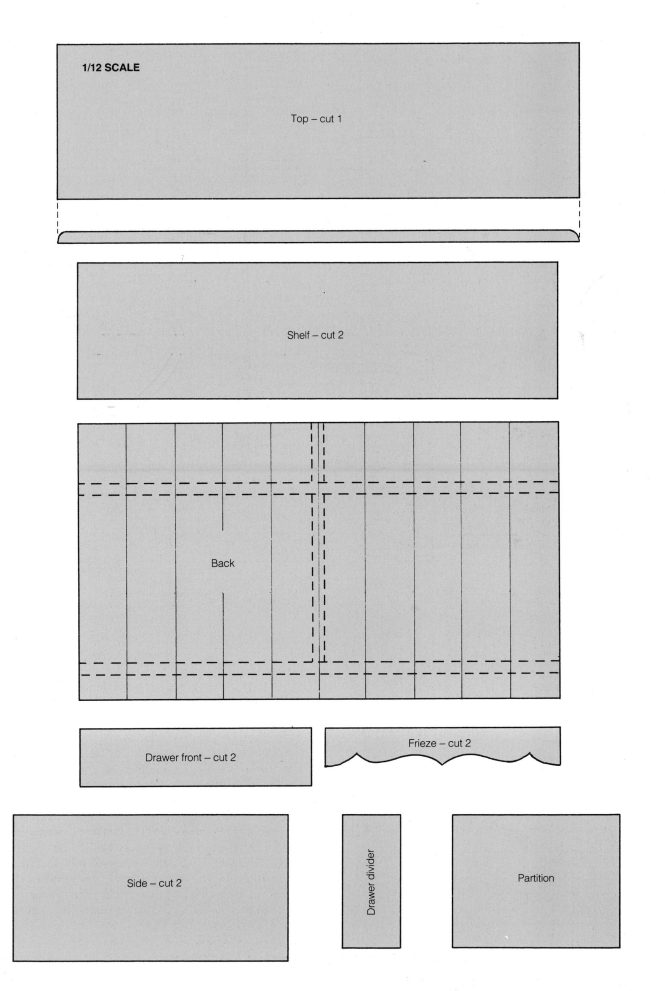

1/12 SCALE

Top – cut 1

Shelf – cut 2

Back

Drawer front – cut 2

Frieze – cut 2

Side – cut 2

Drawer divider

Partition

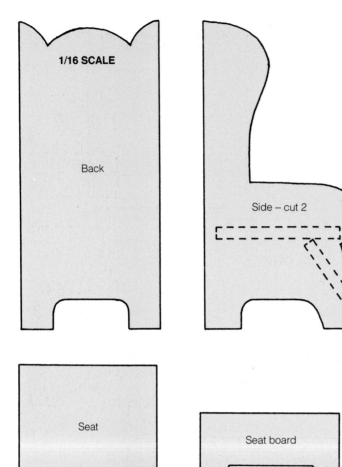

1/16 SCALE

Back

Side – cut 2

Seat

Seat board

or china and a lightly upholstered settee with cabriole legs. The kitchen would have a stoneflagged floor with a large fireplace where food was cooked over an open fire – there would be a clockwork jack to turn the spit and a crane in the chimney to hold the cooking pots over the fire. There might be a water pump (though this was more commonly outdoors) over a stone sink. A wooden table and a few stools and shelves would complete the kitchen furnishings in Queen Anne's day! Accessories such as a warming pan, a spinning wheel and

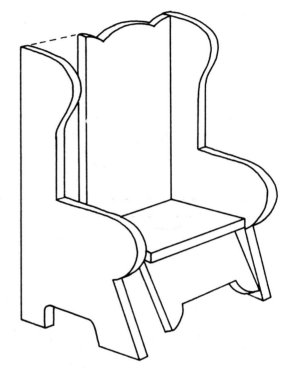

FIG 117 PATTERN FOR THE WOODEN WING CHAIR

Fig 118 Assembling the wooden wing chair

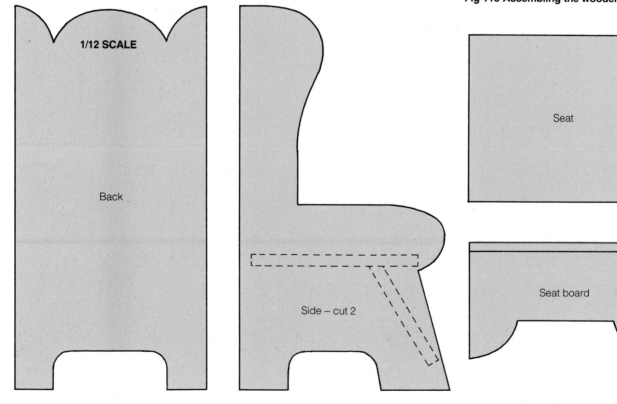

1/12 SCALE

Back

Side – cut 2

Seat

Seat board

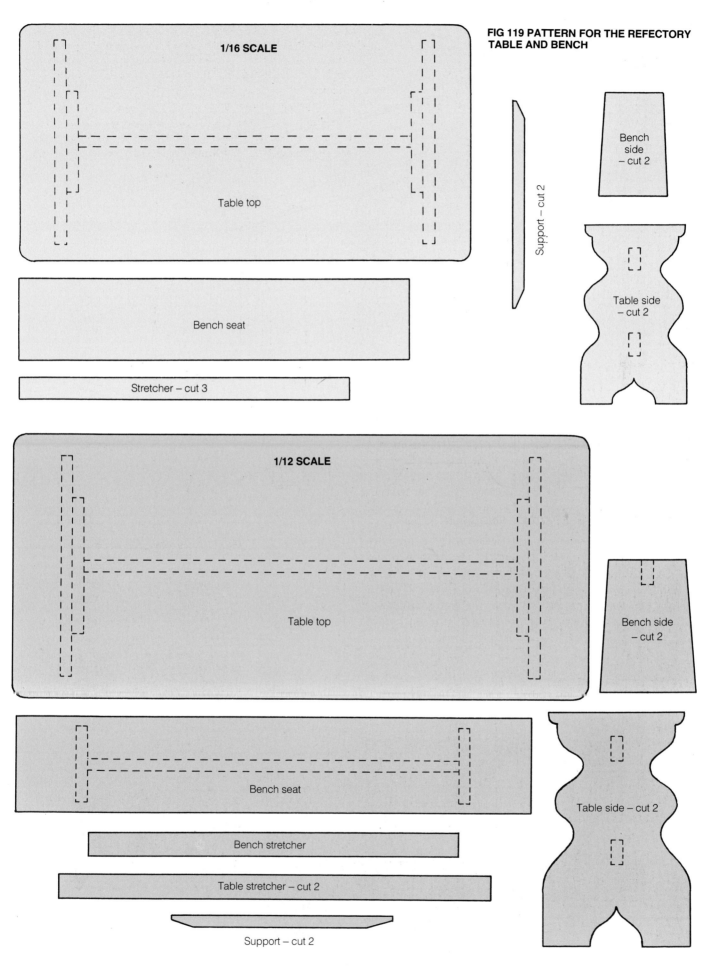

FIG 119 PATTERN FOR THE REFECTORY TABLE AND BENCH

1/16 SCALE

Table top

Support – cut 2

Bench side – cut 2

Table side – cut 2

Bench seat

Stretcher – cut 3

1/12 SCALE

Table top

Bench side – cut 2

Bench seat

Table side – cut 2

Bench stretcher

Table stretcher – cut 2

Support – cut 2

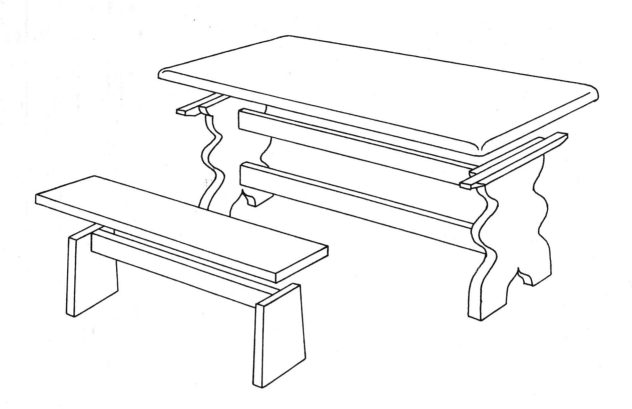

collections of miniature stoneware, Delft or silver would find a perfect home here.

Fig 120 Assembling the refectory table and bench

Alternatively, you might decorate and furnish the interior to correspond with its Tudor exterior. The walls would be lime washed (magnolia emulsion paint over a wood-chip paper would give the right rough texture) and could be 'beamed' with veneer to correspond with the exterior or panelled with wood. In a Tudor house, the front door would open into the hall – a large room with stone-flagged floor strewn with rushes (dried grass) and a large stone fireplace. The furniture would be sparse, perhaps a large table, a buffet, a few stools or chests, and one chair for the master of the house! There might be a display of pewter cups and plates on the buffet, candles in sconces on the walls and pieces of tapestry. The other room

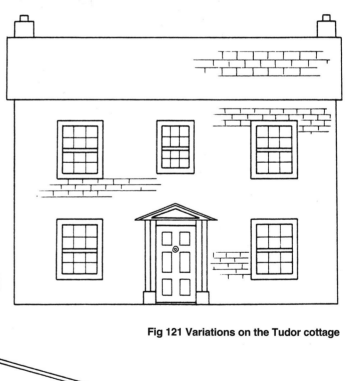

Fig 121 Variations on the Tudor cottage

downstairs would be the kitchen. Again, the floor would be stone flagged and the fireplace very large. There would be a spit by the fire and a crane in the chimney to hold the cooking pots. There might be a brick oven for baking and a brazier for cooking smaller amounts. The furniture would include a trestle table, benches, a few shelves and stools. Upstairs, the main bedchamber would have a planked floor and, possibly, wood-panelled walls. The large four-poster bed would occupy most of the available space with a chest and stool. The other room upstairs might be furnished as a bedroom, or a parlour – here there might be a hooded cradle, an armchair or two, a stool, a chest and the lady's spinning wheel. The Tudors were fond of music (even the owner of a modest house might have a lute),

and embroidery, such as wall-hangings, bed-hangings, covers and cushions.

While this house would have provided ample accommodation for the Tudors who built it, or even the Georgians who lived there later, modern tenants would find it rather cramped. As with a similar life-sized cottage, they would probably build an extension to house a bathroom. This could be done by building a single storey or lean-to extension onto the kitchen side of the house and cutting a doorway through the alcove to the rear of the kitchen chimney breast. The extension might have a hinged roof or front and need only be 6-8in wide. The modern tenants might also find the inter-communicating bedrooms inconvenient, and a build a landing.

12 DOLLS'-HOUSE KITS

One of the most popular and fast-growing aspects of the dolls'-house hobby is the kit. In recent years standards of quality have improved greatly and the range of dolls' houses, furniture and accessories now available in kit form is extensive. Most dolls'-house shops stock a good range and a number of suppliers have mail order catalogues – see Stockists. Most

dolls'-house and furniture kits are available in 1/12 as this is the most popular scale and the kits are intended for adults, although many dolls' houses are quite sturdy enough for children to play with, and some of the simpler furniture kits would also be suitable for children.

DOLLS' HOUSES

For the beginner, a kit can be the ideal way to build a dolls' house as all the measuring and cutting are already done, and

Exterior of a house (from Honeychurch Toys) – one of a wide range of dolls'-house kits and whitewood dolls' houses available

The kitchen of the Georgian house showing the range and pump made from white metal kits and the inexpensive accessories chosen to add period authenticity

the assembly instructions are usually clear and easy to follow. If you do not have the tools or the space to build a house, a kit can usually be assembled on the kitchen table with little more than glue and veneer pins required, and only the minimum of skill needed to produce good results. Most commercial dolls'-house kits are made in good quality plywood, which saves you the bother of finding materials, and in a wide variety of sizes and styles so that you need only choose your 'dream house'

rather than having to plan it. If you like to 'do your own thing', a basic kit can be 'customised' to your taste – perhaps changing the layout of the rooms or placement of the stairs or adding a porch and balcony. Simple houses with the most basic staircases, doors and windows can be elaborated by adding stair treads, banisters and mouldings or substituting better quality doors and opening windows.

Several suppliers also sell their kits ready-made as whitewood houses, ready for you to fit doors and windows and decorate. The choice is extensive, so if you intend to buy a kit (or a ready-made house) do 'shop around' and compare sizes, styles and prices. Some suppliers include doors and glazed windows (opening or non-opening), skirting, cornice, architrave and chimney breasts as part of the house, others do not and these must be added to the cost of the kit. If you buy a ready-made house, a removable staircase is an asset as it makes decorating much simpler; most kits allow you to install the stairs after the house is decorated.

Consider where you will keep the house, how much space you have and need for access. Most British houses are front-opening but there are a number of American kits available and these usually open at the back – this allows an elaborately detailed front but can make access inconvenient. Consider how much time and money you want to spend on decorating and furnishing your house. Large houses in kit form do not cost a great deal more than smaller ones, but you will need more wallpaper, doors, windows, mouldings, lights, and carpets as well as furniture and accessories. Some suppliers sell houses with add-on extensions so you can start with a four-roomed house and add another floor, an attic, basement or conservatory at a later date. If you can, look around at dolls'-house fairs before making your choice as this will show you what is available and perhaps offer ideas you had not thought of. Fairs all over the country are advertised in the specialist publications (see Magazines).

Most of the decorating ideas in the book can be applied to a kit or ready-made dolls' house and the furniture patterns can all be used to furnish it – or you might like to use furniture kits.

FURNITURE

Furniture kits are an excellent option for the beginner as they require only a craft knife, sandpaper, glue and stain or paint to assemble and, carefully made, will produce good quality furniture at a fraction of the cost of ready-made pieces. Of course they do not compare with fine craftsman-made pieces, but most people find it very satisfying to make their own furniture, and kits are a simple way of achieving good results if you have little or no experience. The main suppliers are American (Realife and Craftmark) and German (Mini Mundus) though their ranges are very similar and available from most dolls'-house shops. The range is fairly wide, but mainly in period styles, Chippendale and Hepplewhite being particularly well represented, and the kit comes complete with hinges and handles, if required, and upholstery fabrics. Finishing kits containing stains and polishes are also available or you can use the methods described in the book.

Customising (known as 'kit-bashing') is a popular area of kit making as the pieces from kits are made in the same bass wood and are virtually interchangeable. Thus you might take the fancy trimmings supplied with a Chippendale mirror kit and put them on a wall shelf, or exchange the cabriole legs supplied with one chair kit for the straight legs of another.

Even the most mundane kit cupboard can look quite different and original with a hand-painted or stencilled decoration rather than the suggested stained finish. Furniture kits can be bought individually and as complete room settings and they are not expensive so if you have not made furniture before, try one. If you are making a dolls' house, consider adding a few pieces of furniture made from kits to those you make yourself – carefully chosen pieces can be used in any of the houses in the book made in 1/12 scale.

White metal kits   White metal kits which can be used to make kitchen ranges, fireplaces and a wide variety of accessories are described in Chapter 4, Fixtures and Fittings.

THE GEORGIAN HOUSE

The Georgian house shown on pages 140–1 was designed to be a fairly authentic representation of a small, moderately affluent dower-house built around 1800, and the whole project was to be completed on a limited budget. We chose a four-roomed house from Honeychurch who sell a range of houses as kits, or ready-made, through most dolls'-house shops or direct by post. Though the rooms are a little small for a Georgian house, Honeychurch houses are well made, reasonably priced and sturdy enough for a child which we felt made it a good choice for this book. The furniture is entirely made from kits, all of which are available from most dolls'-house suppliers or from Blackwells by post. The fireplaces, kitchen range and pump are white metal kits from Phoenix and are also widely available from shops or direct by mail order (see Stockists). The accessories are mostly inexpensive items from the commercial imported ranges (Dijon) and are available from almost all dolls'-house shops, with a few finer quality pieces from British craftsmen.

Planning   We chose a small front-opening house as the budget was limited and there was only a small space available to display it. As this was to be an adult's toy the scale is 1/12, and this Honeychurch 'Bold Front' house has a removable roof which is useful if space is even more limited. We wanted to decorate and furnish the house as bedroom, drawing room, dining room and kitchen, so four equal-sized rooms with a central hall and staircase were most suitable and typical of the period we wished to represent. We chose a house which is supplied without window glazing, doors, chimney breasts, cornice, skirting or architraves to allow as much flexibility as possible and ready-assembled to save time.

Building   The house arrived ready-assembled with the fronts hinged and the staircase fixed in place. We removed the fronts but the staircase was too well fixed to remove. The house was very smoothly finished so no sanding was necessary. We installed chimney breasts in three rooms (not the bedroom as the bed would take up so much space) cut to accommodate the fireplaces, and fitted commercial cornice mouldings to the ceilings.

The glazing bars were ready fixed, so these were painted before perspex windows were cut to fit and held in place on the inside of each window, including the fanlight above the door, with frames of dolls'-house picture-frame moulding. We used Honeychurch door kits, and decorated the doors before hinging them in place. Commercial skirting boards were painted and fitted after the walls were papered.

Decorating The exterior of the house was painted with three coats of matt emulsion in honey colour to represent stucco and the doorstep painted stone colour. Glazing bars and window reveals were painted with white satin-finish enamel paint. The roof was papered with a grey slate pattern 'cladding' and the chimney pots painted with terracotta poster colour. We removed the front door to paint it olive green outside and cream inside and replaced it.

The interior was papered with commercial dolls'-house papers in colours and patterns appropriate to the period and the kitchen painted magnolia over lining paper. Ceilings and cornices in each room were painted with magnolia matt emulsion before the wallpaper was applied. As the staircase was fixed, the stairwell was tricky to decorate so we simply applied two coats of magnolia emulsion to the walls and extended it over the front edges of walls and floors. All woodwork was painted with cream Humbrol enamel paint with a matt finish and buffed to a slight sheen when dry – including the stairs. We cut and fitted treads, stained with light oak woodstain, to each stair of the lower flight and the half landing, but found the return flight inaccessible.

The floors were covered with floorpapers, a commercial tile pattern in the kitchen and hall, and light oak woodstained drawing paper (see Chapter 3) in the other rooms.

We added a 'beam' cut from scrap wood, sanded and glued to the kitchen ceiling with small, black-painted pins from which to hang bunches of herbs and joints of bacon.

The inside of the fronts were papered with the pattern used in the bedroom after the window frames were painted, and the fronts were hinged back onto the house when the decorating was complete. The light fitting (from Hobbys) is glued in place, the wire passing through a hole drilled in the ceiling.

Fixtures and fittings The fireplace surrounds in the dining room and drawing room are inexpensive commercial miniatures in cast resin, and the kitchen surround was made in obeche wood and painted cream. The basket grate in the dining room and small hob grate in the drawing room, the open range and the pump are all white metal kits, made up and finished with black lead as described in Chapter 4.

Furnishings As space was limited, we chose furniture pieces which are clichés for the period and kept them to a minimum to convey an uncluttered atmosphere, appropriate for a Georgian house. Reluctant to dispense with the four-poster bed which occupies a disproportionate amount of space, we added only a chest of drawers, a dower chest and chair to the bedroom furnishings. The bed has a canopy made in fabric-covered card to match the bedspread with a pelmet of old tatted edging, and no curtains which would make it more cumbersome. We made the kits up as supplied and finished them with woodstain; light oak for the dower chest and mahogany for the other pieces and wax polish. The sofa in the

drawing room was 'customised' by exchanging the fabric supplied for a prettier, more Georgian cotton print and adapting the method for covering the sofa to give a neater finish. The two chairs were also covered with cotton print. The other pieces were made up as supplied and finished with stain and polish except the tea table, for which we used a commercial finishing kit. For the dining room we chose a small pedestal table and four 'Chippendale' chairs and a sideboard. All pieces were made up as supplied and finished with mahogany woodstain and polish, but we covered the chair seats with woven silk. The kitchen dresser and table were stained light oak and the two ladderback chairs pine. We made woven seats in miniature hatstraw for the chairs rather than using the string supplied to make 'rush' seats.

Accessories The pole screen in the drawing room is made from a kit with a magazine cut-out embroidery panel. The small stool in the kitchen is simply made in obeche wood and stained, and the bedroom rug is a piece of woven fabric, the edges sealed with Fraycheck. The mirrors and pictures, candle sticks and ornaments are all inexpensive items chosen for their 'Georgian' look, including pewter plates, stoneware jugs, wooden bucket and copper pans in the kitchen, the blue and white 'Chinese porcelain' and silver and the warming pan in the hall. The tapestry was made by colour laser printing (see Chapter 6) and is hung by ribbon loops from a brass rod. Tiny dried flowers, modelled foods and a bowl of pot-pourri complete the Georgian effect.

The house has a small garden, made as described in Chapter 7, on a separate base so that it does not impede the front openings.

(Overleaf)
Interior of the Honeychurch house, 'customised', decorated and furnished entirely with kits to represent a small Georgian house

13 THE MODERN HOUSE

The Modern house is the largest in the book and has been designed to accommodate a bathroom – a luxury found in few houses before the twentieth century! The house is not difficult to build – it has a fixed gable roof and the front opens in two pieces below a fixed top edge to show two bedrooms, a bathroom and landing upstairs and two large rooms downstairs. The staircase rises from the larger downstairs room and emerges on the landing behind the bathroom. There are doors to each room upstairs, between the downstairs rooms and a back door into the kitchen, and windows in the back wall to light the landing and kitchen. The layout is realistic and typical of small modern houses but the plans are very versatile and can easily be adapted to make a period house (see the suggestions at the end of the chapter).

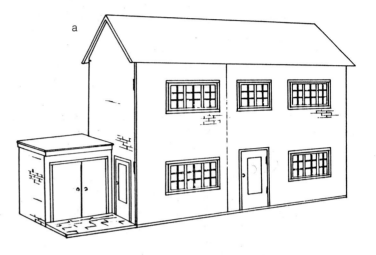

a

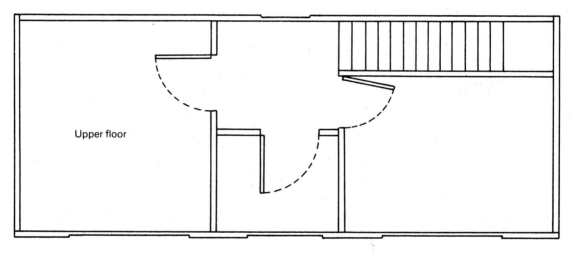

Upper floor

b

Fig 122 Exterior and floor plans for the modern house
A. Exterior B. Floor plans

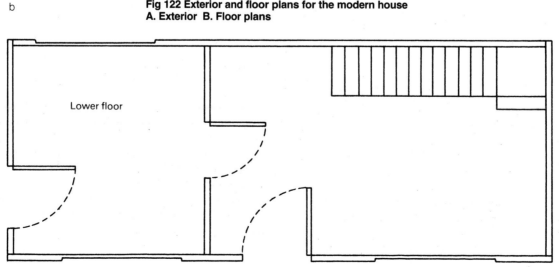

Lower floor

The house shown in the photograph was designed as a child's toy and built in 1/16 scale to accommodate the cheaper ranges of children's dolls'-house furniture and accessories to complement the modern furniture patterns in the chapter.

The house was decorated and furnished simply; we used life size wallpapers for the walls and a hessian pattern as floor covering in the bedrooms and sitting room, and a tile-patterned vinyl paper for the kitchen. The kitchen furniture and bathroom suite were 'customised' from commercial pieces bought in a toy shop – these items are produced by Lundby and Caroline's Home (Bartons) and the styles change every few years as more modern designs are introduced; they are made in wood and plastic and are very modestly priced. Most large toy-shops sell children's dolls'-house furniture, especially around Christmas time, and the range of modern gadgets is extensive. Children love the vacuum cleaner, toaster, coffee maker and television set, etc, just like the ones they have in their own homes.

The house plans are designed to make use of ready-made doors and windows if you wish to do so – but check the measurements before cutting door and window holes. We used commercial, plastic opening-casement windows from Hobbys which are available as single, double and triple windows in 1/16 scale in several styles – and made our own doors. Instructions are given for making your own windows in Chapter 2. If you are building the house in 1/12 scale the range of ready-made doors and windows is extensive, simply choose those most appropriate to the style of house you are planning – but remember to adapt the cut-outs on the back of the house as well as the fronts to accommodate your windows and doors. A ready-made staircase with banisters can be substituted for the open plan stairs described, but will need to be carefully cut and fitted.

The house plans and furniture patterns are given in both 1/16 scale and 1/12 scale, but note that where patterns refer to 3/32in OR 1/8in thick wood, the first measurement is for 1/16 scale and the second for 1/12 scale. Where only one measurement is given it applies to both scales.

MATERIALS
In 1/16 scale:
  1/4in plywood for the house
  1/8in plywood for the roof
  (optional) 5 triple, 1 double and 1 single window
In 1/12 scale:
  3/8in plywood for the house
  1/8in plywood for the roof
  (optional) 7 windows as required
  (optional) 2 exterior and 4 interior doors as required
In either scale:
  1/2in square beading for the ridgepole
  beading or moulding for the bargeboards
  1/8in thick obeche or bass wood for the stairs
  1/4in thick wood (eg spruce) for stair stringers
  woodstrip or moulding for door and window frames
  woodstrip or moulding for skirting board
  six 1in hinges for the fronts
  twelve 3/8in hinges for the doors
  woodwork glue, veneer pins, masking tape

CUTTING (PLANS: FIGS 122-5)
Draw the pattern pieces onto the plywood using a sharp pencil and ruler, and ensuring that the right-angles and measurements are precise. Label each piece in pencil, ie floor, back roof, etc, to avoid confusion when assembling. Cut out the pieces with a saw, including the door and window holes and stairwell. Draw lines onto the inside and outside of the relevant pieces to mark where the upper floor and partition walls occur.

ASSEMBLY
Tape the pieces together to check that they all fit properly (Fig 126). If necessary, make any minor adjustments. Sand all the house pieces thoroughly. Glue and pin the back onto the base. Glue and pin the sides to the back and the base. Glue and pin the lower partition wall (kitchen/lounge) in place, pinning through the base and back. Glue and pin the upstairs floor in place, pinning through the side and back walls. Pin through the floor into the lower partition wall. Glue and pin the partition wall in the left-hand (parents') bedroom, lining it up above the lower partition and pinning through the back.

Glue and pin the top ceiling in place, inside (and pinned through) the side and back walls. Pin through the top ceiling into the parents' bedroom partition wall. Assemble the partition walls for the right-hand (children's) bedroom by glueing and pinning the side-partition (bathroom/bedroom) to the back-partition (bedroom/stairwell). Wallpaper the rear of the back-partition with the wallpaper chosen for the landing and stairwell before putting these walls in place. Glue and pin the partition walls in place, pinning through the top ceiling and the side wall. Pin up through the floor, along the stairwell edge and under the side-partition wall. The bathroom/landing partition is not fixed in place until the house is decorated.

Glue and pin the front-edge strip (chamfered edge uppermost), to the front edge of the top ceiling. Fix the ridgepole by screwing it in place between the tops of the two gables. Pin and glue the back-roof section to the ridgepole and to the top of the gable walls. The back roof overhangs the back and sides of the house by 1/2in. Glue and pin the front-roof section to the ridgepole (butted against the back-roof section), the top of the gable walls and the front-edge strip. The front-roof section overhangs the front-edge strip, so the fronts open freely when they are hinged in place.

EXTERIOR
The exterior of the house is decorated at this stage. We chose red-brick and green-pantile papers. Consult Chapter 3 for suggestions.

Paper the roof, lapping the paper under the gable edges, and the front and back. Paper the house, cutting the paper around the window and door holes, and lapping the sides around to the inside of the house. Cut strips of paper to cover the front edges of the floors and partition walls, lapping them onto the walls, floor, ceiling, and base. Paper the fronts of the house, lapping the paper around all sides to the inside. Cut the paper around the door and window holes. Make sure that the bricks are lined up at the centre join.

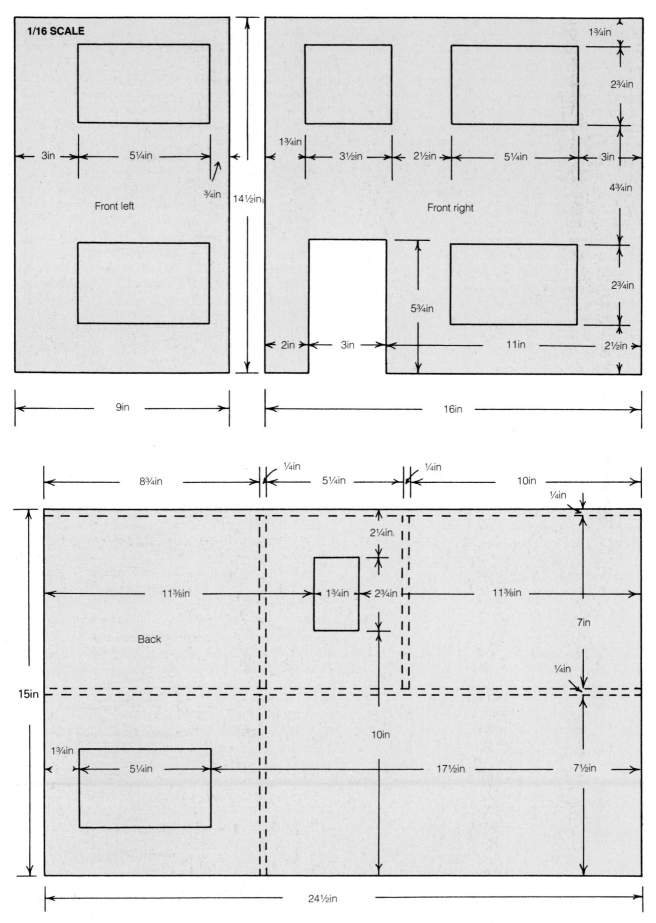

1/16 SCALE

Front left

3in 5¼in ¾in 14½in

9in

Front right

1¾in 2¾in

1¾in 3½in 2½in 5¼in 3in

4¾in

5¾in 2¾in

2in 3in 11in 2½in

16in

8¾in ¼in 5¼in ¼in 10in

¼in

2¼in

11⅜in 1¾in 2¾in 11⅜in

7in

Back

¼in

15in

1¾in 5¼in 17½in 7½in

10in

24½in

FIGS 123, 124 AND 125 PLANS FOR THE MODERN HOUSE

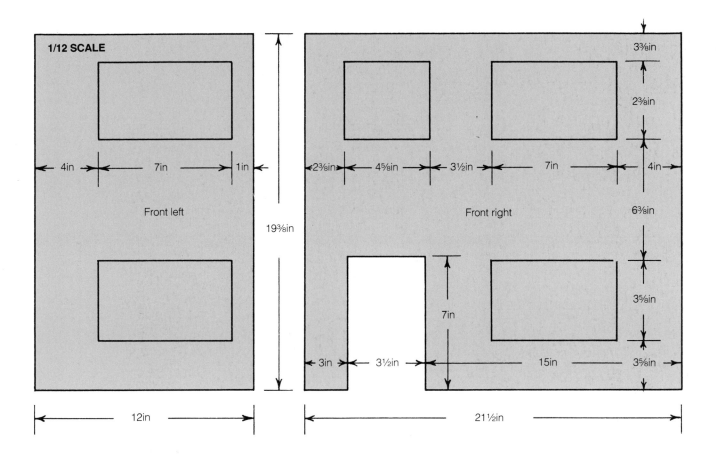

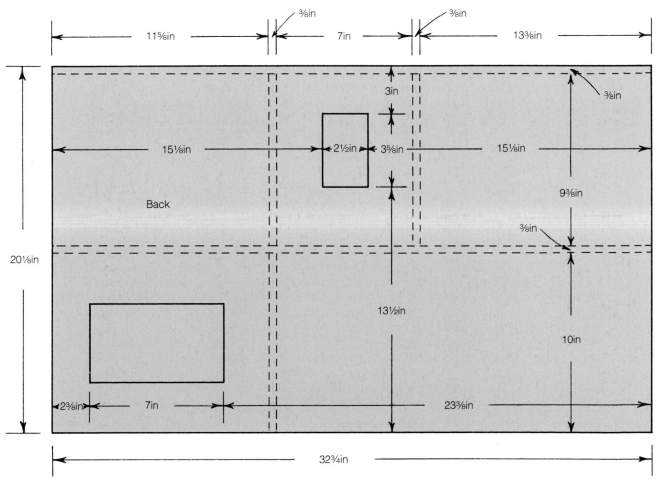

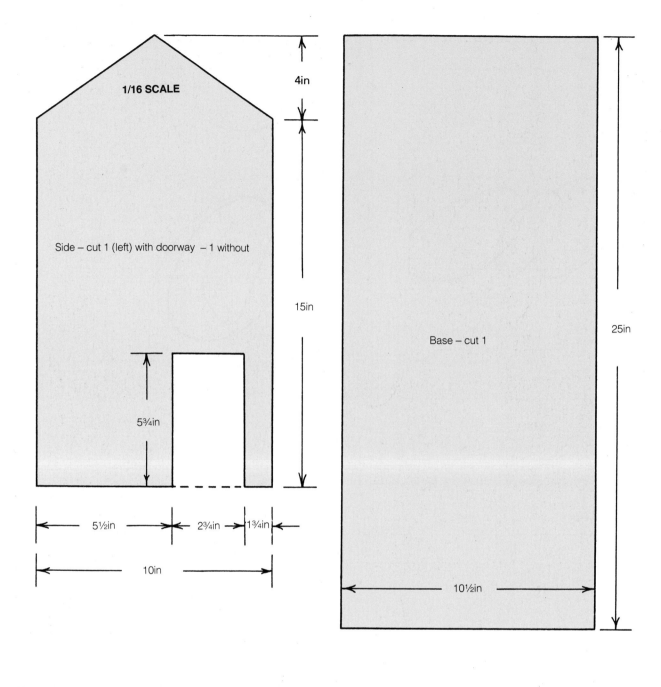

1/16 SCALE

4in

15in

Side – cut 1 (left) with doorway – 1 without

5¾in

5½in   2¾in   1¾in

10in

Base – cut 1

25in

10½in

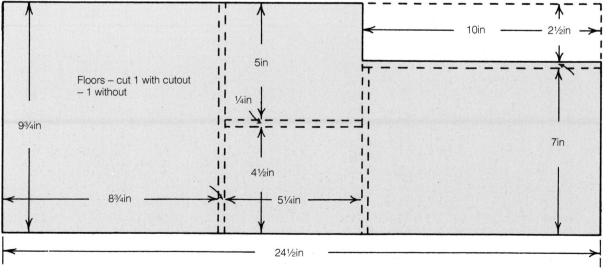

Floors – cut 1 with cutout – 1 without

9¾in

5in

¼in

4½in

8¾in   5¼in

10in   2½in

7in

24½in

146

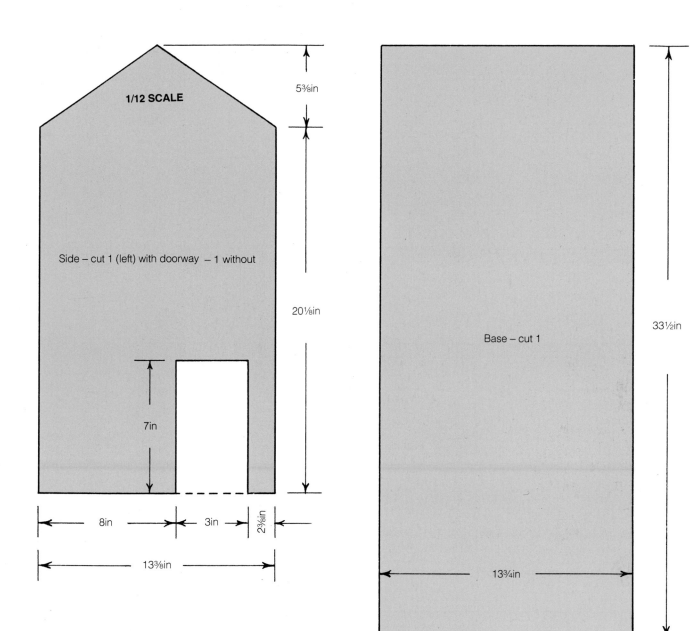

1/12 SCALE

Side – cut 1 (left) with doorway – 1 without

5⅜in

20⅛in

7in

8in   3in   2⅜in

13⅜in

Base – cut 1

33½in

13¾in

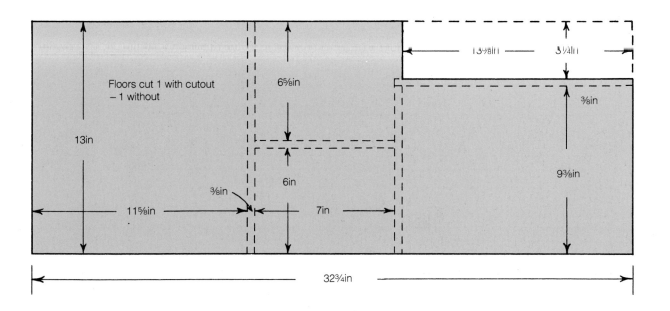

Floors cut 1 with cutout – 1 without

13in

6⅝in

6in

⅜in

11⅝in

7in

13⅛in   3¼in

⅜in

9⅜in

32¾in

147

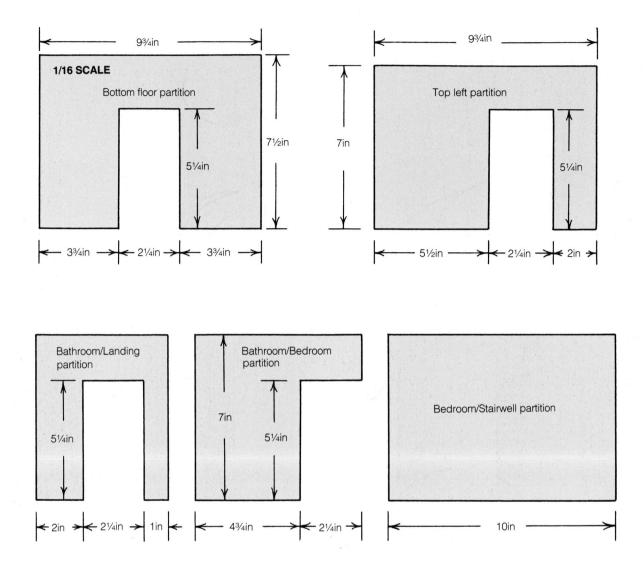

1/16 SCALE

Bottom floor partition

9¾in

7½in

5¼in

3¾in — 2¼in — 3¾in

Top left partition

9¾in

7in

5¼in

5½in — 2¼in — 2in

Bathroom/Landing partition

5¼in

2in — 2¼in — 1in

Bathroom/Bedroom partition

7in

5¼in

4¾in — 2¼in

Bedroom/Stairwell partition

10in

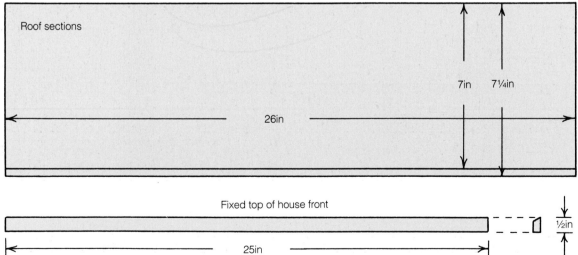

Roof sections

7in   7¼in

26in

Fixed top of house front

½in

25in

Ridge pole

½in

24½in

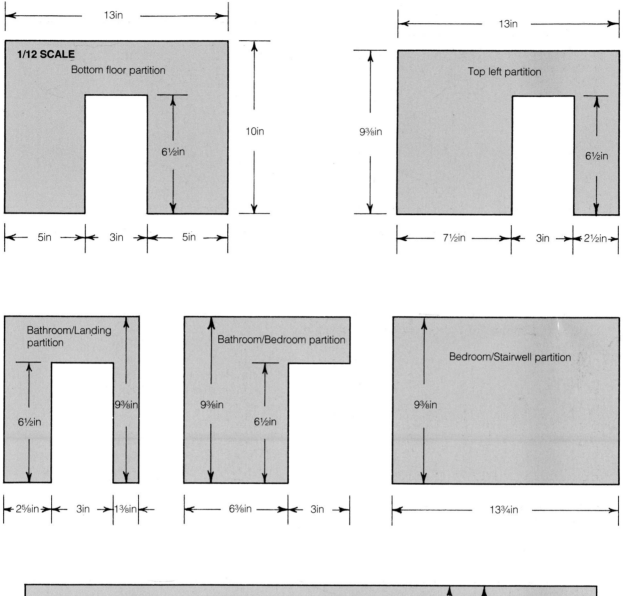

1/12 SCALE

Bottom floor partition

13in

10in

6½in

5in — 3in — 5in

Top left partition

13in

9⅜in

6½in

7½in — 3in — 2½in

Bathroom/Landing partition

6½in

9⅜in

2⅝in — 3in — 1⅜in

Bathroom/Bedroom partition

9⅜in

6½in

6⅜in — 3in

Bedroom/Stairwell partition

9⅜in

13¾in

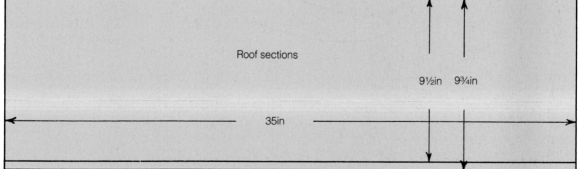

Roof sections

35in

9½in 9¾in

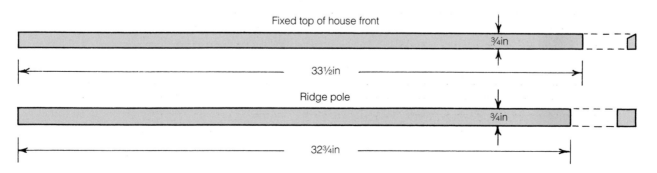

Fixed top of house front

¾in

33½in

Ridge pole

¾in

32¾in

149

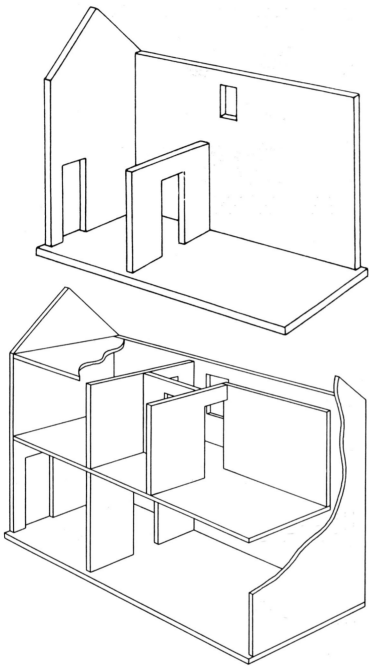

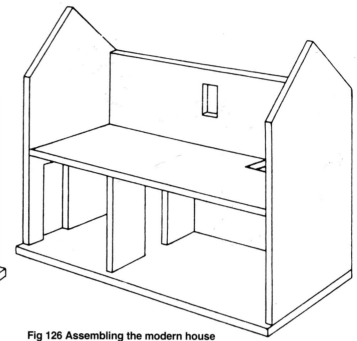

Fig 126 Assembling the modern house

weight until the glue dries. Sand the door with fine abrasive paper and paint both sides. Fit the window into the window hole, using a little UHU or similar glue at the edges.

Hinge the front door on the right-hand side, the kitchen door on the left-hand side, using ⅜in hinges recessed into the wood. These hinges are too small to fix with screws so we use fine pins. To avoid splitting the wood, mark the holes through the hinge onto the door and use a fine drill or dressmaker's pin to drill the holes. Super-glue the hinge to the door, and the pins pushed through the hinges. Repeat this process to hinge the door to the doorway, recessing the hinges into the frame and holding them with super-glue and pins. The handles are map pins – the shanks cut short, glued into fine holes drilled in the doors.

Fig 127 Assembly for the exterior doors and windows

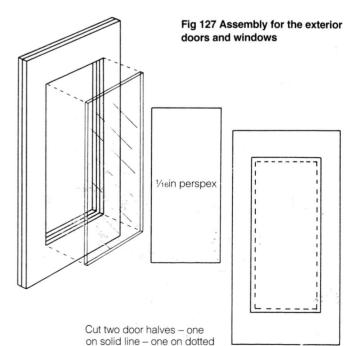

1/16in perspex

Cut two door halves – one on solid line – one on dotted

Windows Glue and pin the windows into the window holes. (We painted the window frames with a coat of white-gloss enamel paint before fixing to match the doors.) When the windows are fixed, paint the inside edges of the window holes with white-gloss enamel paint over an undercoat of matt enamel paint. Paint the inside edges of the doorway holes in the same way. Paint the bargeboards and glue them under the gables, mitring the apex join.

Doors Cut the front door and the kitchen door in ⅛in obeche wood. The perspex windows are cut to fit into the larger window space on the inside of the door (Fig 127). Cut the two door pieces with a razor-toothed saw, the window space with a fretsaw. Glue the two pieces together (sandwiching the cloth hinge if you are using one) and press them under a

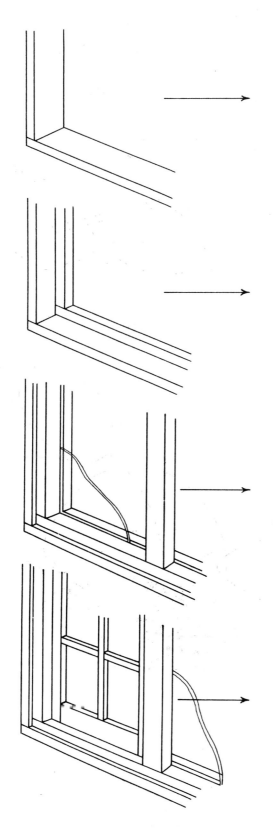

We used transparent Fablon with a ridged pattern over the perspex panels in the doors and bathroom windows to give a reeded-glass effect.

Fronts The fronts can be hinged in place at this stage, using three 1in hinges at each side, recessed into the wood. You might prefer to wait until the interior has been decorated.

INTERIOR

Stairs The open-plan staircase is made of ⅛in thick obeche wood for the stairs, and ¼in thick wood (eg spruce, obtainable from craft shops) for the stringers. It is stained pine colour with button polish and left unwaxed, though you might prefer other finishes. Draw to full size the patterns for the long-flight stringers, using the half-scale diagrams as a guide (Fig 128).

Cut one left and one right-hand stringer from your patterns. The two-step stringers which support the bottom flight have full-sized patterns. Cut all the stringers in ¼in thick wood. Cut fourteen steps in ⅛in thick obeche wood, using the pattern, and round off the front and left-hand edges of each step with abrasive paper. Cut the half-landing from ⅛in thick obeche wood, using the pattern, and sand the front edge round. Sand all the pieces with fine abrasive paper and stain if you wish.

To assemble the stairs, glue the top and bottom steps to the stringers of the main flight, followed by the other steps, with the treads overhanging slightly at the left-hand side and fitting flush with the stringer at the right-hand side (Fig 129). The overall width should fit exactly into the stairwell. Assemble the bottom stair and half-landing in the same way, glueing the stringers under the half-landing as shown on the pattern. Glue the left side of the half-landing onto the stringers of the main flight.

Paint with button polish to represent pine and sand gently with fine abrasive paper. Do not fix the stairs in place until the interior of the house is decorated. Then fit a banister post of square beading. Whittle the top of the post to form a knob, or sand it round, stain it to match the stairs and glue it to the half-landing by the bottom step of the main flight. The banister rail is made of fine woodstrip, sanded, stained and glued to the banister post and into the edge of the stairwell.

Doors   The interior doors are made of ⅛in thick obeche wood. Cut two pieces for each door and glue them together (sandwiching cloth hinges, if used), pressing them under a weight until the glue dries. Sand the fine abrasive paper and check that they fit easily into the doorway holes, allowing for two coats of paint. Paint both sides with a matt undercoat followed by gloss enamel paint, ensuring that the edges are covered. Glue tape-hinged doors to the walls, or use two ⅜in hinges as described for the front door. The handles are coloured map pins, with shanks cut short, glued into tiny holes drilled into the door.

Hang all the doors as described. The bedroom and bathroom doors open into the rooms; and do not forget to

The modern house plans can be adapted to make a period house, decorated and furnished in traditional or modern style as you please

hang the door on the bathroom/landing partition which is not yet fixed in place.

Decorating Before decorating, check for any tiny gaps and fill these with Polyfilla rubbed in with a finger, removing any surplus filler with a damp cloth. Start by painting the ceilings, which can be papered with lining paper first for a better finish.

The bedrooms and kitchen are straightforward – paper the back wall first, then the side walls. Paper them with lining paper if you intend to paint. Next, paper the floors; then cut, paint and fit the door and window frames and skirting boards. (We used fine woodstrip for door and window frames and woodstrip for skirting boards.)

The lounge, bathroom and landing are a little more difficult. As the bathroom/landing partition wall is not yet in place, there is access to the landing, though restricted. We used the same wallpaper as for the lounge, to make the

procedure as simple as possible. Paper the back wall of the lounge continuing up the stairwell to the top of the house (reaching up through the stairwell), and include the landing walls beside and above the bedroom doors. Paper the side walls of the lounge, again continuing up the stairwell to the top of the house on the right wall. Make a window frame for the landing window from fine woodstrip or moulding, with mitred corners – paint it and glue in place. In the same way, make door frames for the bedrooms. Cut, paint and fix skirting boards under the landing window and to each side of the parents'-bedroom door. Cut and stick a piece of carpet paper to the landing floor.

Decorate the back of the bathroom/landing partition to match the other landing walls. Cut the wallpaper to fit exactly, with no overlap, and make and fix the door frame and skirting board as before. Glue the edges of the partition and push it into place. Ensure that it is properly positioned (peep through the landing window to check) and leave until the glue is thoroughly dry. Paper the back wall of the bathroom, lapping the wallpaper an inch onto the side walls and the floor, to strengthen the joins. Then paper the side walls of the bathroom. Cut the bathroom floor and stick it in place. Cut, paint and fix the door frame. Small pieces of skirting board are fitted around the bathroom fixtures when they are fixed in place.

This procedure means that the entire house is decorated, not just those areas which can be seen from the front – most satisfactory when peeping through the landing window! When the decorating is complete, the stairs can be glued into the stairwell, and against the back and side walls. Decorate the inside of the fronts to match or harmonise with the interior.

THE PARENTS'-BEDROOM FURNITURE

The patterns given here are drawn actual size so they can be traced from the book. Before beginning, read Chapter 5, and refer to it when necessary.

Bed The divan bed is made from a block of balsa wood ¾in or 1in thick, covered with fabric. The raw edges of fabric are glued firmly underneath and covered by a rectangle of felt. The bed legs are 1–1½in lengths of fine dowelling or square beading, coloured with black felt pen and tapped gently into the balsa wood with a hammer.

Cut a rectangle of foam for a mattress and make a cotton cover for it. Make a sheet and two pillows and put the sheet over the mattress, if necessary holding the mattress on the divan with double-sided tape. The duvet is a cotton bag filled with terylene wadding, and slip-stitched closed. The 1/16 scale divan is 5¼ × 3¾in, and the 1/12 scale divan is 6¼ × 4½in. Cut a headboard panel in ³⁄₃₂in thick obeche wood and lengths of ⅛in obeche as a frame for the panel. Glue short lengths to either side of the panel, and a longer length across the top, so that the panel is slightly recessed. Sand the headboard with fine abrasive paper and stain with button polish. Sand again, and wax polish. The headboard is fixed on by two upright battens of fine woodstrip which are glued to the back of the headboard and pinned or glued to the divan base.

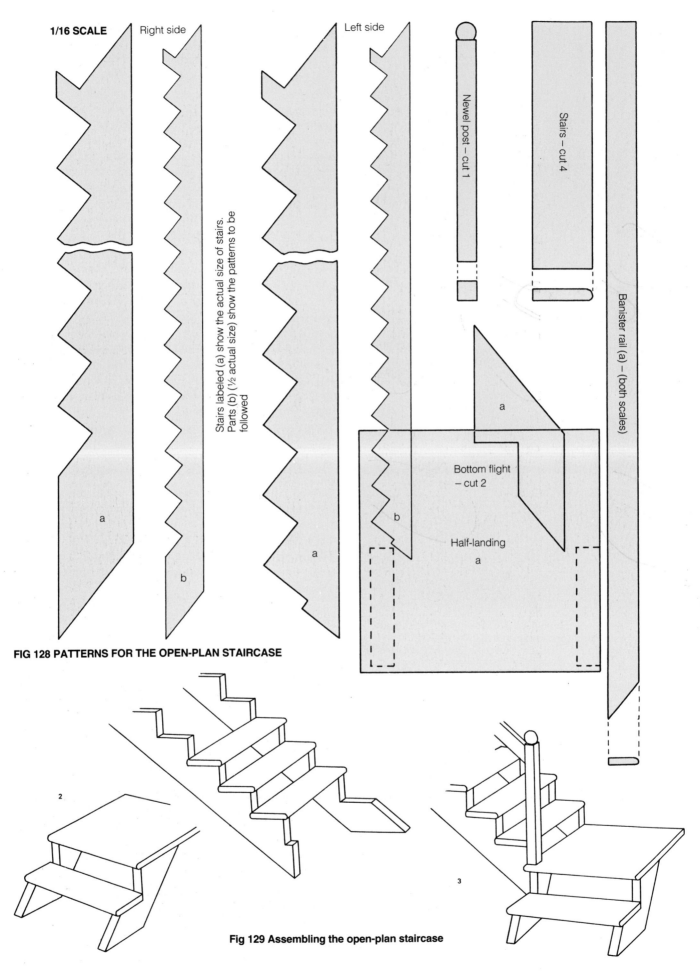

1/16 SCALE   Right side   Left side

Newel post – cut 1

Stairs – cut 4

Stairs labeled (a) show the actual size of stairs. Parts (b) (½ actual size) show the patterns to be followed

Banister rail (a) – (both scales)

a

b

a

a

a

Bottom flight – cut 2

b

Half-landing
a

FIG 128 PATTERNS FOR THE OPEN-PLAN STAIRCASE

2

3

Fig 129 Assembling the open-plan staircase

154

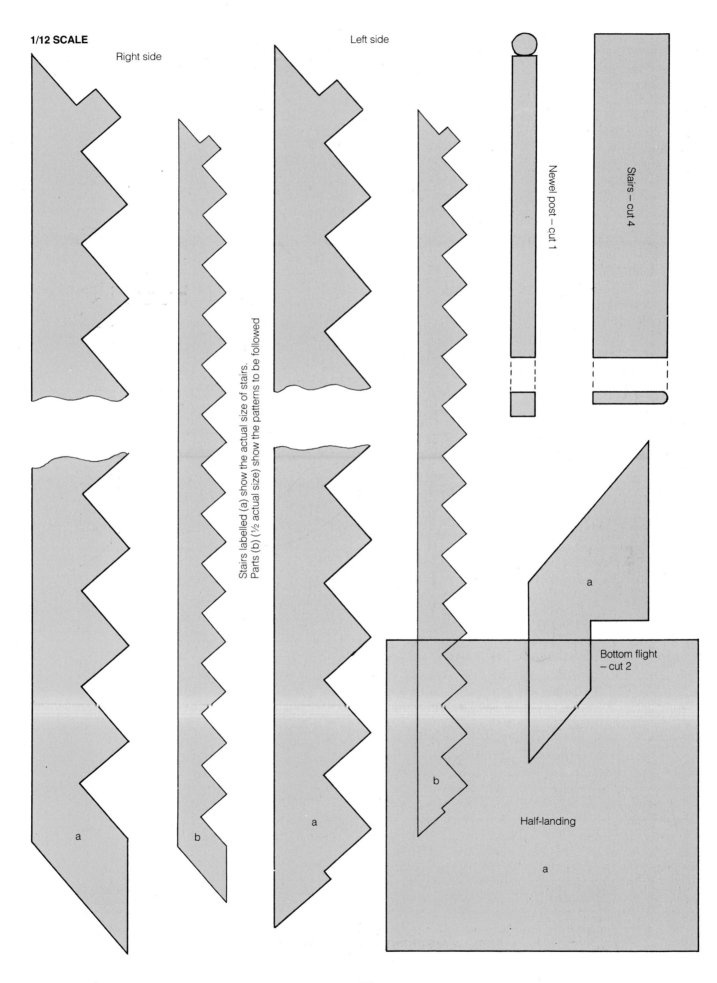

1/12 SCALE

Right side

Left side

Stairs labelled (a) show the actual size of stairs.
Parts (b) (½ actual size) show the patterns to be followed

Newel post – cut 1

Stairs – cut 4

a

b

a

b

a

Bottom flight
– cut 2

b

Half-landing

a

155

Bedside table (Fig 130)   This is made of ⅛in thick obeche wood with legs of 5mm square beading. It is painted with button polish in pine colour.

Draw the pattern pieces onto the wood and cut them with a razor-toothed saw, ensuring that the four table legs are exactly the same length with perfectly square ends. Glue the four frieze pieces in place between the legs, so that the frieze is slightly recessed. Glue the assembled legs to the underside of the top, so that it overhangs slightly at each side. Sand the table with fine abrasive paper. Paint the table with one coat of button polish, sand gently with very fine abrasive paper, and wax polish.

FIG 130 PATTERN FOR THE BEDSIDE TABLE (IN EITHER SCALE)

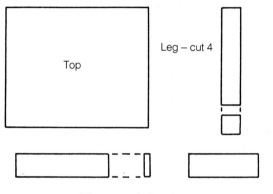

Frieze – cut 2 of each

Wardrobes and dressing table (Figs 131 and 132)   This unit is made of ⅛in thick obeche wood, stained with button polish to pine colour. The handles are white, glass-headed dressmaker's pins with the shanks cut short.

Draw the pattern pieces onto the wood, ensuring that the measurements and right-angles are correct. Cut the pieces with a razor-toothed saw and sand them with fine abrasive paper.

To assemble the wardrobe, glue one side to the back, then glue the base to the side and back. Glue the shelf in place and then the other side. Make fine holes at the top and bottom edges of the doors to receive the pin hinges and sand the hinged edges slightly rounded so that the doors swing open freely. Make fine holes in the base and the underside of the top to receive the pins. When the pin hinges are properly aligned, glue the top in place. Sand the wardrobe with fine abrasive paper and stain with button polish. Sand again with very fine abrasive paper and wax polish. Mark the positions of the door handles and bore fine holes with a small drill or pin. Cut the shanks short on the dressmaker's pins and glue them into the holes. Make the second wardrobe in the same way.

To assemble the dressing-table (Figs 133 and 134), glue the sides and the back to the base, then glue the top in place. Check that the drawer front fits snugly into the space. Cut the bottom, back and sides from unstained wood, assemble the drawer to fit the space, sand, stain and polish it as for the wardrobe, and fix the drawer handles as before. The mirror is cut by a glass merchant and framed with ¼in wide woodstrip with mitred corners. The mirror and frame are stuck to a

backing of thin cardboard. Sand the frame, stain and polish it to match the drawer unit.

Glue the dressing table between the wardrobes, glueing the mirror to the back of the drawer unit. Tape across the back of the mirror onto both wardrobes with masking tape to reinforce the join. The stool in this bedroom is a commercial one, but Chapter 5 gives directions for making one.

THE BATHROOM

The bathroom fittings are from a commercial range of dolls'-house furniture. The original backing pieces on the bath, washbasin and loo were removed by soaking the entire unit in hot water to soften the glue and gently prising the backing away. The pieces were then glued to the bathroom walls and floor. The shower-and-tap attachment was glued to the wall at the head of the bath, and the towel rail with its felt towel glued to the side wall at the foot of the bath. The bathroom

Fig 131 Assembling the wardrobe

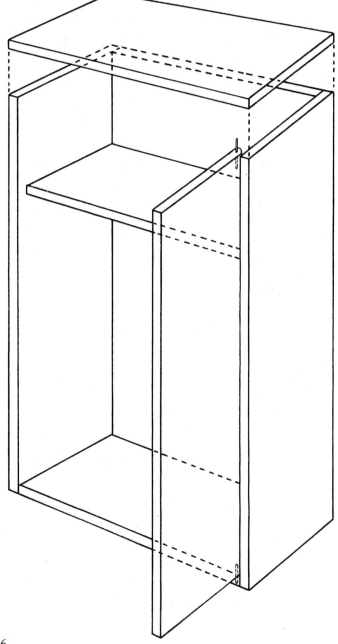

FIG 132 PATTERN FOR THE WARDROBES

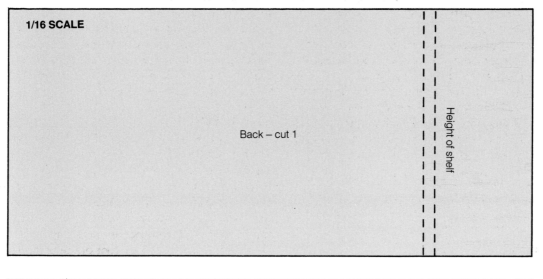

1/16 SCALE

Back – cut 1

Height of shelf

Side – cut 2

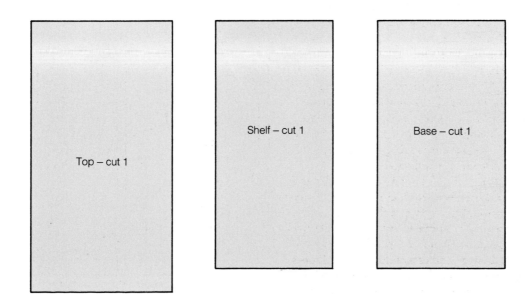

Door – cut 2

Top – cut 1

Shelf – cut 1

Base – cut 1

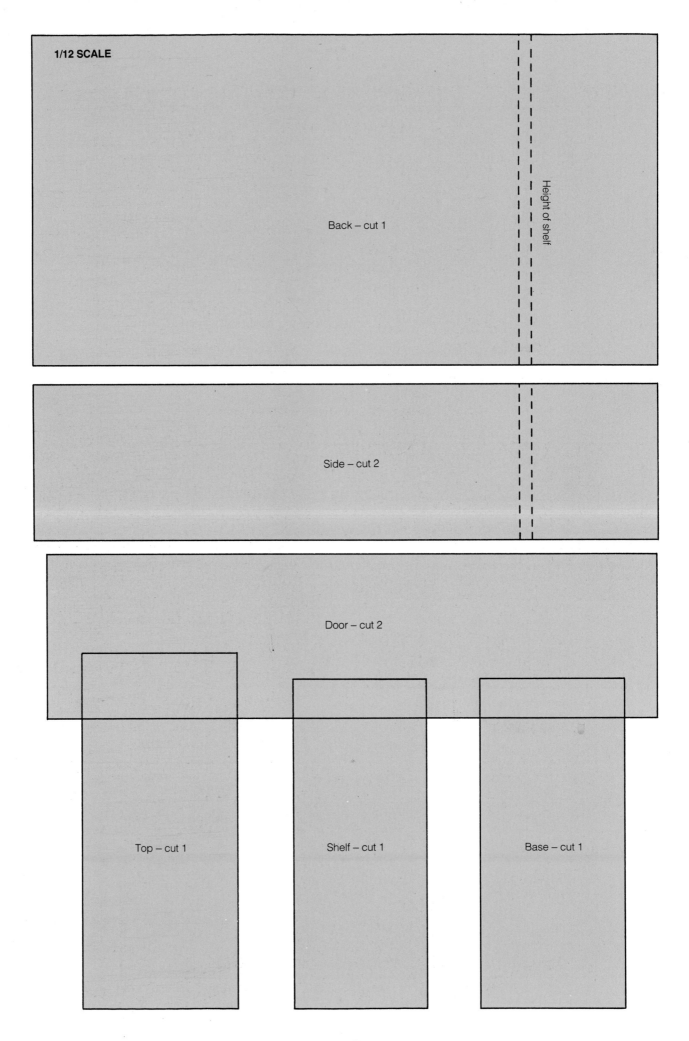

1/12 SCALE

Back – cut 1

Height of shelf

Side – cut 2

Door – cut 2

Top – cut 1

Shelf – cut 1

Base – cut 1

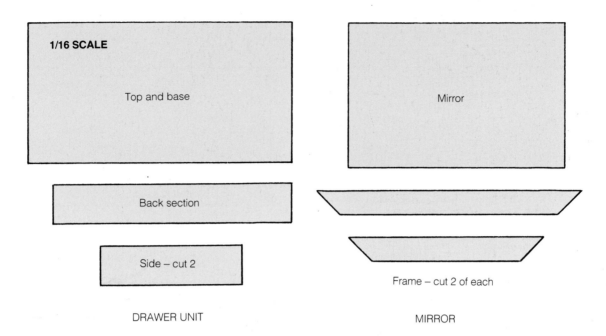

1/16 SCALE

Top and base

Mirror

Back section

Side – cut 2

Frame – cut 2 of each

DRAWER UNIT

MIRROR

FIG 133 PATTERN FOR THE DRAWER UNIT AND MIRROR

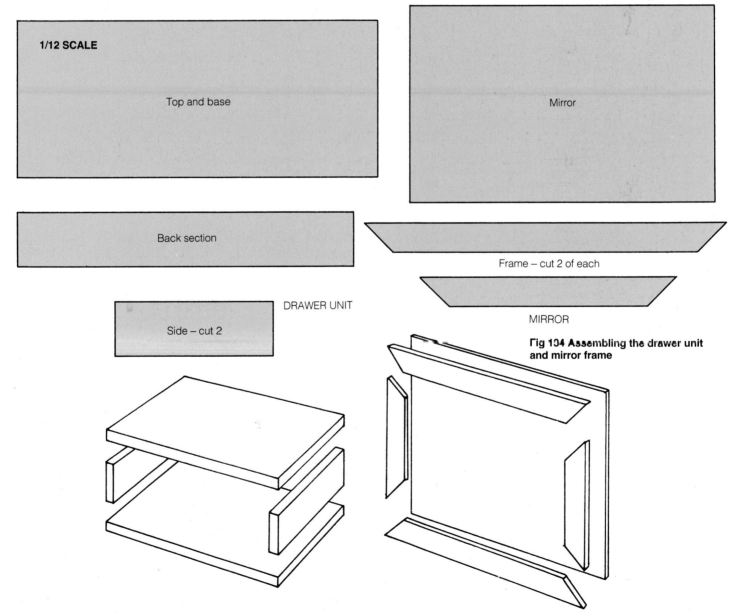

1/12 SCALE

Top and base

Mirror

Back section

Side – cut 2

DRAWER UNIT

Frame – cut 2 of each

MIRROR

Fig 134 Assembling the drawer unit
and mirror frame

FIG 135 PATTERN FOR THE CHEST OF DRAWERS

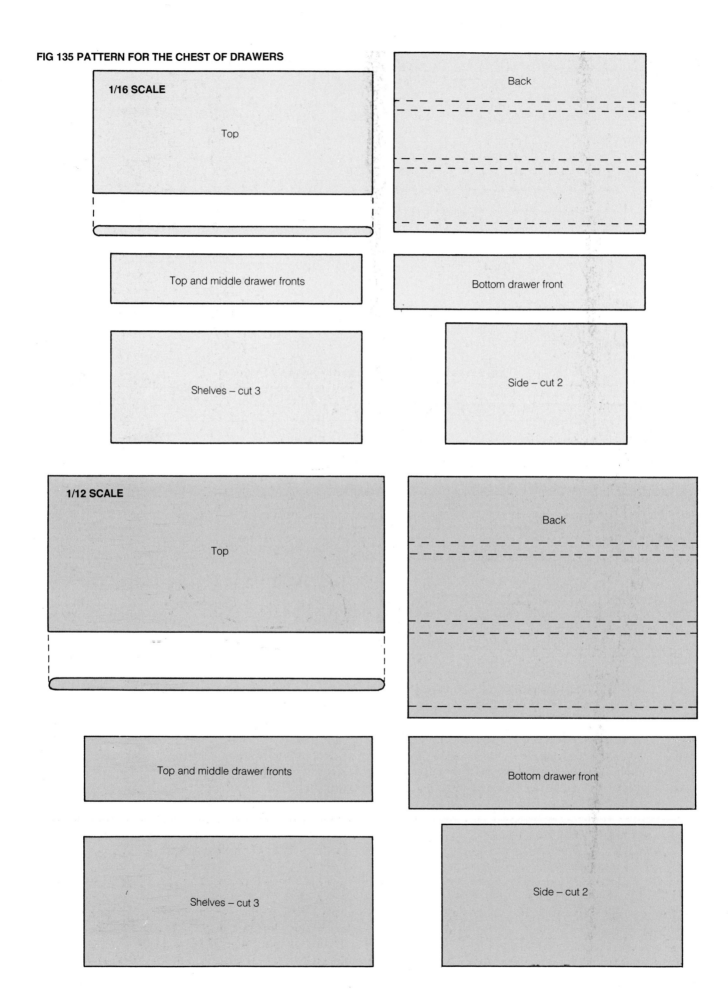

1/16 SCALE

Top

Back

Top and middle drawer fronts

Bottom drawer front

Shelves – cut 3

Side – cut 2

1/12 SCALE

Top

Back

Top and middle drawer fronts

Bottom drawer front

Shelves – cut 3

Side – cut 2

A fine quality porcelain suite (by Ann Shepley) and accessories for the bathroom of the modern house made for an adult

cabinet was glued to the wall above the washbasin. The scales, bath rack and tooth mugs are commercial (Lundby).

If you prefer to make the bathroom fittings, consult Chapters 4 and 6.

THE CHILD'S BEDROOM FURNITURE

Desk   This desk was made from a cupboard-and-drawer unit – a leftover from the commercial kitchen unit which included the cooker. The top is a piece of wood similar to the drawer and cupboard fronts. To make a similar desk, consult Chapter 5. Use ³⁄₃₂in or ⅛in thick obeche wood for the desk, and glass-headed dressmaker's pins, with the shanks cut short, for handles.

Desk chair (see Fig 42)   See Chapter 5 for general instructions on making chairs. This chair has legs of square beading, with an obeche-wood seat. The chair has a seat pad covered in cotton.

Chest of drawers (Fig 135)   This is made of ³⁄₃₂in or ⅛in thick obeche wood, stained with button polish to pine colour. The handles are brass gimp pins.

Draw the pattern pieces onto the wood, ensuring that the measurements and right-angles are correct. Cut the pieces with a razor-toothed saw and chamfer the side and front edges of the top. Sand all pieces with fine abrasive paper. Glue one side to the back, then glue the shelves and base in place, followed by the other side. Glue the top in place, overhanging slightly at the sides and front.

Check that the drawer fronts fit snugly into the spaces. Cut the bottom, back and side pieces for the drawers from unstained wood and assemble them to fit into the spaces. Sand the shell and drawer fronts with fine abrasive paper and paint on one coat of button polish. Sand gently with very fine abrasive paper and apply several coats of wax polish, well-buffed between coats.

Mark the handle positions on the drawer fronts and drill fine holes. Cut the shanks of the gimp pins and push them into the holes, fixing with a dab of glue over the pinhole on the inside of the drawer.

Bunk beds (Figs 136 and 137)   These are made of ⅛in thick obeche wood with posts of square beading. The ladder is made of fine wood-strip with toothpick rungs. The beds are stained pine colour with button polish.

Draw the pattern pieces onto the wood, ensuring that the measurements and right-angles are correct. Cut the pieces with a razor-toothed saw, the sides with a fretsaw. Ensure that the bedposts are exactly the same length with square ends. Sand the pieces with fine abrasive paper.

Assemble both bunks as follows. Glue the side rails, then the head and footboards to the base, leaving corners for the bedposts. Mark onto the bedposts the positions of each bunk as shown on the pattern, then glue the bedposts on one side only into the corners lining up the bunks to the marks on the posts. Leave the bunks on their sides as the glue dries, then turn them over and glue the other side's bed-posts in place. Leave the bunks on their sides until the glue is dry. Sand with fine abrasive paper, and stain with button polish. We also faced the headboards and footboards with white Fablon to imitate melamine.

To make the ladder, cut two pieces of woodstrip. Mark and drill fine holes in both pieces as shown on the pattern. Glue the ends of the toothpick lengths and push them into the holes. Paint the ladder with button polish to match the bunks, and glue it lightly to the footboards.

Use the bed-base pattern to cut mattresses for the bunks from ½in thick foam, and make cotton covers for the mattresses. Make a sheet and pillow for each bunk – we used a plain-turquoise cotton for the sheets and a turquoise-and-white printed cotton for the pillows and duvet covers. The duvets are cotton bags, lightly stuffed with terylene wadding, and the open ends slipstitched.

FIG 136 PATTERN FOR THE BUNK BEDS AND LADDER

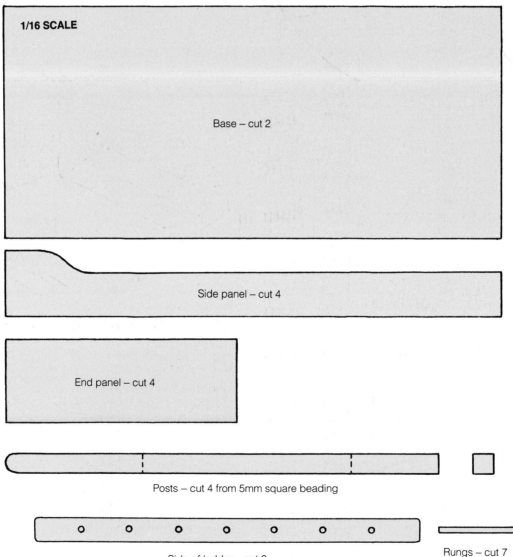

162

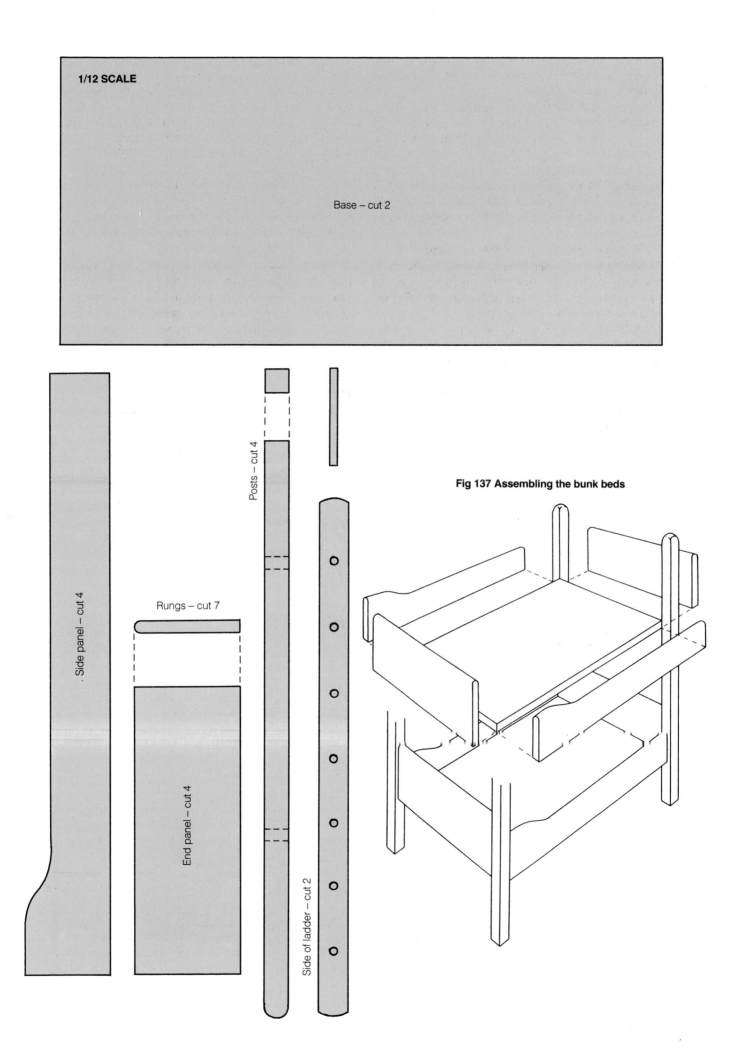

1/12 SCALE

Base – cut 2

Side panel – cut 4

Rungs – cut 7

End panel – cut 4

Posts – cut 4

Side of ladder – cut 2

Fig 137 Assembling the bunk beds

THE KITCHEN FURNITURE

The kitchen furniture and accessories are customised from the commercial ranges of dolls'-house furniture. The top of the sink unit was painted with silver enamel paint to represent stainless steel, (it was originally white). The cupboard unit and fridge were taped together at right-angles and covered with a thick-cardboard worktop, covered with brown Fablon. The washing machine fitted neatly into the space left beside the sink. The cooker was originally glued to a backing, with a drawer unit and cupboard. The backing was removed and the rest used to make the desk in the children's bedroom. The cooker (originally orange) was painted with white-gloss enamel and mounted on a block of black-painted wood. The cooker hood was also painted white and stuck to the wall. The wall cupboard which matches the sink and cupboard units, was glued to the side wall above the worktop. A worktop covered with brown Fablon was glued to the top of the washing machine.

The round, white-plastic table and chairs were bought as a set. The patterned transfer which originally covered the table top was removed by soaking in hot water. The ironing-board, clock, pedal-bin, coffee-maker, toaster, saucepans, and wall shelf are all commercial. When choosing pieces from the commercial ranges, remember to consider the space available, as in a life-size kitchen.

If you prefer to make rather than buy the kitchen furniture and accessories, consult Chapters 5 and 6. A one-portion jam or butter container painted with silver enamel paint makes an acceptable sink, with a silver-painted obeche-wood draining board. A white enamel-painted cupboard makes a passable cooker with black press-studs or washers for rings, glass-headed pins for knobs, and perspex for the oven window.

THE LOUNGE/DINING ROOM FURNITURE

The lounge/dining room contains a combination of bought and home-made furniture and accessories. The matching commercial wall unit, dining table and chairs are made of wood, stained rosewood. The telephone table is also rosewood colour with paper tiles; the coffee table is similar, but stained pine colour. The television set originally had a picture which we replaced with a piece of plain-grey paper; this and the stereo record-player with hinged perspex lid are very realistic. The wooden magazine-rack, stool and yellow-needlecord swivel chair are also commercial pieces.

Sofa and chair (Fig 138) The sofa and chair are made of ⅛in thick obeche wood with stretchers of fine dowelling. They are stained with button polish to pine colour. The cushions are made of rust-coloured needlecord.

The method for both sofa and chair is the same, only the width of the dwelling varies. Draw the pattern pieces onto the wood, ensuring that the grain line is vertical, and cut the dowelling stretchers exactly the same length. Cut the side pieces with a fretsaw, and round the edges by sanding with fine abrasive paper. Drill three holes for the stretchers through each side piece, as shown on the pattern, the same diameter as the dowelling. Assemble the chair frame by glueing one end of the stretchers, pushing them into the holes on one side piece, then the other. When the glue is dry, sand the chair frame with fine abrasive paper and paint on one coat of button polish. Sand gently with very fine abrasive paper and wax polish.

Make one large cushion, lightly stuffed, for each piece. Divide the cushions into 2 or 4 equal sections by stitching across the middle. Fit the cushions to the chair and sofa and secure by oversewing a few stitches at each side around the stretchers.

Record cupboard (Figs 139 and 140) This is made of ³⁄₃₂in or ⅛in thick obeche wood, stained to pine colour with button polish.

Draw the pattern pieces onto the wood ensuring that the measurements and right-angles are correct. Cut the pieces with a razor-toothed saw and sand with fine abrasive paper. Glue one side to the back, the base into the back and side, and the other side to the back and base. Glue the partition to the back and base, then the top into the sides and back, resting on the glued top edge of the partition. Sand with fine abrasive paper and paint with one coat of button polish. Sand gently with very fine abrasive paper and wax polish.

If you prefer to make all the pieces for the lounge/dining room, instructions and patterns are given in Chapters 5, 10 and 11. A television set can be made from a block of wood, faced with grey paper and framed with a piece of plastic packaging (eg empty razor-blade dispensers). Small blocks of wood, appropriately painted, will make stereo speakers and the record-player could be a block of wood covered with a picture of a deck, with a small plastic lid, hinged with tape.

ACCESSORIES

Full details of the home-made accessories are given in Chapter 6.

Rugs The cream fur rug in the parents' bedroom is a rectangle of fur fabric backed with iron-on Vilene. The red rug in the kitchen and the brown-and-green rug in the lounge are both from a commercial dolls'-house range. The bath mat is a piece of felt.

Lights The light fittings in the house are all chosen from the commercial dolls'-house ranges. The wires are taped across the ceilings to emerge from holes drilled through the back wall. There is a ceiling light in each room and on the landing and a lamp on the television in the lounge.

Mirrors and pictures The mirror in the dressing table was cut to the required size at a glass merchant's, as was the mirror in the twins' bedroom which is framed with fine woodstrip stained with button polish. The mirror on the stairs is commercial. The pictures were cut from a magazine and framed with woodstrip. The Mucha poster on the bathroom door was cut from a catalogue, and glued to the door with wallpaper paste. The cork noticeboards in the children's bedroom and the kitchen were cut from a cork floor tile and covered with a selection of tiny pictures from magazines. The football rosette is made from an inch of narrow ribbon

FIG 138 PATTERN FOR THE ARMCHAIR AND SOFA

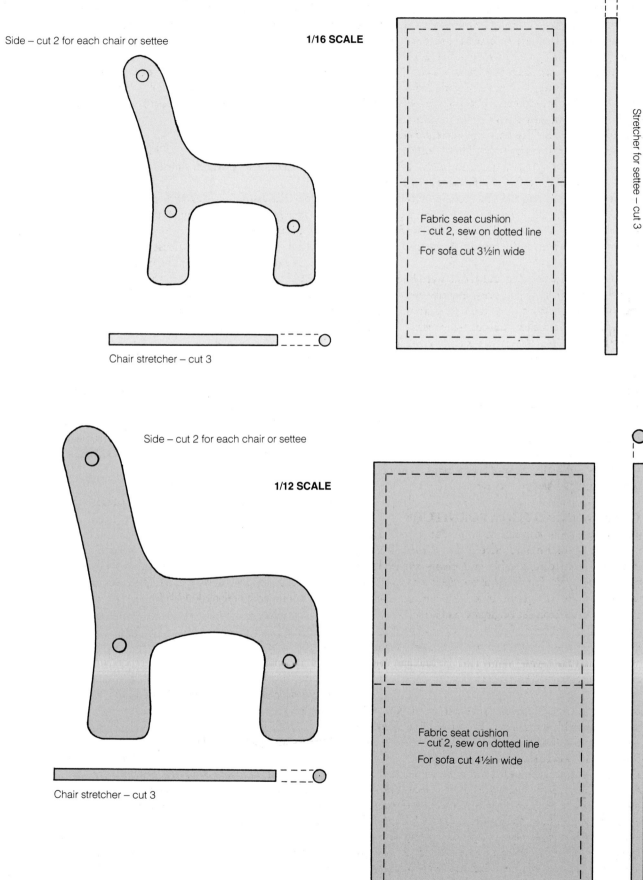

Side – cut 2 for each chair or settee

1/16 SCALE

Chair stretcher – cut 3

Fabric seat cushion
– cut 2, sew on dotted line

For sofa cut 3½in wide

Stretcher for settee – cut 3

Side – cut 2 for each chair or settee

1/12 SCALE

Chair stretcher – cut 3

Fabric seat cushion
– cut 2, sew on dotted line

For sofa cut 4½in wide

Stretcher for settee – cut 3

165

FIG 139 PATTERN FOR THE RECORD CUPBOARD

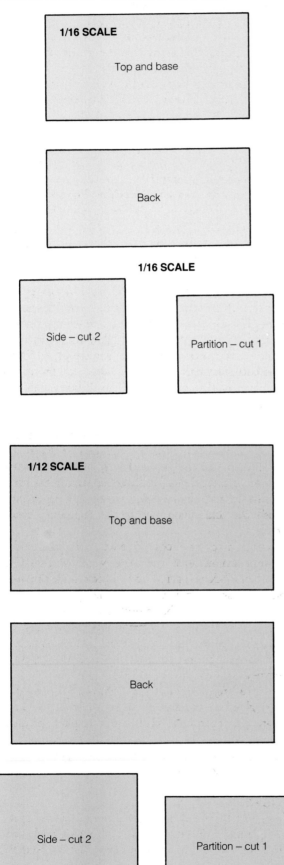

1/16 SCALE

Top and base

Back

1/16 SCALE

Side – cut 2

Partition – cut 1

1/12 SCALE

Top and base

Back

Side – cut 2

Partition – cut 1

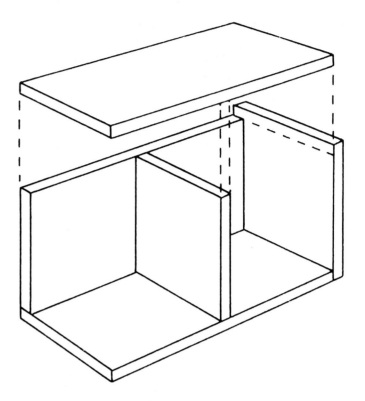

Fig 140 Assembling the record cupboard

gathered tightly along one edge, the calendar is from a catalogue advertisement.

The perfume bottles are glass beads, the lace mats are motifs cut from lace trimming, the records are a magazine advertisement, backed with firm cardboard, and the toys in the children's bedroom are key-ring novelties from the toyshop.

The dolls' house (Fig 141) is a tiny copy of the Victorian town house. It is made of $\frac{3}{32}$in obeche wood, and painted with poster colour. Use the pattern given to cut and assemble the pieces. The roof is made of firm cardboard, the front hinged on with a strip of surgical tape before painting. The truly intrepid might like to try their hands at making furniture!

The mother, father and twins are made from beads and pipecleaners – full instructions can be found in Chapter 14.

THE GARAGE (FIGS 142 AND 143)

The garage is an 'optional extra' for the modern house, it is made quite separately on its own base and can be fixed to the kitchen side of the house if you wish. Made as described, there is a small area in front of the garage which can be covered with brick or stone paper to make a driveway, or the plan can be enlarged to make a larger garden area. The garage is made in plywood and decorated to match the house, the roof covered with dark green, rough-textured sugar paper to represent a tarred, felt roof. The doors are made of obeche wood, pin-hinged to the frames but could be fitted with small hinges at each side if you prefer.

MATERIALS

¼in OR ⅜in thick plywood for the base, walls and roof
⅛in thick obeche or bass wood for the doors

FIG 141 PATTERN FOR THE DOLLS' HOUSE

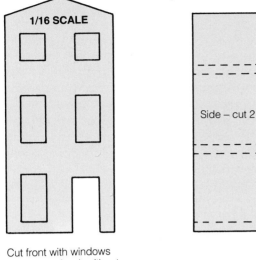

1/16 SCALE

Side – cut 2

Cut front with windows
and door – back without

Floors – cut 3

Roof –
cut from
thin card

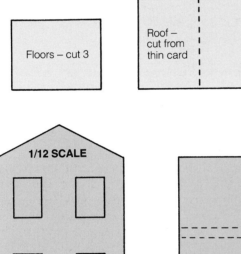

1/12 SCALE

Side – cut 2

Cut front with windows
and door – back without

Roof – cut from thin card

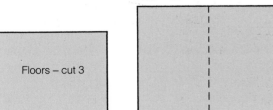

Floors – cut 3

¼in OR ⅜in square beading for the door frame
sugar paper or similar to cover the roof
(optional) four ⅜in hinges for the doors

Draw the pattern pieces onto the wood, cut them with a saw and sand thoroughly. To assemble the garage, glue and pin one side to the base. Glue and pin the back to the side and base, then the other side in place. Glue and pin the front piece between the sides, ensuring that the top edges of the three pieces line up.

Paper the outside of the garage to match the house, and paint or paper the inside of the garage to your taste – we used white emulsion paint. Paper or paint the garage base to represent stone paving, gravel or concrete.

Glue and pin the garage roof in place. The back and right-side edges fit flush with the walls, the front and left-side edges overhang the walls. Cover the garage roof with sugar paper, tucking the edges of the paper under the overhanging sides of the roof.

Cut and paint the three door-frame pieces, and glue them into the doorway, mitring the corners. Cut and paint the under-frame strip, and leave it aside until the doors are complete. Cut the garage doors with a razor-toothed saw, sand the hinged sides slightly round to allow the doors to open freely, and sand the doors with fine abrasive paper. Paint the doors on both sides with one or two undercoats of matt enamel and one coat of gloss enamel. Drill small holes into the top and bottom edges of the doors for the pin hinges. Cut dressmaker's pins and push them into the holes. Try the doors in place and mark the pin positions on the base and the under-frame strip. Drill holes in the base and the underframe strip to receive the pins. Fit the pins in the top of the doors into the holes in the strip, and glue along the top edge of the strip. Fit the pins in the bottom of the doors into the holes in the base and push the under-frame strip, with the doors, into the doorframe.

Cut, sand and paint pieces of fine wood-strip and glue them to the front and left walls under the overhanging roof. Cut a tiny wooden block and glue it to the floor inside the doors to prevent them swinging inwards. Cut the shanks off map pins and glue them into fine holes drilled in the doors, to make handles. The right wall of the garage and the right edge of the base are glued to the left side of the house. Align the front edges of the garage base and house – the back of the garage projects beyond the back of the house.

We used a length of white, plastic farmyard fencing (from a toyshop) glued to the base, a plastic dustbin (originally a pencil sharpener) and two small plastic plants to furnish the yard. We made house signs, drawn with felt pen onto thin slices of log cut at an angle, varnished and glued to the wall beside the front and back doors.

VARIATIONS

As described, this house is typical of modern houses found all over England. However, the basic plan is simple, and the house is large enough to adapt to many different periods (Fig 144).

Using the Tudor cottage as a guide, the exterior could be decorated with brick and timber to make a larger Tudor house.

The interior of the modern house furnished as a child's toy with
commercial, plastic pieces to complement the homemade furniture

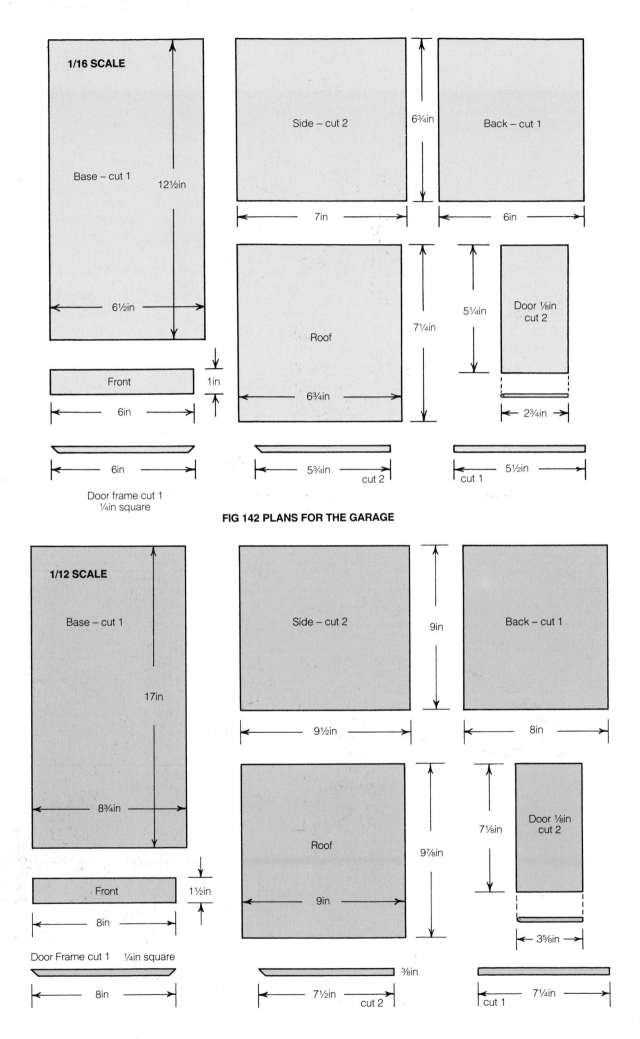

1/16 SCALE

Base – cut 1

12½in

6½in

Side – cut 2

6¾in

7in

Back – cut 1

6in

Roof

7¼in

6¾in

5¼in

Door ⅛in
cut 2

2¾in

Front

1in

6in

Door frame cut 1
¼in square

6in

5¾in

cut 2

5½in

cut 1

FIG 142 PLANS FOR THE GARAGE

1/12 SCALE

Base – cut 1

17in

8¾in

Side – cut 2

9in

9½in

Back – cut 1

8in

Roof

9⅞in

9in

7⅛in

Door ⅛in
cut 2

3⅝in

Front

1½in

8in

Door Frame cut 1   ¼in square

8in

7½in

⅜in

cut 2

7¼in

cut 1

170

Fig 143 Assembling the garage

Commercial windows could be used, but should be painted black or dark brown, and the doors should be planked. The roof would have dark-red tiles, and, as a Tudor house must have fireplaces, there should be chimneys. The garage could be exchanged for a stable, or a garden.

Inside, the house could be partitioned as described but the open-plan stairs should be replaced by a more substantial staircase. The larger room downstairs would be the hall, the smaller, the kitchen. Upstairs, there would be two bedchambers and a small storeroom.

These plans could also be used to make a larger Georgian house. Here again, the red-brick paper and commercial windows would be suitable for the exterior, with grey slates for the roof. The Georgian house also needs chimneys, and might well have a stable with a cobbled or paved yard. The front door should be an imposing panelled one, with a pillared surround and pediment. The interior should be partitioned to make a central hall and staircase, with equal-sized rooms on either side. This would provide a kitchen, parlour and two bedchambers.

The wide, low proportions of this house make it especially

Fig 144 Variations on the modern house

suitable for adaptation to a stone farmhouse. The exterior should be papered with stone paper, or painted to resemble stone using a household-exterior paint containing grit, eg Sandtex. Commercial windows can be used (unless you prefer to make your own) but painted to resembled stone, with characteristic dripstones, cut from thick cardboard, glued above each window. The front door would be fairly heavy, hung from a wooden or stone doorframe, with a dripstone or porch. The chimney stacks might be built of brick at each gable end of the house. The outbuilding might be a large barn, stable or store room, with a larger yard area, perhaps paved or cobbled or laid out as a garden. The roof of such a house might be grey slate, or stone tiles which generally graduated from larger tiles at the eaves to thinner tiles at the ridge.

The farmhouse staircase should be fairly substantial, rising from a large stone-flagged kitchen. The walls would probably be rough-plastered (woodchip paper) and whitewashed (magnolia emulsion). The smaller room downstairs would be a parlour with a planked floor, the walls whitewashed or covered with a small-print old-fashioned wallpaper. The bedrooms also would have planked floors and whitewashed or papered walls. The ceilings throughout the house might be beamed – in the kitchen with hooks to hang hams, bacon joints and onions, etc. Such houses look best with the heavy, simple pieces which are typical of farmhouses – a large oak dresser with a display of pewter, heavy refectory table, and oak settle by the fire. The beds would have patchwork quilts, there would be home-made braided rugs on the floors, a warming pan on the wall, a spinning wheel in the corner and the master's gun above the mantelshelf.

The proportions, especially the fairly shallow pitch of the roof, make this house suitable for a Regency house. The walls should be colour-washed to represent stucco. The roof should be grey slates, and the windows fairly large sashes, with small glazing bars dividing each window into six or nine panes. The front door should be panelled, with a semi-circular fanlight above and pilasters at either side. Inside, the house should be partitioned to make a central hall and staircase, with wide, shallow stairs and a simple banister rail and posts.

The kitchen, parlour and two bedrooms would be of equal size, with fireplaces and chimney breasts on the gable walls. The kitchen would have pale, painted walls, and a stone-flagged or tiled floor. Its large fireplace would contain an open coal fire in a basket grate, with an oven to one side and a boiler for water on the other. There might be a stone sink with a pump for water, a heavy dresser for china, a table and a couple of chairs – though Regency kitchens were still fairly primitive. The parlour would be papered in one of the fashionable, light, pretty papers, perhaps striped or flower sprigged. The polished-wood floor would be covered with a carpet, and the curtains of light-printed cotton or chintz would be looped back to allow light into the room. The fireplace surround would be an elegant wooden affair with a gilt-framed over-mantel mirror. The furniture would also be simple and elegant – a Grecian sofa with striped upholstery and bolster cushions, a bookcase, a sideboard, a dining table and chairs and a small work table. The bedrooms would also be papered in light colours to match the curtains. The polished-wood floors would be covered with rugs, and the fireplaces would have basket grates and wooden surrounds. The beds would be elegant four-posters with chintz curtains and the bedroom furnishings could include a dressing table, bow-fronted chest of drawers and a washstand.

Accessories might include a pole screen by the parlour fire, a bracket clock on the mantelshelf and black-paper silhouettes framed with oval mounts.

14 DOLLS

Most people feel that a dolls' house is not complete until it is inhabited, and the variety of dolls'-house tenants is as wide as the variety of houses. You might prefer a family of mice, teddies or cats but more usually, the tenants are dolls.

The specialist suppliers and dolls'-house shops sell a variety of ready-made dolls and doll kits in all price ranges in plastic, resin, wax and porcelain. They range from the modest families designed as children's toys to beautifully modelled and exquisitely dressed people. If you are a skilled needleperson, a doll kit is not difficult to make-up and dress, and you can choose characters and costume styles to suit your own house – most dolls'-house shops stock a range of kits and the specialist suppliers advertise in the miniatures magazines.

Choose your people carefully to complement your house, and dress them simply if they live in a cottage and more elaborately if they live in a mansion, in styles which are correct for the period of the house. Natural fabrics and tiny trimmings make the best dolls' clothes and The Dolls'-House Draper (see Stockists) can supply everything you will need for miniature dressmaking.

This chapter gives patterns and instructions for simple bead-and-pipecleaner dolls, and clothes patterns which can be adapted to modern or period styles. The method is simple enough for a child to use, but well-made these little dolls will fit into all but the grandest houses. The pipecleaner skeleton makes them flexible so that they will sit and bend easily and, as they are very light, they will stand with the minimum support. Ladies with long skirts can have petticoats made in vilene which will support them very well or, if you prefer, small doll stands (available from the specialist shops) can be used. The patterns are given in both 1/16 and 1/12 scales for adult and child dolls.

MATERIALS

To make each doll you will need:
one round wooden or plastic bead for the head
darning wool, embroidery silk or animal wool for the hair
three 6in pipecleaners
one pair of white shoelaces
approximately 4in of tubular-gauze finger bandage
a little cotton wool for padding
flesh-coloured paint (poster, enamel or acrylic)
felt pens to mark the face

METHOD

To make a 1/16 scale adult doll which will be approximately 4½in tall the bead should be ¾in in diameter. Cut 1in off the pipecleaner which will be used for arms – the other two pipecleaners are used full length.

Fold one full-length pipecleaner in half and push the ends into a 2in length of shoelace. Glue the shoelace-covered pipecleaner firmly into the hole in the bead (Fig 145). Push the shortened pipecleaner into a length of shoelace so that it is completely enclosed. Tuck in the raw ends of shoelace and oversew neatly to form the hands. Stitch the arms to the body ¼in below the head. Push the third pipecleaner into a length of shoelace and oversew the ends as for the arms. Take the looped end of the body and fold it up to just under the arms. Fold the leg length in half and hook it through the body, stitching through legs and body.

Pad the body with cottonwool – the amount determined by whether you want a thin or fat doll. Hold the cottonwool in place by pulling a length of tubular-gauze finger-bandage up over the cottonwool. Stitch the gauze along each shoulder and under the crotch, tucking the raw edges inside, and the doll has ready-made vest and pants. If you want to make a definite waistline, run a gathering thread through the gauze at the waist, pull it up and fasten off the ends. Using flesh-coloured paint, paint the head, neck, hands and any part of the arms or legs which will show when the doll is dressed, and leave the paint to dry thoroughly.

The hair can be made from darning wool or embroidery silk, though the latter usually looks better. For a man's hair, make a parting by backstitching with small, neat stitches through a skein of embroidery silk. Coat the head sparingly with a glue such as UHU and place the hair carefully on the head with the parting where you want it. Ease the strands of silk out so that they cover the head, leaving no bald patches, unless you want them! When the glue is quite dry, trim the hair into shape with small, sharp scissors. Ladies' hair can be made in the same way, whether long or short, loose or tied back. To make a bun, pull the ends of the silk back and tie another strand tightly around to form a pony tail. When the glue is completely dry, plait the pony tail, coil it around on top of the head and stick it in place with a little glue.

Animal wool (available from chemist shops) makes convincing white hair for elderly dolls but is a little difficult to work with. Apply the hair to the head as described and, when the glue is completely dry, spray the wool with hair lacquer to hold it in place. This also applies if you prefer to use the fibre hair sold in art and craft shops.

Draw the features lightly in pencil, and when you are satisfied, colour the eyes, nose and mouth with felt pens. A little pink felt pen, carefully applied, makes rosy cheeks, and a touch of white paint in the corner of each eye gives the face character.

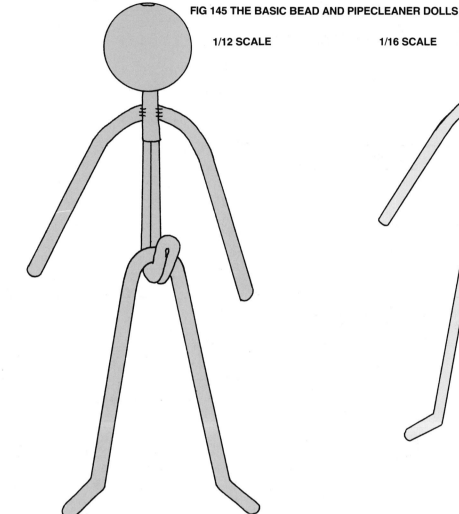

FIG 145 THE BASIC BEAD AND PIPECLEANER DOLLS

1/12 SCALE

1/16 SCALE

OTHER SIZES

To adapt this method to other sizes, measurements are as follows:

1/16 scale child dolls Use a ½in diameter bead, cut 2in off the arm pipecleaner, 1in off the body length and 1in off the leg length. This will make a doll approximately 3½in tall.

1/12 scale adult dolls Use a 1in diameter bead and full-length arm, body and leg pipecleaners. Hook only ½in of the body over the leg length. This will make a doll approximately 6in tall.

1/12 scale child dolls Use the measurements given for 1/16 scale adult dolls.

Babies Babies can be made by cutting the top 1½in off a wooden clothes-peg, sanding it smooth and painting it flesh colour. The baby's face is marked in felt pen, with a little wool or silk stuck to the head for hair. When the baby is wrapped in a shawl or placed in a cradle, arms and legs are not needed!

Babies can also be made using beads and pipecleaners. Use a bead a little smaller than ½in. The body pipecleaner should be 1½in long, the arm length 1½in and the leg length 2in. Proceed as above.

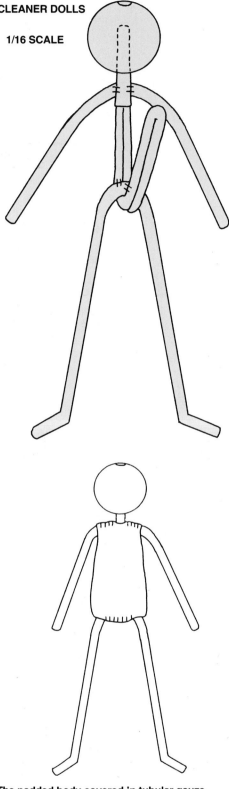

Fig 146 The padded body covered in tubular gauze

CLOTHES

Full-size patterns are given in 1/12 and 1/16 scales. The lines drawn are the sewing lines, so when using the patterns allow

(Pages 176–7) Dolls should be chosen carefully to complement the house or shop they are to occupy – there is a wide choice of ready-made and doll kits available

174

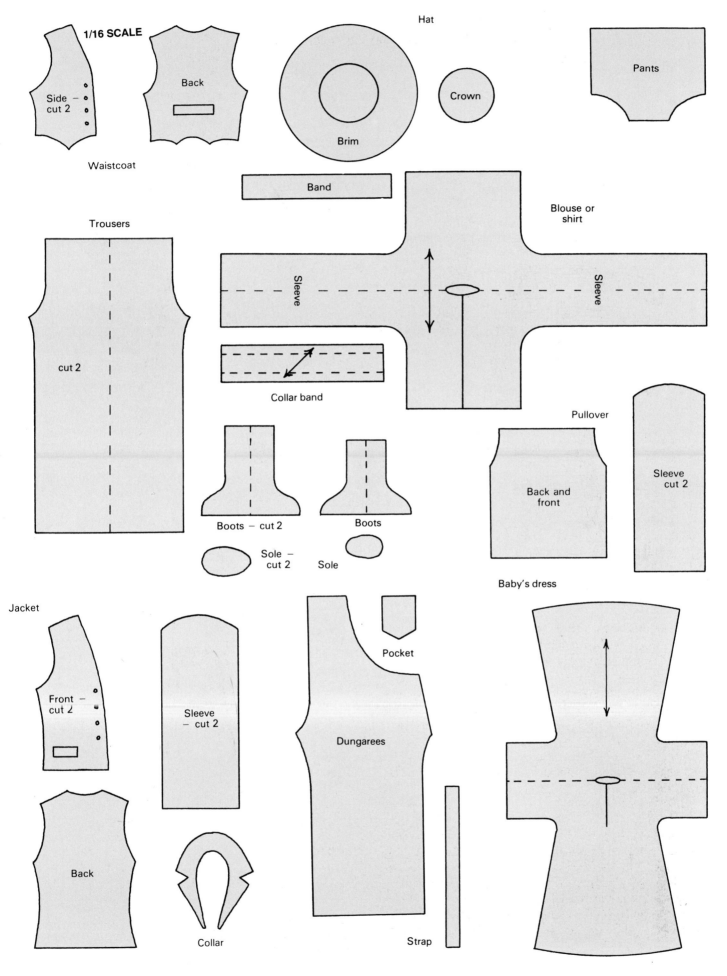

1/16 SCALE

Side – cut 2

Back

Waistcoat

Hat

Brim

Crown

Pants

Band

Blouse or shirt

Sleeve

Sleeve

Trousers

cut 2

Collar band

Boots – cut 2

Boots

Sole – cut 2

Sole

Pullover

Back and front

Sleeve cut 2

Baby's dress

Jacket

Front – cut 2

Sleeve – cut 2

Back

Collar

Pocket

Dungarees

Strap

175

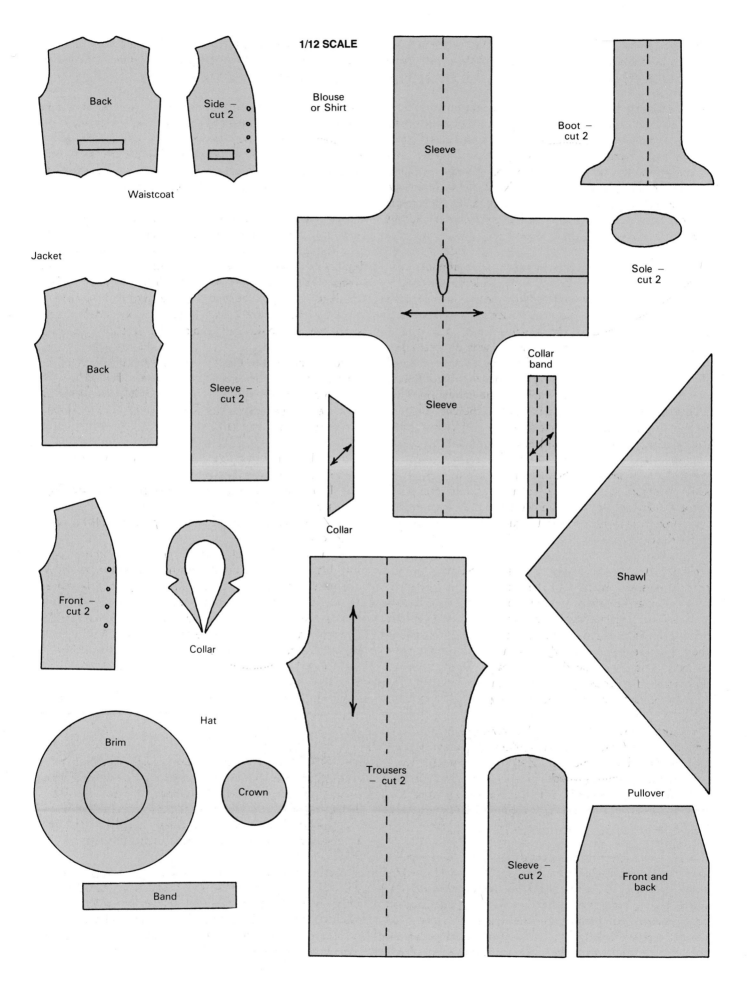

1/12 SCALE

Waistcoat — Back, Side – cut 2

Jacket — Back, Sleeve – cut 2, Front – cut 2, Collar

Hat — Brim, Crown, Band

Blouse or Shirt — Sleeve, Sleeve, Collar, Collar band

Boot – cut 2

Sole – cut 2

Shawl

Trousers – cut 2

Pullover — Sleeve – cut 2, Front and back

178

⅛in extra all-round for seams and hems, except when using felt. Dolls' clothes are fiddly to make, so these are simple garments, though the experienced needleperson may prefer to adapt them.

Materials used for dolls' clothes should be fine and lightweight and should not fray easily. Any design should be tiny and colours should match the period and type of house. Felt is a good choice for trousers, jackets, waistcoats and jumpers as it does not fray and the seams can be oversewn together, making the garment less bulky. Natural cottons are good, especially for blouses, shirts and skirts, as they crease and hang well. Painting edges with Fraycheck will prevent them from fraying.

Shirt This is cut in one piece, using the appropriate scale pattern and adding ⅛in seam allowance. Fold the shirt where indicated by dotted lines and, working on the wrong side of the fabric, sew the seams along the underarms and body. Clip the seams slightly at the underarm curve and turn through to the right side. Slip the shirt onto the doll with the opening at the front. Fold the raw edge of the left-front under and slipstitch the left-front over the right-front. If required, French knots can be worked down the front to represent buttons. Run a gathering thread around each sleeve at the cuff, pull up, tucking the raw edges inside, and fasten off. If necessary, run a gathering thread around the neck edge to pull in the neckline. Fold the raw edges of the collar-band to the inside and press the folds, then slipstitch the collar-band to the neck of the shirt, covering the raw edge. A collar can be cut from white felt and stuck in place over the collar-band. A tiny bow tie, made from narrow ribbon, can be stuck or sewn to the shirt under the collar.

Trousers Cut two trouser pieces in felt, using the appropriate scale pattern. Sew the two pieces together at the centre-front and centre-back seams from waist to crotch. Sew the leg seams – up one leg, through the crotch and down the other leg. Turn the trousers through to the right side and slip them onto the doll, tucking the shirt inside. Run a gathering thread around the top of the trousers and pull up to fit the dolls' waist. If required, a belt, cut from a narrow strip of felt can be stuck to the trousers to cover the gathering thread.

Waistcoat Cut one back and two front pieces from felt. Oversew the fronts to the back at the shoulder and side seams. Turn through to the right side and slip the waistcoat onto the doll, over the shirt. Overlap the left-front over the right-front and make three or four French knots to represent buttons. Cut the pocket flap and backstrap, if required, and stick or sew them in place.

Jacket Cut one back, two fronts, two sleeves and one collar from felt. Oversew the fronts to the back at the shoulder seams. Oversew the sleeves into the armholes, stretching the sleeve head gently around the curve. Sew the underarm and body seams in one. Turn the jacket through to the right side and put it onto the doll. Glue the underside of the collar and position it carefully over the neck and front edges of the jacket. Overlap the left-front over the right-front and sew three or four French knots to represent buttons. Cut pocket flaps, if required, and stick them in place.

Hat Cut one crown, one hat-band and one brim from felt. Oversew the hat-band seam, then oversew or blanket stitch the crown to the top edge of the hat-band and the brim to the lower edge. Trim the hat if required. This pattern can be used to make a lady's hat by cutting the brim larger and trimming the finished hat with ribbons, flowers or feathers.

Boots Cut two boots and two soles in felt. Fold the boot along the dotted line indicated in the pattern. Starting at the toe, blanket stitch the edges together, over the foot and up the leg. Slip the boot up the doll's leg and bend the doll's foot sharply forward into the foot of the boot. Holding the doll upside-down, place the sole over the foot and oversew or blanket stitch it to the bottom edge of the boot. If necessary, secure the boot to the leg with a few small stitches.

Blouse The blouse is made from the same pattern as the shirt, but the opening is at the back. The collar-band can be used to neaten the neck edge, with or without the collar; or use a piece of gathered-lace trimming instead. The cuffs could also be trimmed with lace.

Skirt The skirt is a rectangle of fabric, varying in size for different lengths and scales.

In 1/16 scale: for a long skirt, cut a piece 7½ × 3¼in, for a short skirt, 6 × 2in.

In 1/12 scale: for a long skirt, cut a piece 8 × 4¼in, for a short skirt, 6½ × 3in.

Seam the short edges together and make a narrow hem along one long edge. Run a gathering thread along the other long edge and slip the skirt onto the doll, tucking the blouse inside. Pull up the gathering thread to fit the doll's waist, tucking the raw edges inside, and fasten off. Distribute the gathers evenly and slipstitch the top edge of the skirt in place. If you prefer, the gathered skirt could be stitched to a waistband, but, unless you use a very fine fabric, this can be bulky.

Make a dress by using the same fabric for a blouse and skirt, and hiding the waist seam with narrow ribbon tied in a bow at the back.

Petticoat Medium-weight Vilene makes good petticoats under long skirts, as it is stiff enough to make the doll stand upright. Cut the petticoat ½in shorter and narrower than the skirt, and hem the bottom edge for extra stiffness. Gather the top edge and pull up to fit the doll's waist. A narrow lace trimming can be sewn to the petticoat hem if it is to be visible.

Jumper This can be made from felt, or the top of a sock, using the finished edge of the sock for the hem and cuffs.

Cut a back, front, and two sleeves. Oversew the front to the back at the shoulder seams, ¼in in from the armhole. Oversew the sleeves into the armholes. Sew the underarm and body seams in one and turn the jumper through to the right

Simple bead and pipecleaner dolls, dressed in period or modern styles, will live happily in most dolls' houses

side. Ease the jumper over the doll's head, pushing the arms into the sleeves. Oversew the shoulder seams closed from the armhole seam to the neck.

Apron Aprons or pinafores can be made from small rectangles of fabric, lace or broderie anglaise. Hem three edges of the apron, and gather the top edge. Sew the gathered edge to a piece of narrow ribbon for a waistband and use narrow ribbon for shoulder straps.

Stockings and boots Stockings are made by pushing the doll's legs into shoelaces of the required colour, tucking the raw edges inside and oversewing the shoelace to the top of the

centre-front seam from the bib to the crotch. Sew the centre-back seam from the waist to the crotch. Sew the leg seams up one leg, through the crotch and down the other leg. Turn the dungarees through to the right side and slip them onto the doll, tucking the jumper inside. Stitch the straps, one each side at the top of the bib front, pass them over the shoulders, crossing them at the back, and sew the ends inside the waist at the back. Stick or sew the pocket to the centre of the bib front.

Baby's dress   The baby's dress is cut in one piece from white felt, cotton or wide broderie anglaise trimming. Fold the dress along the dotted line indicated on the pattern, and, working on the wrong side of the fabric, stitch the underarm and body seams. Turn a hem at the bottom edge. Clip the seam at the underarm curve, if necessary, and turn through to the right side. Slip the dress onto the doll with the opening at the back. Slipstitch the back opening closed. Gather the cuffs and pull up, tucking the raw edges inside. Trim the neckline with a piece of narrow ribbon tied in a bow.

PETS

Dolls'-house pets traditionally come in all shapes and sizes. Cats, dogs, rabbits, etc, in resin, china or plastic, can be found in most dolls'-house shops and in toy and gift shops, and many will fit happily into the dolls' house. Plastic cats and dogs can often be improved with careful painting. Felt or fur-fabric animals are sold as key-ring mascots, and porcelain and china miniatures are sold as collector's pieces in china shops. The white-plastic doves sold as wedding-cake decorations will make reasonable budgies, given a coat of paint! Or you might try making a fish tank, using a clear-plastic box for the tank, cutting the fish from orange or gold metallic foil, and adding a little sand and a few plastic water weeds in resin 'water'.

Modelling your own animals in Das or clay is quite a challenge, but it can produce some amusing results. Find a picture to use as a model and work the clay into the right shape. When dry, paint the animal with poster or acrylic paints, using your picture as a guide. Consider plastic farmyard animals, especially for a cottage – or how about a 'Vietnamese pot-bellied pig' in the 1980s yuppie house!

If your pet requires a basket, consult Chapter 6 and don't forget the blanket and feeding bowl!

leg and toes. This method is useful if you feel that your doll's legs are too thin – another shoe lace fattens them quite considerably.

The ladies and children's boots are made the same way as the men's, in a colour to match the clothes.

Dungarees   The children's dungarees are made in felt. Cut the dungaree pieces, two straps and one pocket. Sew the

15 RENOVATION

Old dolls' houses are now regarded as antiques, and valued accordingly. A Victorian or Edwardian house in reasonable condition will fetch a high price in an auction or antique shop and is therefore beyond the means of most people. Even the commercial post-war children's dolls' houses like the Triang models are no longer cheap, though obviously not as expensive as the older ones. However, it is still possible to find a dolls' house, in a junk shop or country sale, which the antique dealers have missed, perhaps because it is 'home-made' and of less value than the old commercial houses. It is possible that the old dolls' house of your own childhood is still around, tucked away in some family attic and long forgotten.

Whatever the source of your old dolls' house – auction or attic – it will probably need some restoration work. Over the years, dirt, damp, woodbeetle and central heating can reduce any once-proud mansion to a shabby looking derelict. Unless you are an expert on the restoration of antique furniture, it is possible to do considerable damage by over-enthusiastic renovation. It is therefore wise to give some serious thought to the age, appearance and value of your dolls' house first.

ANTIQUE HOUSES

These are Victorian or Edwardian houses (rarely older) perhaps home or carpenter-made, or one of the commercial houses made for children at this time. The house itself might appear crudely made, badly proportioned, even ugly, but if it is in reasonable condition it is potentially valuable and should be treated with respect. Stripping the original paints and papers and removing any fixtures will not only reduce the financial value but would be an act of vandalism similar to sticking Formica on top of a Regency table! The rule for an antique house should be careful preservation rather than renovation.

Cleaning The first stage is to clean the house, gently but thoroughly. A solution of soap flakes or washing-up liquid in warm water will do the job efficiently, but the old-fashioned cabinet-maker's recipe is a solution of equal parts of linseed oil, vinegar and turpentine with a few drops of methylated spirit. Dust the house with a clean cloth first, then use cottonwool, wrung out in the cleaning solution, to remove dirt from the interior and exterior. This will clean loose dirt from the wood and paintwork but will not affect the patina of old age.

The exterior of the house might be polished wood, in which case a good beeswax polish, well-buffed, will be all that is required. If the exterior is painted, the cleaning may reveal chips and cracks. It is probably best to leave these, but if you feel that you must paint over them, use small tins of enamel paint, mixing carefully to match the colour as closely as possible and apply with an artist's paintbrush.

If the exterior is brick papered, even if the paper is torn, leave it. The modern brick papers are quite different in colour and design from the old ones and stripping off an old paper to replace it with a new one contravenes the first rule of preservation! The exception to this rule is if the paper has obviously been applied later over a house that was originally painted. If this is the case, and you feel that the paper is sufficiently torn to justify removing it, soak it carefully with tepid clean water applied with cottonwool, so that it peels away quite easily. The paintwork underneath can then be cleaned as described.

The interior of the house will probably be papered, quite possibly with several layers of paper. The problem here is in deciding whether to peel away the top layers to reveal the older papers underneath. If the top layer of paper is badly torn and that underneath looks better, soak the wall carefully with tepid clean water applied with cottonwool, and use nothing more drastic than your finger nails to peel it away. Work slowly and carefully, and with luck, removing the torn and dirty top paper might reveal a better one underneath. If there is only one layer of paper on the wall, or you prefer not to excavate, rub gently with a soft pencil rubber or pieces of fresh bread, which will remove most dirt and quite nasty stains. If there are immovable stains or torn patches of paper, these can be concealed by pictures and mirrors or careful placement of furniture. You might feel that the wallpaper in a room is in very bad condition or impossibly ugly and be tempted to replace it with a new one. If this is the case, rather than stripping the old paper, leave it and line the room with thin cardboard, held in place with small pieces of double-sided tape, and carry out the new decorating scheme on the cardboard. This method can be used if you do not feel able to clean or peel the old paper as described, and will protect the paper while allowing you the freedom of decorating the rooms as you please. The dolls'-house floors might be polished wood, painted or papered, and should be treated as the walls.

Repairs Exposed to damp and heat, wood will crack, and joints come apart. Cracks and holes can be filled with plastic wood of the appropriate colour, smoothed with the fingers and then painted if necessary to match the fabric of the house. If the old animal glues used in the joints get damp, they no longer hold. The old glue can be carefully scraped off with a knife blade and a woodwork glue applied to the joint, which will probably need clamping until the glue dries.

Rusty old hinges and locks, if they are still holding firm, can be cleaned with rust remover, metal polish and an old toothbrush. If the hinges have worked loose, they should be removed, the old holes filled and, if necessary, new hinges, as similar as possible, fitted. It is a good idea to keep the original hinges and anything else you might remove from the house.

Broken pieces of woodwork, turning or carving might be difficult to replace, but if you can find or make replacements, keep a note of the new pieces. The simplest way of recording any replacements and repairs is to take before and after photographs of the interior and exterior, and keep them safely with the pieces you have removed.

The golden rule with an antique dolls' house is to do nothing irrevocable. If you need help, there are good books on antique restoration available from the library, and firms which specialise in repair and renovation of antiques. Your local museum is often a much underrated source of advice and information. They are in the business of preservation and therefore generally sympathetic to anyone with similar aims.

OTHER OLD HOUSES

The second category includes all those other old houses which, though not antiques, are still worth preserving. Commercially-made dolls' houses of the early part of this century are rapidly becoming valuable, and, if in good condition, it is probably wise to treat such a house as a potential antique and do nothing drastic. It is a sad fact, though, that the majority of children's dolls' houses in this century have been badly treated and are in a poor condition – if they have survived at all! A house in such condition is obviously not worth preserving as previously described, so complete renovation is quite justifiable. However bad the condition, by stripping the house down to its basic parts, repairing and remaking it, almost any house can be saved.

Drastic repairs We were recently given to repair a house in a sad state of dereliction. It was a small Triang house, made in 1928, which had been a toy for many years, then stored in an attic for another twenty. It was crudely made of pine, with a cardboard roof, but even in its battered state it had charm. Woodbeetle had feasted on the base, the hinges were torn out, the windows were missing, the roof was broken and some child with a passion for decorating had plastered hideous 1950s wall papers all over. All in all, a sad sight!

We began by stripping all the wall and floor papers, sighing over the remaining tiny scraps of original paper. Then we cleaned the house thoroughly inside and out. The base was removed and a new base made of plywood, painted a similar green to the original. The roof, which was torn and broken along the seams, was repaired with many layers of masking tape until it was firm and strong again. All the cracks in the wood were filled with plastic wood and the joints between walls and floors re-glued with woodwork glue. The old broken hinges were removed, the holes filled and new hinges fitted. Broken woodwork around the windows was replaced and the front door was re-hung with new hinges so that it closed properly. The house was now a clean bare shell and we painted it all over with Rentokil fluid to prevent future attacks by woodbeetle. The exterior had originally been cream, so we gave it two coats of cream emulsion paint and papered the roof with green-pantile paper. The interior was decorated with wall and floor papers as similar to the originals as we could find (the parquet floor paper was almost identical). As the house was a commercial one, we used commercial windows, similar to the original ones, though plastic instead of metal. The paintwork was given a fresh coat of ivory gloss, the ceilings ivory emulsion and the front door green gloss. The finishing touch was the flower-garden effect on the front of the house which had originally been crudely painted in oils. As most of this had been rubbed off, we replaced it with flower transfers to resemble a border.

The finished house looked almost new. Very little of the original remained beyond the basic wooden shell, but the owner was delighted and thought it looked much as it had when new. It now has another lease of life with her grandchildren, who, she hopes, will treat it more respectfully than she did.

This kind of drastic restoration is easier, and more fun, than the measures recommended for antique dolls' houses, but it should only be carried out on a house which is obviously quite beyond preservation. It would be tragic to destroy a genuinely beautiful, antique dolls' house simply because it is shabby.

FURNISHINGS

Similar rules apply here. If you are fortunate enough to own an antique house with antique furnishings, aim for preserving rather than re-making. Use small tools such as cotton buds and toothbrushes, and a very gentle touch.

Fabrics Curtains and upholstery tend to deteriorate through dirt and moths rather than fading or hard usage, and generally only need cleaning to look good again. Curtains, bedclothes and other fabric items should be washed in a mild solution of soap flakes in warm water (squeezing gently rather than rubbing) rinsed in clean water, squeezed out and dried flat. If necessary, iron very carefully with a warm iron. Beware with old cottons, especially blue colours, as the dye might not be stable. Unstable colours should not be washed, but you can dry-clean them by spreading the fabric out flat, spraying it with a dry hair-shampoo and brushing gently with an old, clean toothbrush.

Upholstered furniture, carpets and rugs generally need only a good brush with an old toothbrush to remove the dust and dirt, but, if there are grease marks, try dry shampoo or a gentle dabbing with cottonwool wrung out in a mild soap solution.

If the old fabrics are wearing thin or fraying, a piece of lightweight iron-on Vilene, carefully applied to the back will strengthen and help to preserve them.

FURNITURE

Wooden furniture, usually glued together with animal glue, is subject to the same joint trouble as houses. Clean the furniture with the same solutions, using cotton buds to reach the awkward parts, and re-glue the pieces with woodwork glue. Polish the furniture gently with beeswax polish on a soft cloth. Broken chair legs, rails or drawer handles, etc, can be replaced

A furniture restoration workshop could be housed in the Antique shop premises

if you can find or make a good match, or the broken piece could be placed in the house with the defective part discreetly hidden.

Metal   Many of the older dolls' houses have metal furniture or accessories. Silver, brass, copper, pewter, Brittania metal or tin can all be cleaned in the same way as life-size items, using the commercial metal-cleaners and polishes. Again, an old toothbrush is useful for cleaning the fiddly bits.

Broken metal furniture is difficult to mend as even super-glue will not join all metals. Soldering is possible on some pieces if the metal is suitable, and fuse-wire can be used to wire a small part such as a chair leg in place. Cleaning these small metal items regularly will prevent future tarnishing, or they can be lacquered with one of the commercial metal lacquers.

Bone and ivory   Furniture and ornaments in bone and ivory were once very popular in dolls' houses. To clean them, wipe gently with methylated spirit on cottonwool or a cotton bud. Very yellowed ivory or bone can be bleached with a stiff paste of whiting and hydrogen peroxide. Coat the piece with this paste and leave it outdoors to dry. When dry, remove the paste with a damp cloth and polish with a soft dry cloth. Cracks in bone and ivory can be filled with melted candle wax, rubbed smooth over the crack with a finger.

Glass   Glass items, obviously, must be treated very gently – usually washing them in warm water and detergent is sufficient. A few drops of ammonia in the water will remove stubborn marks. Broken glass pieces can be mended with an epoxy resin. Roughen the edges of the glass slightly with glass paper, then join the broken pieces with glue, holding the join with sticky tape until the glue sets.

China Glazed china crockery for dolls' houses was made in quantity during the last century, and surprisingly large amounts have survived. Most pieces need only to be washed in warm water and detergent and dried. Small stains can usually be removed with a little bicarbonate of soda. The coarse china, which is porous and can become badly stained, should be immersed in household bleach for a few hours, then rinsed. Broken pieces can be mended with an epoxy resin or super-glue, taping the join until the glue is set. Gummed brown-paper tape is best for repair work of this type, as it shrinks slightly as it dries, holding the join very tightly.

Oil Paintings. If you are lucky enough to have miniature oil paintings in your dolls' house, they might well be dark and dirty. If the painting will come out of its frame easily, remove it, otherwise, clean it in the frame. Either turpentine or white spirit can be used and cotton buds are excellent tools. Work carefully, changing the cotton bud as soon as it gets dirty. When the painting is clean, if it is still murky and brownish, you might wish to remove the old varnish. This is done with a swab of cotton wool, wrung out in acetone (or nail-varnish remover). Have ready another swab, wrung out in turpentine. Wipe quickly and carefully over the picture with the acetone swab and then wipe over again immediately with the turpentine swab. Re-varnish with picture varnish, using an artist's paint brush. When the painting is thoroughly dry, replace it in the frame.

Leather Leather-upholstered furniture will become shabby if it is not cared for, but it can be restored by the following treatment. To clean the piece, make up a mixture of three parts castor oil to two parts surgical spirit and wipe it on with a cottonwool pad or cotton bud, leaving it for twenty-four hours. Then wipe with a piece of cottonwool wrung out in castor oil. If the leather has become hard, rub in a leather cream, then polish with a soft wax polish on a soft cloth, using a coloured polish if necessary. Regular polishing with a soft wax will keep the leather furniture in good condition.

STOCKISTS AND SUPPLIERS

It would be impossible to list all the dolls'-house shops in the country so the suppliers listed here are those mentioned in the book. For a comprehensive, county by county list of shops, we recommend that you contact:

The Dolls'-House Information Service
Avalon Court
Star Road
Partridge Green
West Sussex RH13 8RY

Please note that all enquiries to addresses listed here should be accompanied by a SAE or you cannot reasonably expect a reply, and all firms make a charge for their catalogue.

Blackwells of Hawkwell, 733 London Road, Westcliffe on Sea, Essex SS0 9ST
Extensive range of furniture kits and ready-made doors and windows and lighting etc. Available on the premises, or from most miniatures shops or direct by mail order. Catalogue.

The Dolls'-House Draper, PO Box 128, Lightcliffe, Halifax, West Yorkshire HX3 8RN
Miniature haberdashery and small-scale fabrics, including ribbons, hat straw, lace and trimmings, cotton prints, silk and velveteen. Available by mail order. Catalogue.

W. Hobby Ltd, Knights Hill Square, London SE27 0HH
A range of wood mouldings, doors and windows, papers and claddings, furniture kits and lighting etc. Available by mail order. Catalogue (Hobby's Annual) available from newsagents.

Honeychurch Toys Ltd, Woodlands, Ledge Hill, Market Lavington, Wiltshire SN10 4NW
A range of good quality dolls' houses, ready-made or as kits. Available from many dolls'-house shops or direct by mail order. Catalogue.

Gable End Designs, 190 Station Road, Knowle, Solihull, West Midlands B93 0RR
Aga cookers moulded in plastic resin as kits or ready-made to order in all Aga colours. Catalogue, by mail order.

Vale Dolls' Houses, 'Wayside', Church Street, Whatton in the Vale, Nottinghamshire NG13 9EL
A wide range of good quality whitewood dolls' houses; and dolls' houses made to commission. Available by mail order. Catalogue.

Phoenix Model Developments, The Square, Earls Barton, Northampton NN6 0NA
A wide range of white metal kits for kitchen ranges, fireplaces and accessories. Available from most dolls'-house shops or direct by mail order. Catalogue.

Thames Valley Crafts, Mere House, Dedmere Road, Marlow-on-Thames, Buckinghamshire SL7 1PD
A very large range of shop fittings, accessories and miniature packages etc. Available from most dolls'-house shops or direct by mail order. Catalogue.

US SUPPLIERS
In the US, because both the country and the interest in miniatures are so large, there are literally thousands of suppliers. The beginner is advised to look first for a local supplier who will probably stock most things you need or will be able to advise you

This local supplier will also carry *The Miniatures Catalogue* which is a comprehensive guide to sources for everything the miniaturist could need, including box rooms, building components, lighting kits, furniture and accessories. It is a mail-order shoppers 'dream book', published (and up-dated) annually. If you have any difficulty finding it, it may be ordered from: Hobby Book Distributors, 3150 State Line Road, No. Bend, OH 45052.

AUSTRALIAN SUPPLIERS (courtesy of Wendy Benson)
In Australia miniatures are a fairly new hobby, growing steadily in popularity. There are now a number of suppliers, and the following list includes shops, mail order suppliers and specialists. All suppliers listed offer a mail order service.

North East Models (Russell Asprey), PO Box 588, Wodonga, NSW 3690
Milled basswood, structural shapes, stripwood angles, tees, beams, columns, weatherboard siding, scribed sheathing, corrugated siding, roofs and floors. This firm has placed a range of its products in a shop in Melbourne called 'Nancraft', 289 Elizabeth Street, Melbourne, Victoria 3000.

Crafter's Timbers (Trevor Crafter), Edmund Road, Silvan, Victoria 3795
Special Australian scale timbers for furniture and dolls'-house joinery, including wild cherry, blackwood and huon pine.

Bustle and Bows (Heather Hall), Shop 3, 10-14 Railway Avenue, Ringwood, Victoria 3135 (Tel: 03 870 5994)
Extensive range of ribbons, cotton lace, fabrics and unusual trimmings in miniature, including narrow hat straws. Miniature petit point sometimes available.

Alan Waters Miniatures, Lot 7, Bucca Road, Lower Bucca, NSW 2450
Superb quality handcrafted furniture and accessories, including the most complicated designs. Fine hand-painting on many items, including clocks and plates. Mostly Georgian and Victorian, but any item can be made, to any scale.

Greg Cranwell, 23 Cresdee Road, Campbelltown, South Australia 5074
Handcrafted Australian colonial furniture.

Gulliver's Wonderful World of Miniatures (Bryan Fraser) 13 Walker Road, Caringbah, NSW 2229 (02 524 3591)
Brass furniture and accessories – also silver and copper.

Dimity Dolls (June Newman), 86 Skyline Terrace, Burleigh Heads, Queensland 4220 (Tel: 075 358 269)
A range of original dolls'-house dolls dressed in Victorian or modern costume. Adults with cloth bodies, children, all bisque.

Small Pleasures (Nerida O'Callaghan), 2 King's Place, Carlingford, NSW 2118 (Tel: 02 630 2804)
Goods are stocked by several good miniatures shops in Sydney, and 'Just Miniatures' in Canberra. Exquisite food, plants, toys and accessories.

Just Miniatures (Mandy Perry), Cnr. Gladstone & Victoria Streets Hall, ACT 2618 (Tel: 062 302 642)
Huge range of quality furniture, kits and accessories, both imported and from top local craftspeople. Probably the best miniatures shop in Australia, certainly the best mail order service.

Toy Parade Toyworld (Sylvia Martin), 182 The Parade, Norwood, South Australia 5067 (Tel: 08 332 3319)
A comprehensive range of furniture, accessories, plans and building requirements for dolls' houses.

Houseworks (Jackie Bell), 229 Canterbury Road, St Kilda West, Victoria 3182; 21 Carlos Road, Artarmon, NSW 2064 (Tel: 03 534 7063-Vic; 02 419 4013-NSW)
Furniture; ready-made or DIY kits. Building components; including doors, windows, plans, lights, corrugated iron, bricks, transoms, wallpaper and hardware. Many accessories, including porcelain and pewter from UK.

Miniature World (Shirley Putnin) 12 Parliament Place, West Perth, Western Australia 6005 (Tel: 09 322 2020)
Dolls' houses and locally made dolls'-house kits, building supplies, lighting, furniture and accessories (some imported), and Western Australian pottery

Fisher Discount Workshop Machinery (Tom Fisher), 68 Barrier Street, Fyshwick, ACT 2609 (Tel: 062 804 105)
Stocks Dremel and Emco miniature power tools, and a full range of full-size woodworking tools.

Parra Power Tools, 280 Paramatta Road, Granville, NSW 2 (Tel: 02 637 9055)
Stocks Dremel and Emco miniature tools, and also full-size woodworking equipment.

Colin B. Walker, 1 Campbell Street, Collingwood, Victoria 3066 (Tel: 03 417 2281)
Superb selection of woodcarving and woodturning tools, also books.

BOOKS AND MAGAZINES

BOOKS

For a wide-ranging catalogue of books on dolls' houses, miniatures, dolls, architecture, furniture and crafts contact:

The Mulberry Bush,
9 George Street,
Brighton,
Sussex BN2 1RH

You may find the following books useful:

Atkinson, S., *Making and Dressing Dolls' House Dolls* (David & Charles, 1992)

Calloway, S., *The Elements of Style* (Mitchell Beazley, 1991)

Dodge, V., *The Dolls' Dressmaker* (David & Charles, 1987)

Dodge, V., & M., *Making Miniatures* (David & Charles, 1989)

Hardyment, C., *Home Comfort* (Viking/National Trust, 1992)

Nicholls, B., *Making Dolls' Houses* (David & Charles, 1991)

Yarwood, D., *The English Home* (Batsford, 1979)

FAIRS

The two major fairs in Britain are Miniatura and the London Dolls' House Festival. Practically everything the miniatures world has to offer can be seen at either of these fairs.

Miniatura is a two day event, covering the whole spectrum of miniatures in every price range, held in Birmingham every year in the spring and autumn; and Scottish Miniatura is held in June. For full details contact:

Bob & Muriel Hopwood, 41 Eastbourne Avenue, Hodge Hill, Birmingham B34 6AR

The London Dolls' House Festival is a three day event held in Kensington in May each year, it offers an enormous range of fine quality miniatures. The festival also publishes a directory of shops and craftsmen covering the whole country. For details of the festival or the directory contract:

Caroline Hamilton, 25 Priory Road, Kew Green, Richmond TW9 3DQ

MAGAZINES

The following magazines are specialist dolls'-house publications which contain a wealth of information including articles, how-to projects, advertising and listings of dolls'-house fairs. They are available on subscription from the address given – please enclose a SAE with all enquiries.

Dolls House and Miniature Scene, 7 Ferringham Lane, Ferring, West Sussex BN12 5DN

Dolls' House World, Ashdown Publishing, 104 High Street, Steyning, West Sussex BN4 3RD

Dolls' House World (US Office), Heritage Press, 3150 State Line Road, Cincinatti, North Bend, Ohio 45052.

The Home Miniaturist, Ashdown Publishing, 104 High Street, Steyning, West Sussex BN4 3RD.

The International Dolls' House News, Nexus Special Interests Ltd, Nexus House, Boundary Way, Hemel Hempstead, Hertfordshire HP2 7ST

Both these fairs exhibit the best of British miniatures and also include a number of guest exhibitors from abroad. They both have 'limited entry' days with tickets bought in advance, and 'open' days when tickets can be bought at the door.

(Please enclose a SAE with all enquiries)

There are also smaller events all over the country, some of which specialises in miniatures, others which combine miniatures with dolls or toys.

Smaller fairs are usually one day events and generally have a range of exhibitors, including craftsmen, suppliers and often local dolls'-house clubs.

There are now so many fairs that it is not practical to list them, but they all advertise in the specialist magazines – giving details of the dates, venue and organiser. Some fairs have pre-paid 'limited entry' tickets for the first hour or two, and these are an excellent idea if you dislike crowds.

INDEX

Page numbers in italics denote illustrations